EAST-WEST ENCOUNTERS

FRANCO-ASIAN CINEMA AND LITERATURE

Sylvie Blum-Reid

WALLFLOWER PRESS
LONDON AND NEW YORK

First published in Great Britain in 2003 by Wallflower Press
5 Pond Street, London NW3 2PN
www.wallflowerpress.co.uk

A catalogue for this book is available from the British Library

ISBN 1-903364-67-1 (paperback)
ISBN 1-903364-69-8 (hardback)

Printed in Great Britain by Antony Rowe, Chippenham, Wiltshire

EAST-WEST ENCOUNTERS

Contents

List of illustrations

Acknowledgements

Thanks to: Julia Lesage, who was my first reader of 'Returning to Vietnam' for *Jump Cut* in Paris; Christine Holmlund for organising the special SCS session on Francophone cinema where I delivered a talk on Rithy Panh; Nadine Dormoy and *Europe Plurilingue* for publishing a shorter version of my chapter on *L'Odeur de la papaye verte*; the University of California's visual series program (Davis) for giving me the opportunity to present one of my earliest papers on the topic; Kuan Hsin Chen for his continuous support over the years; Nafei Ding, David Desser, Panivong Norindr and Chris Holmlund for their editorial suggestions and encouragement. I wish to thank my departmental chair Geraldine Nichols who over the years encouraged me and provded me with a semester off after four years of teaching at the University of Florida so that I could devote my time to finishing the project, along with the sustained guidance and support of my mentors Bill Calin and Bernadette Cailler. Thanks to the department of Romance Languages and Literatures and the College of Liberal Arts at the University of Florida that supported my research with three summer research grants providing the necessary impetus to conduct research abroad. Thanks also to the international studies and Asian studies program for helping me to go on a research seminar in Vietnam in 2001 and to the University of Florida English Department Film & Media Studies program and Robert Kay (Chair). My gratitude to the University of Florida's librarians for building the collection in Franco-Asian studies, Frank Di Trolio and David Hickey.

My special thanks to the people who generously gave their time, some of whom I interviewed and/or met over the course of several years, others only once. All of them gave me directions to follow: Lam Lê, Rithy Panh, Patrick Barberis, Louise Ernct, Nguyen Khanh Hoi (tonton), Sean James Rose, Do Khiem and Viet Linh.

I also wish to acknowledge the help of foundations, associations, archives and videotheques that gave me access to their collections, among others the Albert Kahn Foundation, the Forum des Images (formerly the videotheque de Paris) that gave me the status of Chercheur Associé (Autumn 2000), the Association d'Amitié Franco-Vietnamienne, the Ecole Louis Lumière and Mr. Thé, the BIFI, bibliothèque du film à Paris, where I was able to read important documents and scenarios from archives, Catherine Dussart Productions for lending me documents on Rithy Panh, Lazennec Productions, Mars films, Renn films and Eric Heuman and JBA (Jean Luc Bidou) productions, Jean de Calan, the Ateliers Varan and Chantal Roussel.

I wish to express my gratitude to the following, for their long and unfailing support over the years it took to write the book: first of all, my thanks to Jacqueline Stora-

Burstin for giving us a warm place in Paris, over the years, not to mention her counsel. Thanks also to Denise and Camille Cholot, to my father and Sarah and to Mark A. Reid who keeps pushing me. I also wish to express my thanks to Geneviève Zondervan for giving me some of her time, rare books from her collection and contacts with some of the film-makers.

Thanks in particular to Khan Hung Ding Chu, a student from Vietnam, now living in the US. Thanks to Lotta Rao for her proofreading job, and to Sujata Varma for editing the manuscript. Thanks for the technical support I have received over the years from Eric Sanders. Thanks to my friends and relatives for their understanding on both sides of the Atlantic and Pacific. My thanks to Del Cullen and Yoram Allon for their patient editing.

For Mark.

INTRODUCTION

For many Western nations Vietnam still symbolises the rallying cry of the 1960s and it exists as a country that has come to embody a national fight for freedom and independence.[1] European and Western powers fought long wars in Indochina, and destroyed many of its people in the name of ideology. The vast destruction of the American conflict did not end until 1975 with the withdrawal of US troops from Saigon, and the earlier European conflict ceased in 1954, with the defeat of the French army at Diên Biên Phû. The repercussions of these wars echo through the Indochinese diaspora, and the effects are still present in the infrastructure of the countries of origin, such as the results of large amounts of exfoliate spread over the land of Vietnam, and the still-deadly landmines there and in Cambodia.[2] A large diasporic group of Vietnamese and Cambodian people now live outside their respective countries – the largest concentration is located in the US, with about 1 million Vietnamese immigrants.

In 1990, France officially reported 4.19 million immigrants (Tribalat 1996b: 64). A person born abroad, who resides in France and has acquired French citizenship, is still considered an 'immigrant' in the census. Children of immigrants and 'second-generation' children whose parents were born in France amount to 4.4 million and 5.3 million respectively, and all are classified as French (*Ibid.*). Asians in France, originating from such diverse countries as China, Vietnam, Cambodia and Turkey, formed 12.5 per cent of the immigrant population in the 1999 census (Insee 2001) and are a rising group, with 8 per cent in 1990 compared to 5 per cent in 1982 (Tribalat 1996b: 65).

Ignoring the displacements and repercussions of these wars would amount to burying one's head in the sand. For French (or American) children who were born after the 1960s, Vietnam no longer signifies what it did for their parents and grandparents, who have been referred to as the 'génération Vietnam' (Guillebaud 1993: 14).

However, if the 1960s image of Vietnam has been shelved away or historicised, a series of films and a vast body of literature have recently emerged from both East and West and have put Vietnam, Cambodia and other South East Asian countries back on the contemporary (cultural) map. Commemorations now point to the opening of Vietnam to the West and possibly the strengthening of a French presence in Asia. This book concerns itself with the renewal of interest in South East Asia; is it, as historian Benjamin Stora (1992) proposes, a symbolic closure of the mourning process over the loss of the colonies, or the opening of these countries and the reclamation of their autonomy and legitimacy, after the fall of the Berlin wall and the end of Stalinism?

We will examine the renewal of the relations between a segment of the former French Empire called Indochina and its colonisers, as seen under the cinematic and literary magnifying lens. Our study is mostly concerned with the decade of the 1990s, as it witnessed a re-emergence of fiction and ensuing scholarship about the East. Many scholars have previously turned their attention to the historical and socio-political situation of Indochina or Vietnam during colonial times (see Yoshiharu Tsuboi 1987). For instance, Lisa Lowe's *Critical Terrains* (1991) compares Orientalist practices in British and French literature, while Panivong Norindr (1996) explores the construction of Indochina as a phantasmic Eurocentric projection since the nineteenth century, through French literature, film and architecture and increasingly, now, through Franco-Vietnamese films. Marie-Paule Ha's study (2000) proposes an off-centre reading of the Asian 'other' in metropolitan (French) literature, and Penny Edwards (1998) concentrates on male and female relations in colonial Cambodia. An anthology covering various configurations of Vietnam in literature and devoting two segments to cinema, focusing on Tran Anh Hung and Lam Lê's films, was published in 2001 (Bradley, Ollier & Ollier 2001). A study of *Cyclo* (Tran Anh Hung, 1995) by J. Paul Narkunas (2001) appears in an anthology devoted to urban spaces in the global era.

This book maps out the more recent filmic, and occasionally literary, relations between East and West, limiting itself to France on the Western side and mostly Vietnam and Cambodia on the Eastern, with a few extraterritorial incursions. This particular area of study is not yet established in film history books, and is still developing. One type of film covered in this study has been categorised by some as 'third cinema' (Gabriel 1989), as 'cinema from the periphery' (Hayward 1993) and more recently as an 'accented cinema' (Naficy 2001). My purpose is not to write an exhaustive historical survey of all the films produced by Franco-Asian directors or French directors about Asia, but rather my interest in this area of French cultural and postcolonial studies is primarily to initiate a dialogue between recent films and other texts, ranging from fiction to documentaries.

Unusually, the vast and rich artistic/intellectual production coming from the Indochinese diaspora is the leading popular conduit for disseminating cultural/political/socio-economic information about the former colony. For instance, spectators – before watching *Indochine* (Régis Wargnier, 1992) or *Cyclo* – were not necessarily readers of fiction by Pierre Loti, André and Clara Malraux, Andrée Viollis or Linda Lê. I do not claim that these same spectators are going to read up on Vietnam or Cambodia and its people after watching the series of films that were released in 1992–93. However, a large audience fosters the renewed interest in the literature and media on the subject that flourishes today. Or maybe it is the other way around. In a market economy, books and films are commodities and are often treated as such – that is, as objects of desire that must generate profit and a consumer desire for more. Some publishing houses in the West focus and specialise entirely on the Orient. In fact, books written by Vietnamese writers are more readily available in the West than in the East. Editions Kailash ('Editions et diffusion de livres sur l'Asie'), for example, based in Paris and Pondicherry, India, are reprinting some of the early travel narratives as well as publishing books spanning the entire Asian continent, from India to Vietnam. Philippe Picquier, based in Arles, publishes a collection of recent Vietnamese prose in translation, and Sudestasie, based in Paris, produces books in French and Vietnamese among other South East Asian languages. Paris is now not only a base for Asian publishing and film-making but also for the music industry originating in the Asian community, further extending the influence and impact of Asian culture and art (Raulin 2000: 192).

A similar phenomenon is taking place in North America with the publication of Asian series, such as that produced by Penguin. At the same time, French writers coming from the 'majority population' have recently ventured into a fictional colonial Indochina with, for example, Régine Deforges, Christophe Bataille, and Jean-Luc Coatalem, among others.[3] They constitute signposts of a new Orientalist wave.

In their approach to postcolonial French cultures, Alec G. Hargreaves and Mark McKinney (1997) distinguish three different groups in the French population. The first group is based in the former colonial periphery; the second group is composed of minorities of Third World (ex-colonial) origin, now settled in France; and the third group is the 'majority population'. French children of the 'majority population', growing up in a now largely multi-ethnic society (above all in the larger cities), are accustomed to relating to people of different ethnic ancestry, be they of North African, Sub-Saharan, Middle Eastern, Far Eastern, or South Pacific origins. The French are familiar with migrant communities and sometimes participate in their 'rituals'. What used to be 'exotic' has now become 'ethnic', and if one were to accept Anne Raulin's sociological investigation of ethnic consumption, signs of the exotic have become common at least in certain parts of France: 'The exotic is today a daily practice for the city dweller. It is now part of his habits and representations; it somehow became popular' (2000: 9–10). Immigrant communities, detached from their place of origin, are now reactivating or cultivating an 'ethnic visibility' that Raulin locates in the third generation of immigrants. She devotes one chapter of her study to the Parisian Asian community's media consumption and the importance of images conveyed in the culture.

Thus a sizeable segment of France's population consists of people of Asian origins and their children, be they first-, second- or third-generation. Asian migrations to France took place in two waves: the first wave was linked to decolonisation and was between 1945–54; the second wave was the result of the Cold War, between 1965–75, when Communist regimes settled in Cambodia, Vietnam and Laos (Fourgeau 1998: 7). Based in the (former) immigrant population and their children, an entire generation of European-Asian artists has emerged in countries including Belgium, Switzerland and Germany, absorbed with various art forms like dance, painting, sculpture, fiction, documentary, experimental films, music and photography, that more often than not plunge deeply into their parents' or ancestors' past and identity. 'Postcolonial cultures are indeed implicitly defined, even if only antithetically, with reference to current or former relations among former imperial nations and their overseas dominions' (Hargreaves & McKinney 1997: 5). The Franco-Asian community, in its diasporic position, remains connected to its European or American diasporic counterparts and its country of origins. The circulation of people between France, the United States, Canada, and now Vietnam, constitutes a network of informational exchange that historian Georges Boudarel likens to capillaries (1988: 254). Concurrently a circulation of images and texts accompany these movements, along with increased electronic travelling. Some of the most visible representatives of Asian cultures in France are located on the Internet with, for example, the webzine Eurasie which covers art exhibitions, conferences, books and courses pertinent to the Asian world.[4]

The example of a Vietnamese (script) writer who lives in France and California, and is able to navigate between these two experiences, is not uncommon; transnational travel and exchanges are common among diasporic and exilic communities. The segment of population that travels back and forth is not limited to an intellectual elite. Distance does not break the ties between communities. When relocated, members of the community will characteristically adapt to the country of adoption yet will always maintain a Vietnamese 'character' (see Hoàng Bich Son in Boudarel 1988: 249–50).[5]

The French Republican colonial ideals encouraged assimilation over exclusion; yet they are not all-inclusive in France. If I am reluctant to apply the (all-American) grid based on the old binaries of colour/race, East/West, North/South, my goal is to identify and analyse some of the artistic contributions of Franco-Asian citizens, or people of Vietnamese, Laotian and Cambodian origins living in France. These ethnic differences are intensified in critical discourses, as I will demonstrate in this study, yet film history books tend to overlook any discussion of films made by Franco-Asian directors. Such boundaries and labels will ultimately collapse and disappear from our maps in the not-so-distant future. However, as historical and present considerations inform us, racial differentiation and profiling have been present since the beginning of French colonisation, if not before, and their effects endure. As Max Silverman suggests in his study of France, racial discourses have moved from nineteenth-century preoccupations with racial purity and hierarchy towards those based on cultural difference and cultural essentialism, the point at which one confronts Etienne Balibar's notion of 'racism without races' (Silverman 1999: 44–5). Looking at this very difference as it is practiced today will help us to locate diasporic identities and discourses in terms of the space they occupy in France. The suggestive term of hybridity best designates that particular position. It is urgent, in view of the increased racism in France, or the multiple faces it is taking, to be aware of some of the problems that have paved French history and which resurfaced around the turn of the millennium. French social scientist Michel Wieviorka reminds us that 'European racism was formed, even before it received its present name, out of the encounter with the Other – most often a dominated Other (colonialism) – and out of the invention, against the background of the rise of nationalisms, of modern anti-Semitism' (1991: 5). This preoccupation with growing xenophobia is not absent from the Franco-Asian world. In autumn 1983, an anti-racist march (and movement) took place in Paris and united France's minorities. This march for equality and against racism has been called the 'Beurs march', yet was composed of many of France's ethnic groups, including members of the Franco-Asian community.[6] Kim Lefèvre sends a warning call at the end of her autobiographical novel, *Métisse blanche*, the story of a biracial person who grows up in Vietnam and decides to emigrate to France:

> What Vietnam had refused me, France gave to me; it welcomed me and accepted me … If I say that I am Vietnamese, people take me as such, if I tell them that I am French, they ask me about my origins: That's all. Of course, I do not forget that the racist currents directed against Maghrebian communities and maybe tomorrow, against Asian communities, are more and more numerous. (1989: 405)

When reading historical and/or travel accounts, missionaries' reports or fictionalised versions, the link forged between the colonised and coloniser does not simply translate into a one-way monolithic relation. The colonial text and film inform the reader that the colony urgently required the arrival of the French in order to prosper from an otherwise apathetic, degenerative condition; the French colonial order apparently brought everything that the Indochinese people lacked and more. The grand oeuvre of France was primarily conducted as an exploratory and pacifying mission of a region that was seemingly 'constantly at war' with its neighbours (Russier 1931: 116).

One of my underlying claims that runs throughout this book is that France and Europe were, and still are, to learn and gain from the East. But that knowledge cannot be gauged since it has taken place psychologically and we do not have the instruments to measure it. This 'something' resides in the realm of an intellectual and spiritual exchange. I use the word 'spiritual' in its broadest definition, expanding it to include Catholicism, but also Buddhism, Taoism and Zen. In this context, France's multi-ethnic, multi-cultural and, by extension, multi-religious nation, encompasses Catholic churches but also synagogues, temples, mosques and pagodas as significant places of worship. French television programming on Sunday mornings has for years featured programmes on Islam, Judaism and Buddhism, addressed to a general audience.[7] For several years now, France's leading magazines (*Nouvel Observateur*, *Le Point*) have devoted at least one issue a year to the effect and growth of Buddhism in France, which in the year 2000 counted approximately 2 million adepts and 5 million interested people.

Yet the encounter between East and West has been commodified. Vietnam, China, India, Japan, Tibet and Thailand exert a surprising fascination for the West. Although my intention is certainly not to collapse all these nations into one geographic area, it is worth noting that in France there is confusion concerning these places, that are conveniently amalgamated into a homogenous whole. French intellectuals of the 1970s would travel to China or Japan and publish their travel notes – a practice with its origins at the turn of the century or slightly before (Pierre Loti, for instance) and then again in the 1920s and 1930s. For some, the journey East meant (and still means) regeneration.

Roland Barthes, in *L'Empire des signes* (1970) proposes to imagine a fictional people, a Romanesque object in Japan that along its diverse signs can be read as a system. His book speaks of an East/West encounter, under the mode of resistance, producing an unrestrained passion for everything Japanese, although disavowing it from the start: 'The Orient is indifferent to me.'[8] However, his approach to China proves much less passionate (see 'Alors, la Chine?' (1974)).

Many intellectuals of the 1960s and 1970s suddenly took Asia as a model, which they immediately contrasted with the occidental model that they rejected. Gayatri Spivak explains this trend as a rejection of Western metaphysics:

> French theorists such as Derrida, Lyotard, Deleuze, and the like, have at one time or another been interested in reaching out to all that is not the West, because they have, in one way or another, questioned the millennially cherished excellencies of Western metaphysics: the sovereignty of the subject's intention, the power of predication and so on. (1988: 136)

Sinologist Jean Chesneaux contends that:

> China also met a basic aspiration ... which I would describe as political exoticism, that is, the tendency to look for a political homeland

and model of reference in distant, exotic countries. At times in Cuba, at one time in Algeria, in Vietnam, then in China; each provided a substitute for the ideal society France was unable to develop at home, especially after the failure of the May '68 movement. (1987: 12)

Vietnam is never too far from these philosophers' preoccupations, and if its borders were closed, in the eyes of the profane, its political situation was then comparable to China. There have been many interrogations and extrapolations on Chinese culture, women or language. Roland Barthes (1974) and Julia Kristeva (1974) were also among the first French observers of a Chinese society in transformation. In cinema, Louis Malle would travel to Asia and try to grasp Indian society with several films. He would subsequently move to the US, and devote several films to its Vietnamese and Laotian immigrant community (*Alamo Bay* (1985); *And the Pursuit of Happiness* (1987)).

Barthes' reflection on Japan turns the country and its characteristics into a tautological imaginary unit called the 'Orient'. Lisa Lowe has argued that both Barthes and Kristeva, despite their obvious anti-colonialist politics, were somehow orientalising the East, in reverse. Following this same perspective, but in a different mode, Duras' texts located in Calcutta (*Le Vice-consul*, 1965; *India Song*, 1973) are nothing more than a way out of discussing Indochina by transposing it to India.

The earliest colonial venture of the French into Vietnam intended to go to China and conquer it. Vietnam (Indochina) was only a gateway to the future French empire in Asia. Francis Garnier, the navy officer, on his mission to Indochina, was exploring ways of entering China through the Mekong before the English could do so (see Franchini 1994: 21). Similarly, India counted French territories in Bangale, Madras and other areas.[9]

What some critics have termed an appropriation of the Orient still constitutes the strategies of many writers or film-makers, and inevitably results in a self-reflexive stage, where the country becomes a mirror for the writer. Pierre Loti's opening remarks about writing *Madame Chrysanthème* (1885), the story of his summer in Japan and marriage to a Japanese woman, insist that his three main characters in that text are 'me, Japan and the effect that this country has produced on me'. Contrary to the intimations of the title, his intentions are not to discuss the Japanese woman. His visions of late nineteenth-century Nagasaki remain forever tinged with his own preoccupations, his 'spleen' and his foreignness. He tries to understand the country but more often than not criticises it for what 'he' thinks it means. The system of signs offered him is sometimes undecipherable. There is also a fear of disappearing within the system that manifests itself at various intervals. Both Loti and Barthes share common ground; one example is the apparent ability (and audacity) to understand a system, and a language, after only a short stay, and acquiring a few rudiments of the language. Both also fear contamination by the Other's system, fear their own systems being corrupted, cannibalised and radically changed, and fear becoming other. As travellers, they cannot resist the need to decipher signs in what I will call 'cultural texts' and vignettes ranging from food to architecture, smoking and performances. Their designated position essentially inscribes the 'us versus them' discourse.

In view of this, I believe that the West should rethink its position with the East, and specifically its former colonies, but not necessarily in terms of binaries. Barthes denounced the lack of understanding of the Orient by the West, and the appalling misinformation, but he also aptly signaled the learning that one could gain from studying it. He fails to explain how he could decipher these signs without knowing how to read the language.

Many Western critics share the fact that the Orient transforms them and changes their life by suggesting a new consciousness and an introspective look into oneself. This approach has not exactly ceased. Luce Irigaray's recent study, *Entre Orient et Occident* (1999), testifies to a profound transformation in her thinking, and a turn to Eastern philosophies. Régis Airault's *Fous de l'Inde*, ('Crazy about India', 2000) interrogates the attraction as well as the consequences experienced by Westerners when they visit India. André Malraux, in the 1920s, suggested a transformative process but modulated the outcome. 'The object of the quest of Western youth is a new notion of man. Can Asia teach us? I do not think so. Rather, it can show us who we are.'[10]

The question of one's positioning is crucial. To illustrate this, one might ask such questions as who is speaking in Kristeva's *Des Chinoises* or in Barthes' text on Japan, *L'Empire des signes*. What is the position of the critic/intellectual from the West when approaching these works? Indeed, in my own case, what should be the position of a Western-taught French academic, living outside France in the US when approaching these texts?

My examination of the return to/of Asia in French national cinema crisscrosses different fields and does not follow a singular path. For example, this book has a sociological perspective; it practices close film and textual analysis, including some novels, sometimes venturing into psychoanalysis and music. It also examines recent French modes of film production. The overall perspective is feminist, or 'womanist', as it pays attention to the treatment of women, in general, by the respective directors under scrutiny. The first part explores the 1992 release of two blockbusters, *Indochine* and *L'Amant* (*The Lover*, Jean-Jacques Annaud) next to the earlier film model that I select in *Emmanuelle* (Just Jaekin, 1974). Both 1992 films celebrate a moment of splendor and empire-building located in the 1930s, yet they gloss over the fall of the Empire. These epic sagas constitute cultural events or markers of the 1990s. I contrast them with two other fictions stemming from the French colonial past located in Africa, directed by female directors: *Chocolat* (Claire Denis, 1988) and *Out-remer* (*Overseas*, Brigitte Rouan, 1990). These two directors cast a seemingly critical look on France's colonial past in their semi-autobiographical texts.

The second and third chapters cover immigrant film-making from diasporic artists, first scanning the early career of Lam Lê, whose contribution, in terms of postcolonial French cinema, is crucial. His position is that of an in-between, or a 'passeur' negotiating between two cultures, France and Vietnam. *Rencontre des nuages et du dragon* (1979) and *Poussière d'empire* (1983) are critically and culturally analysed.

Next, an analysis of Tran Anh Hung's *L'Odeur de la papaye verte* (*The Scent of Green Papaya,* 1993) is offered. I approach the film-maker who is now considered the voice of Franco-Asian cinema, yet represented Vietnam at the Oscar ceremony. This chapter explores the cinematography of the film and its implicit messages, as well as the critical response that this first film generated in France and abroad. I subsequently look at his second feature film, *Cyclo*, where a literal return to Vietnam took place. Both films are contrasted in terms of production and reception. My reading considers critical responses stemming from the Asian community in France, culled from letters to the editor, reviews, and a recent, yet short-lived, French journal, *Cyclo*. The chapter concludes with Tran's film *A la verticale de l'été* (2000), also released in the United States.

Various documentary films made in France about Vietnam present resistance voices to dominant discourse or open an interrogation into the way Vietnam has been represented. Some of these are lesser-known films, yet they are accessible to the public. One of the film-makers studied here is Robert Kramer, an American who lived in Paris until his death in 1999. His 1993 film, *Starting Place*, constitutes another 'return' to a country that has deeply touched the film-maker's life. The last part of the chapter focuses on Vietnamese dissident writer Duong Thu Huong, whose texts have influenced writers and film-makers discussed in this project.

The chapter entitled 'Khmer Memories' is devoted to the contribution of Cambodian documentary film-maker, Rithy Panh. I examine some of his films, such as *Les Gens de la rizière* (*Rice People,* 1995) and look at the way he is working out his own traumatic past. As an exiled film-maker living in France, Panh continually negotiates between two cultures. My study goes into the financing of his films, as it has been the focus of different criticisms. An interview with the film-maker is transcribed in an appendix that closes the book.

The Conclusion proposes to look at the tropes of métissage and translation acts that take place in the films discussed but also in literature from diasporic writers. My approach is informed by Trinh T. Minh-ha's theories about translation practices in film-making. The chapter articulates theories about métissage as it weaves itself culturally in the literary texts of two contemporary French women writers from the Vietnamese Diaspora, Linda Lê and Kim Lefèvre. Literature is explored at different intervals throughout the book, as most films plunge into legends, myths or travel narratives at the core of the film-makers' culture. The last part interprets the various translating acts that arise in the films and novels under focus, and questions the positions that are assigned to film-makers of the diaspora as well as the position that French cinema has taken in a postcolonial era.

CHAPTER ONE

A Return

For general Western spectatorship, Vietnam does not exist outside of
the war. And she no longer exists since the war has ended, except as a
name, an exemplary model of revolution, or a nostalgic cult object for
those who, while admiring unconditionally the revolution, do not seem
to take any genuine, sustained interest in the troubled reality of Vietnam
in her social and cultural autonomy. The more Vietnam is mystified, the
more invisible she becomes. (Trinh T. Minh-ha 1992: 100)

Indochina is back on the map, or at least France as a whole has finally decided
to look back on its past in colonial Indochina. A series of novels and films
– avant-garde, documentary and reportage – have appeared, projecting images
of that part of Asia in France and outside. Novels are published that are written
by Vietnamese writers; some of these writers live in Vietnam, and their books
are first translated then published in France. A new generation of Franco-
Vietnamese writers, painters, photographers and performance artists is finding
its voice and offering new readings and interventions in France's multi-cultural
and multi-ethnic population. An extensive study devoted to early Vietnamese
novels written in French rightly deplores the lack of exposure of some of the early
writers who were already producing in the 1950s and 1960s (Yeager 1987: 87).

French production houses and government-funded agencies are backing
the productions of film-makers of Vietnamese or Cambodian origins living
in the diaspora, some of whom are second-generation children born to
Vietnamese or Cambodian immigrants. There is renewed interest in the region
that hosted the Francophone Congress in November 1997 (Hanoi) and which

is now part of the ASEAN organisation. Some of its aspects borrow from the rhetoric of 'francophonie', attempting to establish that French is still spoken in Vietnam, Cambodia or Laos, and the ties linking these countries earlier in the century were never broken off. The term 'francophonie' is best defined as the 'group of people who can express themselves and communicate in French, ultimately, it is a cultural and moral ideal, about a métisse creativity, dialogue and synthesis' (Frandjis & Cassan 1997: 13). Some of the most glamorous films made by nostalgic film-makers participate in this rhetoric, lamenting the loss of a country for which France was the 'mother'. We will first approach three films that celebrate the elegiac moment of return that I have deliberately located in the early 1990s, since it was during 1992 that cameras seemed to converge on the East.

In 1992, Vietnam became the locus of three major French films, with the release of Jean-Jacques Annaud's *L'Amant*, Régis Wargnier's *Indochine,* and Pierre Schoendoerffer's *Diên Biên Phû*. Many reviews noted the convergence of interest. French scriptwriters, film-makers and production houses had negotiated a return to France's colonial past, involving a collaboration with Vietnamese authorities and film crews that was unprecedented since the independence of the country. Earlier Franco-Indochinese film productions typically took place in colonial times (with Parisian companies financing a number of films in 1935) but only on a minor scale (Sadoul 1949: 487).

Vietnam's *doi moi* (renovation) politics reopened its borders to Western trade, and despite the American economic embargo that ended in 1994, the French nation resumed collateral trade beginning with President Mitterrand's visit in February 1993. Tourism in Vietnam is increasing, with two million tourists visiting the country in 2000–01. The 'Maison de l'Indochine' in Paris offers travel brochures and tours to 'mysterious Indochina' and in spring 1998 housed part of a large exhibition of paintings and photographs by Vietnamese artists, Le Printemps vietnamien. The Maison de l'Indochine is now paired with the Maison de la Chine; both are located on the prestigious Place St. Sulpice (Paris). It is conveniently called the Orientalist House.

Recent postcolonial screen representations of the French colonial experience in Indochina meet at a particular moment, the 1980s and early 1990s. However, this return to a colonial time in Indochina has largely been neglected or is absent from earlier French commercial pictures, with only a few exceptions. Discussions of films about colonial Indochina are remarkably absent from film history books. For example Pierre Boulanger devotes most of his study of colonial cinema to films shot in the Maghreb region (*Le Cinéma colonial* (1975)).

In the Anglophone film world, critics have also observed a recent 'wave of elegiac narratives about the closing of the imperial period' (Shohat & Stam 1994: 123). The attempt to theorise about filmic representations of colonial Indochina encompasses several discourses and compels one to reconsider the history of 'orientalisms' or the European fascination with, and appropriation of, the Orient. In *Critical Terrains*, Lisa Lowe investigates the different aspects of French and British Oriental discourses in literature from the eighteenth century on. Distinguishing differences between the French and British situations, she argues, in the footsteps of Edward Said, that French orientalism has a long tradition in literature that preceded some of its manifestations and that 'colonialism is often not named or addressed' in such texts (1991: 107).

The Albert Kahn project and the shaping of the East/West gaze

Before turning to the 1990s films *Indochine* and *L'Amant*, we will briefly examine some of the early films and pictograms originating from Europe, looking in at Asia. Albert Kahn's technicians shot the first films ever made in Indochina in the 1920s. Entire crews of ethnographers travelled to the region to record views of 'native' inhabitants and their customs. Similarly, the Lumière family sent entire teams to collect films of far-away places as well as to project early Western films. The first Vietnamese movie house, which opened in Hanoi in 1920, was a Pathé frères theatre (Kanapa 1989: 287). Film historian Pierre Leprohon believes 'colonial' documentaries lacked in foresight and design and were 'scenes recorded by rushed travellers, general vistas deprived of originality, or without power' (1945: 232). Yet he noted that the resident general of Indochina, Albert Sarrault, created a special cinematographic mission, destined to record pictures of people and landscapes, and to show films to the native population. This mission covered the different regions of Annam, Tonkin and Cambodia.

The film collection found at the Albert Kahn museum in Boulogne sur Seine spells out how early film form and narrative relayed and captured Eastern images and tailored, or 'framed', them for the Western imagination. Kahn, a Jewish Alsatian banker, was instrumental in preserving photographic and filmic images of the world in a large collection. Between 1910 and 1931, Kahn sent teams of operators to 48 countries. After his bankruptcy in the 1929 crash, his Boulogne mansion was sold and his collection scattered, and it was only in 1974 that museum curator Jeanne Beausoleil started to work on his collection, rehabilitating 72,000 autochrome images (glass plates) – a process that had been invented by the Lumière brothers in 1907 – with 170,000 metres of films. The gallery, named 'Les Archives de la Planète', opened to the public in 1990. Some of the archives are thematically organised around sociopolitical events, arts and culture, religions, costumes, transportation and habitat. This archival project could not see completion owing to Kahn's bankruptcy, which meant that large areas of the world were left unrecorded. Kahn, a private man, had a passion for the arts; he knew and associated with such artists as sculptor Auguste Rodin and composers Vincent D'Indy and Manuel de Falla. He remained a lifelong friend of Henri Bergson, who had been his professor, and died in his house in 1940 just as the Vichy laws about the special Jewish status had been voted (see de Roux 1995).

France's colonial venture in the regions that were to become part of the Confédération Indochinoise started in the middle of the nineteenth century. Missionaries had already travelled to the area much earlier. According to historian Marc Ferro, three forces were behind the colonisation of the region: the church, traders (in such as silk and weaponry), and a rampant Anglophobia that could be found in the navy, especially with Francis Garnier, one of the French naval commanders (Ferro 1994: 145). Asia had been, by and large, the territory of British colonisation, with India the 'jewel in the crown'. Yet by 1885, the Confédération Indochinoise had become official, and counted one colony and four protectorates – Cambodia and Laos included. Contrary to other French colonies, Indochina was not a settlement colony – as was the case for Algeria, for instance.

Cinematographers and ethnographers, whose practices started around the same time, at the end of the nineteenth century, were inspired by the urge to preserve, collect and archivise the world; their enthusiasm to go out and record shots of 'primitive' people was strong. The recorded images could be transported, and shown to an audience whose Western position and centrality remain evident. These moments, according to Marc Henri Piault, remove the various obstacles of time and distance in the technician's recollections:

> The animated image ... captures a transitory duration, and goes beyond the subjectivity of travellers' suspicious testimony; it takes away from the vagaries of memory: the fleeting lived moments, and the singularities and differences of the Other, become transportable and therefore, can be observed at wish, like the Luxor obelisk, Egyptian mummies, or Parthenon frescoes. (2000: 10)

The appointed head of the archives, geographer Jean Brunhes, a professor at the Collège de France, designated Léon Busy as the chief operator to be the permanent correspondent in Indochina. Bruhnes shared Kahn's passion for human geography, and his book *Géographie Humaine* (1910) attempts to describe human activity and habitat in order to classify it. He favoured the medium of photography and called himself a 'geo-photographer'.

The archives, now open to the public, present the earliest snapshots and moving pictures of Indochina. A lengthy research project entirely devoted to the archives has been conducted by Paula Ahmad.[1] A segment entitled 'undressing and dressing of a young Vietnamese woman', taken in 1921, specifies that the 'operator deliberately shot this scene blurred'.[2] During this short sequence of 1 minute 7 seconds, a static camera faces a young Tonkinese woman while she is undressing, appears nude, then quickly gets dressed again. One of the focuses is on her hairpiece, a sort of long scarf. The film-maker has opted for a deliberately blurred shot yet the entire scene is more revealing of Western voyeurism about a female native than an interest in science. There are, of course, many ways of reading this film text and, in retrospect, the camera does more than record images; it puts together a 'narrative' that entails the subject photographed and the person behind the camera, not to mention the audience for whom these films were destined to be screened. The composition of the shot is not altogether different from the more recent *mise-en-scène* of the young Vietnamese female character whose breast is unveiled by a male protagonist in Wargnier's *Indochine*. Fatimah Tobing Rony's discussion of the same archives intimates that such scenes showed 'that the body landscaped was not only racialised but gendered … It is clear that the absolute voyeurism and scopic possession of the native female body was palatable to a white audience; if conducted on the white female body, the same technique would have been declared pornographic' (1996: 82). A similar voyeurism is recorded in recently printed archival documents, with a presentation of nude pictures of Cochin-chinese and Moi women, printed along with the 1882 report of A. T. Mondière entitled 'Monographie de la femme de Cochinchine'. Mondière, a doctor, would measure women's breasts, collect their temperature, inquire on their sexuality, and 'studied' 1,244 women in the region (Borgé & Viasnoff 2001: 98–104).

Inderpal Grewal, while studying the influence of landscape on nineteenth-century travel narratives, has denounced the fact that indigenous people were not considered as individuals: 'What is noticeable in the passages from nineteenth-century travel narratives that include the description of foreign landscapes as beautiful is that the people of these lands are not seen as beautiful' (1996: 44). Instead, these countries appear as 'blank spaces that await the colonizer' (*Ibid.*). When it comes to Asian women, they are usually, if portrayed, seen in erotic poses and have to be civilised and stripped of their veil. This practice is now commonplace in film.

The sequence described is unique to the collection and therefore stands out. The focus of the collection classically rests on rituals, ceremonies, and street scenes. Another segment, a ritual ceremony to the gods, points to the relationship between land and people. Many people are shot in a frontal position, looking at the camera, a forbidden look in narrative films with, for instance, street scenes including a large crowd (#143),[3] shot in Indochina (1921).

A large portion of the films Léon Busy shot in Phnom Penh, Cambodia, involve the royal palace dance troupe and the Apsaras 'Royal classical khmer dancers at the Royal Palace' (1921). These dances feature some of the longest segments to be shot by Busy, with one sequence lasting 16 minutes, and came to embody the entire Cambodian nation, often being used to represent their country abroad. Scenes of daily life in Cambodia and Vietnam cover rice-growing, fishing and street scenes. The visit to the town of Angkor Vat attests to Busy's interest in architecture. One of these segments was reportedly shot during the 'colonial week'. The catalogue description of these scenes reflects predominantly Eurocentric concerns: 'For the colonial week, 1,200 bonzes are going up the pagoda in these famous ruins and enact[ing] a ceremony in honour of France.'

A steady camera captures a large crowd going up the stairs then moving to a courtyard where people are praying. The title indicates a 'Buddhist ceremony to honour France in a 3rd level gallery of the sanctuary' (Cambodia #159). A 1925 Madrolle tour guide praised the French mission for successfully renovating the ancient temple that had been abandoned: 'The site of Angkor Thom, the ancient Khmer capital, was abandoned for five centuries. Its monuments were invaded by vegetation until 1908 when the archeological section of the Ecole d'Extrême Orient was requested, by the Indochinese government, to preserve these medieval constructions.'[4]

Angkor Vat, and the fascination for its ceremonies or its architecture found in the films, confirms the tone and message present in Pierre Loti's contemporary travel narrative in Cambodia *Un Pélerin d'Angkor* ('A Pilgrim from Angkor', 1912). The last images of the Archives of the Planet appeared in 1928, for after this date Kahn could no longer afford to send his operators outside France. Ironically, the last moments of Asian life captured by his operators were seized at the 1931 Exposition coloniale of Vincennes, with shots of Angkor Vat, in its (partial) reproduction format, with images of Asian women as well as the temple by night. Kahn would eventually have to acquire footage from other companies to continue his collection.

A question relating to these early silent films: did the cinematographer have his 'actors' perform, and re-enact scenes according to his direction, or were people comfortable enough with the camera that they could perform their ceremonies and undress? The debate surrounding the Lumière brothers and Georges Méliès in the context of early cinematography (which has been called 'primitive') is informative in view of what were considered the first documentary films. Louis and Auguste Lumière, who shot the earliest documentary footage of their factory workers leaving work, apparently also directed them, having prepared them for the coming event. Workers did leave the factory but all dressed up in their Sunday best. Composition and *mise-en-scène* went through careful elaboration. Watching these early ethnographic films and stills made in Indochina is a lesson in orientalism and exoticism that unveils early attempts to appropriate the native and construct his/her image. Barthes' critique of ethnographical expeditions 'as object and site of the myth of exoticism' (*Mythologies*, 1957), pointed out this aspect (cited in Lowe 1991: 154).

Boosting the interest in the colony

The French population was not particularly enthusiastic about colonial Indochina at the turn of the twentieth century and, because of this apathy, the government took several measures to foster and stimulate the interest in going overseas. If French children had to memorise colonial geography with names of rivers, towns and people from distant lands, 'the French rarely heard of the colonies which were never mentioned at political meetings and were generally forgotten by the daily papers or the radio. Some magazines published good illustrated reports but they were expensive and, until the Second World War, few people bought them' (Sorlin 1991: 135). Film houses, museums and colonial exhibitions remained the preferred channels, where the outside world could find a way into the French person's experience, and transport them outside France. The 1931 colonial exhibition constituted a grand lesson addressed to the French public about the colonial effort. In his inaugural discourse, Maréchal Lyautey reformulated the goal of colonial conquest: 'Colonial conquest … is a working organisation. It works at manifesting strength in order to avoid its use; its goal must not be the destruction of one's opponent, but his attraction.'[5]

In other words, French colonial policy was not antagonistic to the colonised, but on the contrary praised itself for attracting the natives and seducing them into French-style colonisation. That claim was further supported by the argument that French colonisers were 'beautiful'. In his geo-political study of the region conducted in the 1930s, Henri Russier boasts that:

> France may not have the most beautiful colonies in the world but she can boast some of the most beautiful colonisers. They are, however, in Asia or Africa, a small elite that has been able to combine Latin fervor with a tenacious reflection, and Anglo-Saxon boldness, while adding a warm soul, and a gift of sympathy so unique to the French race. (1931: 114)[6]

Commentators did remark on the lack of French films made in the 1930s on Indochina:

> The absence of fictions on Indochina is surprising since France spent a large amount of money on its Far Eastern territories and since French business was prosperous there. It would be incorrect to say that the cinema ignored Asia. However the films which were made dealt only with China and Malaya, two countries which were of little importance for French trade and policy. (Sorlin 1991: 137)

These observations echo Geneviève Nesterenko's earlier essay 'L'Afrique de l'autre' (1986). Unfortunately, the Vietnamese response to these colonial films is not readily accessible. A rare 1984 article on Vietnamese cinema reported North Vietnamese president Ho Chi Minh's complaint, made in 1962, about the colonialists' use of picturesque images in films:

> Colonialists would use cinema to denigrate our people. Thus, at the Marseille exhibition, besides posters representing a crowd of Annamite Mandarins bowing in front of some puppet king and his big dog, the governor-general and resident, and bare-breasted coolies who would

push cyclos, there were films. In these films, one could see old women with lacquered teeth chewing betel leaves, emaciated peasants in rags, men climbing coconut trees, all these baptised Images of Annam.[7]

The representation of history in Indochina is seriously lacking in the narratives that we will discuss first. Instead of exposing the fabric of colonialism, the two stories instill feelings of intense nostalgia for something that eludes the spectator. These films expose directly the colonial situation from the position of the colonialist, whom Albert Memmi, in his analysis of the colonial situation, identifies as the 'the colonizer who agrees to be a colonizer … [He] agrees to legitimize colonization' (1965: 45). They espouse the discourse of colonialism but refuse to condemn it, and through their nostalgic rhetoric, the scenarios are infused with colonial mores, justifying the presence of French settlers and their superiority. A reviewer of *Indochine* denies this nostalgic perspective: 'To see in *Indochine* a nostalgic gaze on the colonial world would be a mistake. The film instead shows the inevitable break between France and Indochina, as shown by the two female characters' (Férenczi 1999: 138).[8] Forty years after the facts, Indochina still seduces spectators with its colonial charms, and feeds a fascination that is sometimes commercially exploited. The use of eroticism and sexual attraction among the races is inscribed in both scenarios, as well as the fascination for the other, be it a geographic or human landscape. Both *L'Amant* and *Indochine* are located at the historical juncture immediately preceding the end of the colonial era. Whereas most historians concur in identifying the first blows given to French colonisation at the time, in the 1930s, when the Vietnamese nationalist party was founded, both Wargnier and Annaud conclude with the physical departure of the French presence in South East Asia, even if the realisation of such a moment is not formally acknowledged on screen.

French historian Henri Rousso interrogates the function of memory in France after World War Two. According to his analysis, the 1970s witnessed the resurgence of lost memories, or what he calls 'the return of the repressed' – a process that culminated in 1974 (1987: 19). The need to purge the past is evidenced in cases like the Klaus Barbie trial, the Touvier affair, and in autumn 1997 and spring 1998, the Papon trial (the former, a Nazi war criminal, the latter two, French collaborators, all three diligent government officials responsible for the deportation of French Jews to Germany during World War Two), or more recently, the excavation of François Mitterrand's troubled background during Vichy times and the recognition of torture used by the French army in Algeria. France is still processing the conflict in Algeria, which continues to have repercussions in both countries.

Colonial history enters the chiaroscuro zone of France's repressed histories. Aside of Frantz Fanon's body of work on the subject, it is only recently that queries about colonial and postcolonial subjects have surfaced and that such history became part of the French high school curriculum. Kristin Ross's 1995 study of 1950s and 1960s French culture, *Fast Cars, Clean Bodies*, examines and reconciles the two otherwise separate histories, namely that of colonisation and decolonisation and that of modernisation in post-World War Two France. Few films in France have addressed colonisation from an objective historical standpoint, indicating the impossibility of dealing effectively with this specific past. French cinema counts few mainstream/commercial texts, films or novels on the war or colonial experience in Indochina and North and West Africa. The 'return to reality' – a trend qualified by film historian Roy Armes in his attempt to periodicise French cinema for the years 1969–74 (1985: 207) – seems only to be applicable to the parameters of the 'hexagon' – a name that designates France as seen through its geographic mapping.

Examples of more politicised films are to be found in independent productions both fictional and documentary, such as *Avoir 20 ans dans les Aurès* (René Vautier, 1972), *Le Petit Soldat* (Jean Luc Godard, 1960–63) – films that were either banned, and/or not widely distributed. *Loin du Vietnam* (*Far from Vietnam*, 1967), a collective film made by Chris Marker, Alain Resnais, Claude Lelouch, Joris Ivens, William Klein, Marceline Loridan, Agnès Varda and Michèle Ray might be the exception to this rule, as it exposes 'the problems of the war in Vietnam seen from Europe' (Armes 1985: 45). The film combines both documentary and fiction and is a product of the 1968 collective organising spirit. *Loin du Vietnam* denounces the American imperialist war in Vietnam and is definitely pro-North Vietnam. The voice-over commentaries attest to a deep solidarity with the Vietnamese people in their fight against the US government. Rare footage of protest demonstrations are shown taking place on Place de la Concorde in Paris. On the whole, the French past is represented in one brief 'flashback' sequence of newsreel images showing French soldiers leaving after Diên Biên Phû. Godard's *Letter to Jane* (1972) touches on Vietnam as it analyses a still photograph of Jane Fonda in Vietnam, for 45 minutes. Oblique references were made to these conflicts in Alain Resnais' *Muriel* (1964). If French cinema of the 1960s witnessed the rise of independent productions against the Vietnam War, it was mostly after the French withdrawal from Indochina. In Hollywood and America, documentary images of the Vietnam War coming from Europe and Vietnam were banned, and *Loin du Vietnam* was banned from the US. However, Vietnam 'prompted film-makers in many countries to produce advocacy works, almost all of them opposed to United States involvement' (Sklar 1993: 411). This may explain why an American film-maker like Robert Kramer is not included in most film history books.

It has taken approximately forty years for French mainstream cinema to approach the topic of decolonisation and its treatment in a non-oblique fashion. On the other hand, independent militant cinema in France has, since the 1950s, exposed the situation of colonisation and postcolonisation in Algeria, Africa and Indochina, mostly in documentary forms. Francophone African and Arab film-makers had targeted the history of colonialism and its products in postcolonial Africa and North Africa. In fact, many film projects were never produced because of their reflection on postcolonialism and colonialism and their dependency on French capital.

French cinema of the 1950s stands out as a stagnant period dominated by studio production that was heavily criticised by *Cahiers du cinema* critics for the emphasis on plot and literary adaptations.[9] Immediately after the war, when France reorganised its cinema to focus on literary adaptations, American productions that could not be seen during World War Two also started flooding the market. It was difficult for the younger generation of French film-makers to be too innovative, 'given the climate at the time of political immobilism and strong censorship, especially on what was happening in the colonies' (Hayward 1993: 159).

The 1960s witnessed a 63 per cent drop in attendance at theatres in the US, and Hollywood film production dropped dramatically, from a yearly average production of five hundred until World War Two to a total of studio-produced films of two hundred (Sklar 1993: 344). The French New Wave directors looked up to American directors and in a particular sense contributed to their revival in their articles and film quotes. Film critics of the *Cahiers* tradition admired Hollywood and B-movies' *mise-en-scène*, editing techniques and style, and tried to emulate some of the directors. Hollywood, on the other hand, was focused on developing new technology and not so much interested in 'auteur theory'. Hollywood approached Vietnam mostly with the war film genre in the late 1970s; the significant period being 1978–79 with *Coming Home* (Hal Ashby, 1978), *The Deer Hunter* (Michael Cimino, 1979) and *Apocalypse Now* (Francis Ford Coppola, 1979), not long after the American withdrawal. French film historian and theoretician Raymond Bellour distinguishes a rupture in classical American cinema that took place in the 1960s. Vietnam was one of the factors in the destabilisation of American cinema and its prestige overseas, and the fact that people started to look at its images differently (1980: 7–8).[10]

The treatment of colonialism in fiction films started in the late 1970s, a period of historical introspection for France, with films like *La Victoire en Chantant*, later renamed *Noirs et blancs en couleurs* (*Black and White in Colour*), a Jean-Jacques Annaud film (co-produced by France/Ivory Coast, best foreign film Oscar, 1977), where white settlers in Africa come into view through the merciless objective lens of the camera, Francis Girod's *L'Etat Sauvage* (*The Savage State*, 1977), and *Coup de Torchon* (*Clean Slate*, Bertrand Tavernier, 1981). All three films are set in West Africa and reveal some of the appalling aspects of French racism and the colonialist mentality.

Several recent films made by French women film-makers seemingly cast a critical look on the colonial era. Three women directors share the fact that they were born and grew in various parts of the empire and wrote about it before adapting their experience onto film. Ella Shohat and Robert Stam, in their study of eurocentrism, see these film-makers as re-examining the colonial situation:

> Some of the few critical colonial 'nostalgia' films which, interestingly, have been made by French women (Claire Denis' *Chocolat*, Marie-France Pisier's *Bal du Gouverneur*, and Brigitte Rouan's *Outremer*, all from 1990), shift their focus from male aggressivity to female domesticity, and to the glimmerings of anticolonialist consciousness provoked by transgression of the taboo on interracial desire. (1994: 123)

These female-oriented colonial scripts depart from the traditionally male-centred imperial narratives constitutive of Orientalism, yet the position of the female colonial is sometimes ambiguous or complacent about colonial rhetoric and practices.

Claire Denis, who grew up in Cameroon, wanted to explore white guilt, and *Chocolat* (1988) exemplifies the attempt to come to terms with the end of the colonial world. Stuart Hall's reading of the film has suggested that '*Chocolat* … may be the only kind of film European film-makers should be making about Africa just now. It may be time for Europeans to confront what colonisation has done to them rather than instantly taking on the white man's burden, once again, of speaking for the other' (1992: 51).

Chocolat is a story of a return to one's native land, seen from the ex-coloniser's perspective and recounted in the autobiographical mode. 'It was like writing a journal until I decided to add fictional elements to it' (Denis in Reid 1996: 68). A young French woman named France is travelling back to Cameroon. In one major flashback, the film reconstitutes a moment in her childhood immediately preceding independence. Although evoked only once, during the search for a native doctor found at a night school meeting, but mostly off-camera, the nationalist struggles for independence are foregrounded by several elements throughout the film. France fails to see her old house and never meets up with her childhood male servant ('boy') Protée, with whom she had a close but conflictual relationship as a child. The luxuriant landscape is visually explored and the film's present-tense journey becomes a pretext for rediscovering the past.

Entirely constructed in flashback, the last sequence shifts back to the present, jumping in time from the previous point of view shot, originating from a departing airplane's take off that carries Europeans away from the Mindif region. The temporal gap is bridged by Abdullah Ibrahim's smooth jazzy musical score (Ibrahim is from South Africa), juxtaposed to fast-moving images of the landscape.

Brigitte Rouan's first feature film, *Outremer*, proposes an incursion into the colonial geography of pre-independence Algeria, then a French department. The war between France and Algeria leading to the independence of Algeria started right after the war with Indochina in 1954. The Evian agreements would be signed in 1962, and the autobiographical signature is mediated through the perspectives of three sisters. The film's structure interestingly re-enacts several moments, seen from each woman's point of view. Almost a demonstration of the importance of point of view in films, the structure teaches the spectator how events can be seen, sometimes omitted, and interpreted differently according to the person who is seeing – a structure that is close to the French Nouveau Roman practice. Native Arab people are present though not given any large part in the film. The narrative focuses largely on three white adult women in a soon-extinct 'colonial féminin' world (see Portuges 1996). The powerful marked face of an older Algerian woman, Zohra, enters the frame twice. However, the sisters are unable to decipher her face or to engage in any dialogue. Her fleeting onscreen presence reveals just how much native women are excluded from these colonial narratives which are mostly preoccupied with the fate of white settlers, male or female or, as the American ad bluntly put it, 'The story of three women with man problems'.

In the 1980s, with feature films by francophone African film-makers, Maghrebian film-makers, and now Franco-Vietnamese film-makers like Tran Anh Hung, the production of postcolonial fictions and autobiographical testimonies was growing. As far as the treatment of colonial conflicts in South East Asia on film is concerned, Schoendoerffer remains the precursor, with *La 317e section* (*The 317th Platoon*, 1965), *Section Anderson* (*Anderson Platoon*, 1967), which deals with an American patrol in Vietnam, and *Le Crabe-Tambour* (*Drummer-Crab*, 1977). *Diên Biên Phû*, released in 1992, is the only film that stages the infamous battle where the French army was defeated in 1954. The Vietnamese government and film-makers collaborated on the making of the film.[11]

La 317e section was shot in Cambodia by cinematographer Raoul Coutard and benefited from the assistance of the Khmer army. Unlike the feminine worlds of Rouan and Denis, Schoendoerffer's space is largely male-dominated. *La 317e section* is structured around diary entries related to the life of a doomed French patrol a few days before the fall of Diên Biên Phû. Jacques Perrin, one of Schoendoerffer's favourite actors, who is now involved in producing and making films in Vietnam, plays young lieutenant Torrens, in charge of a native troop. On their way into North Laotian territory, he is assisted by the Alsatian soldier Wilsdorf, a character who resurfaces in *Le Crabe-Tambour*. Wilsdorf is one of the career soldiers who fought in Indochina, just as he fought in World War Two, and in the Russian campaign enlisted by the German army. Wilsdorf's career will eventually end in Algeria, the next armed conflict involving France. The postscript announces that 'the 317th Platoon is no longer' and that Wilsdorf will be killed in Algeria in 1960.

History is at the centre of Schoendoerffer's preoccupations but so is Vietnam, a country that has deeply marked him;[12] he insists that France never ceased to be at war between 1939 and 1962 although the areas of conflict were displaced from France onto the 'colonies'. Wilsdorf, a figure of admiration for Schoendoerffer, expresses a genuine interest in the area, which he apparently knows well. Despite the fact that it is a war film the Indochinese regions shot by Coutard seem almost dreamlike and hypnotic. Wilsdorf, in the tradition of characters found in André Malraux's Asian novels, as well as in Joseph Conrad's *Heart of Darkness*, speaks the native language and has a deep understanding of the mountain or highland people's culture and traditions. He is critical of the war and its machinery.

Following the nostalgic formula encountered in *Chocolat* and *Outremer*, the two blockbusters of 1992, *L'Amant* and *Indochine*, pick two French women born in the colonies as their chief protagonists. Both films rely on fictional dramas that seem to be inspired by a childhood in Vietnam during the colonial times and the tradition of popular melodramas, or what E. Ann Kaplan calls 'maternal melodrama' (1987: 125). The plots are set during the 1930s, at the height of the colonial era.

The depiction of Indochina on film is far behind the production of films about, for instance, Algeria. These two conflicts are linked in many ways, and only seven months went by between the resolution of the Franco-Vietnamese conflict and the beginning of the Franco-Algerian war. Benjamin Stora pairs North Africa with Indochina but differentiates between the respective cinematic treatment of both regions:[13] Algeria was the object of documentary film-making in the 1990s, whereas Indochina's reality was mostly reconstituted through fiction; 'The representation of Indochina is behind in French cinema (this is the case for colonial "black" Africa) whereas the Algerian period has given over twenty fiction films' (1992). By the 1990s, the mourning process that France had undergone seemed to be complete.

How Emmanuelle set the stage

What does the East in cinema and literature connote for a French person at the turn of the century and the beginning of the new one? How is it invoked? Ado Kyrou remarked on the hypnotic and sensuous qualities of Asian films (1957: 129).[14] Besides Hong Kong's kung fu action films and a few Japanese classics, or animation films, the Asian person displayed and sometimes displaced on French screens is viewed as an exotic and mysterious other most likely located in the confines of an imaginary French 'Chinatown'. Yet, if the Indochinese male character has never been a dominant figure in French cinema, the French soldier who did 'L'Indo' came out as a virile hero, typified by such actors as Alain Delon or Maurice Ronet in the 1960s (see Jeancolas 1992: 87).

However, there has been a growing passion for Asian cinema in the West, with films like *Crouching Tiger, Hidden Dragon* (Ang Lee, 2000), *In the Mood for Love* (Wong Kar-wai, 2000), and *What Time is it There?* (Tsai Ming-Liang, 2001), to name the most recent ones. The Cannes film festival reported as many Asian as American film screenings in May 2001 (see Lancelin 2001: 136).

In 1974 the release of two films – Bertrand Blier's *Les Valseuses*, and Just Jaekin's *Emmanuelle: The Joys of a Woman* – created a stir in the French film industry and are still considered essential films. They have generated many debates about censorship and the representation of sexuality on screen. Two minor production companies, Trinacre and Orphée, produced *Emmanuelle* – Trinacre, formerly specialising in the advertising business, bought the rights to *Emmanuelle* and decided to enter the feature film business. Critics dismissed the film directed by a newcomer to film-making – former fashion photographer Jeakin – for being shot like a fashion shoot. We, however, are interested in the confluence of East and West that meet here under the pornographic and/or erotic film genre. The East, located in Thailand (Bangkok), becomes the privileged colonial site enabling the sexual initiation of the white French woman called Emmanuelle – a representative of all French women. Asian males, who are scarce in the plot, become the unlikely subordinates to her initiation into the pleasures of sex and eroticism. The 'Orient' is the ideal terrain for such scenarios. However, the script is far from being typical, at least in commercial mainstream cinema. *Emmanuelle* became a model for subsequent films, such as Jean-Jacques Annaud's *L'Amant*. In fact, film critic Serge Daney aptly criticised *L'Amant* for being a remake of *Emmanuelle* (1992: 14–16).

Guy Austin connects a relaxed censorship in post-May 1968 France with the increase of erotic/pornographic films being released. This sudden phenomenon would last until the late 1970s. '*Emmanuelle* eventually became the best-attended film of the decade, attracting nearly nine million spectators' (Prédal 1991: 404). 'Its phenomenal success legitimised the porn film, and was followed by other hits' (Austin 1996: 46). The porn wave preceded another wave of post-porn films, some of these films tactfully questioning the representation of sex onscreen, for instance Godard's *Sauve qui peut (la vie)* (1979). One can reasonably argue that *Emmanuelle* set the stage for some of the films that we will discuss: *L'Amant, Indochine* and *L'Odeur de la papaye verte*, albeit in different styles.

We can read, in *Emmanuelle*'s scripted version of an 'East meets West encounter', the proposition of the erotic, sexual encounter of the French (colonial) with her European counterpart – played by an older Alain Cuny – mediated by an Asian other partner. Mario (the same actor played in Marcel Carné's *Les Visiteurs du soir* (*The Devil's Envoys*, 1942)), the aging French male and presumably pederast – as one gathers from the novel – coaches Emmanuelle into the realm of eroticism. Mario becomes the designated sexual initiator but takes the last twenty minutes of the entire film. Some of his dialogue redefines eroticism in an esoteric and exotic context.

Emmanuelle is intriguing in that it reverses the traditional formula found in fictional and historical accounts of the French white European male engaging in sexual encounters with an Asian woman – the Asian woman typifying land to be conquered. The colonial trope, when it comes to France, and it may be different when considering the United States, usually implies a sexual, romanticised relation which takes centre stage over a discussion of politics, wartime conflicts or economic accounting of colonisation. Novels abound on these sort of ties: Jean Hougron is one prolific writer to discuss and fictionalise his personal experience with Asian women in his 1950s cycle of novels on Indochina, *La Nuit Indochinoise*. Contrary to Emmanuelle's auxiliary, albeit minimal, initiation by Asian men, French men were supposed to bring pleasure and sex to Asian women. 'Male infallibility was maintained by the myth that Europeans had taught Asian women passion. Such stereotypes bolstered notions of the sexual prowess of the white man, emasculated the Orient, and cast the congaï as a purely physical object incapable of the tender emotions and material instincts of *la Française*' (Edwards 1998: 117). A rare semi-fictional text that transcribes a passionate relation between a white woman and an Asian man is Marguerite Duras' *L'Amant* ('The Lover', 1984). Duras' novel in many ways instigates the sudden return to the East. The precedent in non-fiction would be Clara Malraux' friendship with a Cambodian man during her Indochinese stay.

Emmanuelle develops a white French female's adventure in an Eastern country but adopts a male perspective on women. The plot transports the main character from Paris to Bangkok, after a short opening scene in her Paris apartment, looking onto a postcard-like view of the Sacré Coeur. Emmanuelle (Sylvia Kristel), a newlywed, according to her husband, a French diplomat, cannot be compared to any woman yet; she has to be taught about eroticism in order to become 'a real woman'. Left by herself in their large Thai countryside mansion, Emmanuelle meets other white colonial French women by the pool, and engages in different adventures of a Sapphic nature. Her first teacher, or initiator, is a 15-year-old girl called Marie-Ange (Christine Boisson). The shots frame Emmanuelle in soft focus and pastel colours, reinforcing the childlike

Figure 1   *Emmanuelle* (© *Studio-Canal, Just Jeakin*)

Figure 2 *Emmanuelle* (© *Studio-Canal, Just Jeakin*)

status conferred upon her by men and women. Emmanuelle finally opts to follow Mario's initiation, and is offered to Asian men as a prize in a boxing match and at the opium den. These sequences are fast-paced. Mario devises erotic situations, out of the ordinary, or out of the typical white colonial realm into indigenous zones, yet everything concludes to a return to the familiar, comfortable white world, especially in the montage of these scenes that are almost immediately cut once introduced. Emmanuelle's body is offered to Mario through a third party, a young Asian male. The film stops on a freeze-frame of Emmanuelle, looking at herself in a mirror, possibly imagining these fleeting scenes that, for once, are not given in a realist mode.

The age of *Emmanuelle* corresponds with the crisis of masculinity located in the early 1980s. According to Phil Powrie (1997), who has proposed a unique approach to masculinity in French cinema, the advent of feminism in France and the arrival of women in the workplace mediate the crisis of masculinity in film. Such a crisis, then, loomed largely before the 1980s, as French women entered the workforce after World War Two. Powrie covers an impressive array of film genres, ranging from the nostalgia film to the detective film and comedy. He convincingly argues that men increasingly exhibit signs of 'hysteria' and are excluded only to be replaced by powerful female roles, at least on screen. *Emmanuelle*, not unlike the Eliane Devries character found in *Indochine*, enters this atypical yet strongly colonial scenario, displaying a woman in control, the wife of the French ambassador in Bangkok, in a world that has been traditionally controlled by white males – colonial Indochina, here conveniently recast in Thailand.

Catherine B. Clément's Marxist reading of *Emmanuelle* underscores the latent ideology contained in the film (and its sequels) as well as its marketing. The system of references in the film's visual iconography takes the spectator on a journey from the classy bourgeois Parisian apartment to the Air France first-class trip to Bangkok (not to mention the illustrious rattan armchair that was prominently displayed on the *Emmanuelle* poster worldwide). The aeroplane sequence parades Air France as one of the film's unofficial sponsors. The space reconstituted in *Emmanuelle* is thus seeped in the white colonial world even if the context is not French and therefore removed from its colonial history: 'Everything prepares for the world of Whites in Asia, at the margins of the script; colonial mansions, colonial servants, pools for colonisers, the colonial car moving through a crowd of curious children, and erotic colonial "boys"' (1975: 25).[15] Clément observes that most communications take place among whites, and that even Asians 'act white'. The non-whites are merely servants, destined to serve and act as objects, sometimes sexual toys to their white masters. Clément picks up André Bazin's thesis on the embalming act represented by photography, a concept Barthes would take up in his writing on photography.

The adaptation of Emmanuelle Arsan's novel *Emmanuelle. Livre I: La leçon d'homme*, written in 1959, is infused with exoticism and orientalism. The writer of the book, Arsan, interestingly of Asian (Thai) origins, gave her name to the novel written by her French diplomat husband.[16]

Emmanuelle, an exercise in embalming acts, is accompanied by signs of colonial decadence and degeneration whose decaying representations can equally be found in Marguerite Duras' texts and her film *India Song*. Other critics have expanded on the concept of degeneracy in the colonies and the way European women supported the colonial enterprise and 'the solidification of racial boundaries' (Stoler 1997: 355).

L'Amant and the eroticized Asian body

L'Amant, a Franco-British co-production (Renn Productions, Burrill Productions), adapted from Duras' 1984 best-selling novel, is a partially autobiographical narrative. The protagonist is a 15-year-old girl, the daughter of two French schoolteachers who left France to resettle in Indochina with the hope of bettering their social status. Instead, the widowed mother raises her three children by herself in a state of poverty.

Having failed in a land-exploiting scheme, and duped by the French colonial administration that gave her land by the Mekong delta, the mother falls into semi-madness, and leaves her children entirely free to do as they wish. This story is continually reworked in other Durassian narratives, and found in her 1954 play, later transposed into a film, *Des Journées entières dans les arbres* (*Entire Days Spent in Trees*, Duras, 1976). In the 1980s version, the young girl has an affair with a 32-year-old wealthy Chinese man, who in turn will help to pay for her sea-voyage back to France. Earlier versions of the story never covered the racial component. Annaud organises the narrative around the interracial romance between a young French girl and a Chinese-Indochinese man during the 1930s, and in so doing drops the melodramatic dimension that constitutes half of Duras' story, articulated around the mother/daughter intense relationship. He blots out the photographic dimension that permeates the text and constitutes its genesis.

Duras has written extensively about her family ordeal in Indochina, where she was born. *Un Barrage Contre le Pacifique* ('The Seawall', 1950) was a formative novel in its attempt to write about the experience of growing up in Vietnam. More information regarding Duras' childhood has been recently uncovered by Laure Adler (1998) in her painstakingly detailed biography – some of it showing a more realistic picture of Indochina and Duras' affair. With, and despite, the enormous body of critical work written on Duras, clearly no one who writes about Indochina and colonial history can avoid her. She has written about her native country in eloquent, poetic terms, and even if what she wrote is removed from her actual biography, and therefore, if the autobiographical signature is contested by some critics, the writing remains and attests to a deep-rooted love of a place and a people.

Annaud, at first rightfully reticent to touch such a 'national monument' as Duras, decides to make the film and goes back to Indochina, now Vietnam, to recreate the atmosphere of Indochina in the 1930s. In itself the physical return to 'Indochina' does not seem possible. The 'return home' (the nostos) intrinsic to any nostalgic scenario, according to Vladimir Jankélévitch's definition of nostalgia, is further complicated by the fact that the past, or home, cannot be reached if the latter has been destroyed or changed. Indeed Indochina no longer exists, except as imaginary, historical, colonial and linguistic concepts – all of them closely intertwined.

Both *L'Amant* and *Indochine* focus on Vietnam, a fraction of the colonial territories of French Indochina. The country has been devastated and divided by wars, internal and external, and is economically just emerging and rebuilding itself. Annaud's venture parallels that of earlier French settlers. To make the film, he had to build roads and bring in the necessary infrastructure. He did research into the Chinese lover's background and family, enough to infuriate Duras and provoke her break with Annaud.

Gérard Brach, Annaud's collaborator and scriptwriter, insists that without the love scenes, the colonial nostalgia and the costumes would not have been substantial enough for the making of the film 'for, despite colonial nostalgia, costumes and light, if the love scenes at the bachelor's apartment did not take place, there would not be any film' (in Achard 1992: 53). *L'Amant* is faithful to some extent to Duras' story and text, and the special vision she has given of Indochina. Duras would have liked to make the film herself but she would have shot it in the French countryside. During Annaud's film-making, Duras rewrote the text and added filmic directives, turning the former *Lover* into the *North China Lover* (*L'Amant de la Chine du nord*, 1991) and explicitly developing aspects that she had only previously touched on. Duras, a film-maker herself, recreated India, a displacement for Vietnam/Indochina, on location in France for *India Song* with smaller means. This theoretical approach to the recreation of the past on film and the cinematic potential to reconstruct situations anywhere constitute two of the many differences at the base of the rift between her and Annaud.

Duras' native land is schematically outlined, its inhabitants acting as extras next to her characters' intense passion and suffering that play at centre stage. When one considers Duras' narrative treatment of the colonial question, the Orient figures as a mental landscape, with a native population functioning as a backdrop. Duras is more interested in focusing on the degenerating colonial milieu, with which she was familiar. In Annaud's adaptation, the chief characters, the girl, her mother and brothers, and the unnamed 'Chinese' man, are detached from interaction with the natives and always distant from them. The Indochinese people are usually shot as silent domestic workers or in a crowd. Characteristic of the colonialist mentality, any European settling in a colony became a coloniser and was above the natives. However, a discussion of power might need revising since it could be construed as what Homi Bhabha calls 'a historical and theoretical simplification' (in Holmlund 1991: 8). If the scenario (and novel) insists on the extreme poverty of the settlers' family, the race and social status of these French colonials set them apart from native people and struggles. The Vietnamese officials apparently appreciated the fact that it showed a family of deprived colonisers, but a 'dignified' Chinese man.[17]

Duras' vision of her native land is inscribed in Annaud's film. He did not reproduce on screen his astonishment at what he witnessed upon his 'return' to Indochina, or what Jane March, the lead actress, characterised as the poorest country she had ever seen. What went on in 1930s Indochina, besides the love affair between a young French girl and a 32-year-old Chinese-Indochinese man, remains a mystery. Duras avoids the topic of the nationalist indigenous struggles for independence to concentrate on the fact that she, a poor 'white-trash' girl, braved both French and Chinese cultural taboos and had sex with a member of the Vietnamese-Chinese ruling class (long-time colonial rulers of the Indochinese population and now considered as one of the 54 ethnic minority groups in Vietnam). The film examines the parameters of an exotic passion between two people from different social and racial backgrounds, and is limited to the geography of the Cholon bachelor's bedroom, turning it into a 1990s *Emmanuelle*. Gabriel Yared's dreamy musical score haunts the film in its rendition of the sounds of '1930s Indochina' (see Achard 1992).

This plot follows the formula already established in eighteenth-century popular imperial narratives of transracial love, where the 'allegory of romantic love mystifies exploitation out of the picture' (Pratt 1992: 97). The narrative underlines the class difference between the young French girl and the Indochinese/Chinese man as one of the major components of their relationship or, at least, one she uses to justify the relation with a new twist to it: she is the daughter of a deprived coloniser in need of money, and he is the wealthy French-educated son of an opium-smoking Chinese merchant. Once this distinction is established, there is no attempt to construct a political statement about the colonial system; the exploration of interracial desire does not provoke a re-examination of anticolonial consciousness in this text but at least it sets its limits.

Textual bricolage in Indochine

Régis Wargnier's script merges elements culled from photo-novellas, melo-dramas and a vast body of colonial literature and imagery that can be seen as bricolage and patchwork. These elements will be discussed in our reading of the film. Wargnier is no newcomer when it comes to using the Indochinese area as a backdrop to his films. However, by 1992, his career had developed since his debut, in 1987, with *La Femme de ma vie*. His film *Une Femme française* (*A French Woman*, 1995) covers the fate of a French woman and her family, during the various decades when France was at war with Germany or with its colonies. However, there is no in-depth comment about or return to these countries, especially since her husband is an army officer and therefore constantly off to these pockets of colonial struggles. Instead the historical drama of France, during and after World War Two, is filtered and diluted through the woman's numerous liaisons and fate. She stands on trial for France's colonial enterprises.[18]

Indochine juxtaposes several layers of stories and points of view, which add texture to an otherwise shallow narrative. Read as a maternal melodrama, it involves a scenario of separation between a mother and her daughter, then a separation and return, and an eventual rupture with the mother. But in spite of its jagged nature, the narrative remains closer to the conflictual rapport played out between Indochina and France and contains allusions to politico-historical events such as the Yen Bai mutiny of 1930. *Indochine* is an epic vehicle for Catherine Deneuve who plays a French woman, Eliane Devries, born in the colony. *Indochine* is a 1990s rewriting of a fantasy plot designed to place a woman in a position of power, heading a plantation, clearly a historical aberration or exceptional situation when women in France and Europe as a whole were rarely able to access leadership positions in the workforce. She is not married but adopts and raises a young girl, Camille, the daughter of her two closest Indochinese friends who have perished in an airplane accident.

The story borrows from fairytales and religious myths that can be traced back to colonial stories where the natives either have 'European affiliations or, renewing an older motif, are "really princes or princesses"' (Pratt 1992: 100).

Camille belongs to the royal family. The two-fold narrative follows Eliane at first, then Camille and her love for Jean-Baptiste, a young French navy lieutenant. Eliane's sexual life is hidden from her daughter whom she wants to protect, although the spectator does not know from what. Eliane's interest in the navy officer fails; the young man becomes in turn the love interest of her teenage daughter, who accidentally meets him in a rescue attempt. The French man severs the strong bond that once was between the mother and daughter. Camille leaves Eliane to join Jean-Baptiste who has been banished to an island.

Both imposing female roles catalyse the dualistic opposition between France and Indochina in epic proportions. This vision is constantly reinforced by the grandiose musical score of Scottish-born Patrick Doyle, which adds to the suture effect on the spectator. An in-depth analysis of colonialism underlines the Hegelian-like association between the coloniser and the colonised as intertwined, and of mutual dependency; for without the colony the coloniser would not exist, nor would the colonised. This association is played out here under the familial trope where Eliane, a distinct representative of a colonialist, adopts a daughter of the colony, Camille, just as France claimed to take under its wings the country it occupied. The role of the mère-patrie (motherland) and therefore that of the 'peuple-enfant' or 'colonised people as children' is invoked more than once, and best depicted when Eliane decides to punish a worker at her rubber-tree plantation. After she is done, the worker who was a deserter recognises and praises both her maternal and paternal fibres.[19] Next to the eroticisation of the colonial 'other', the trope of infantilisation is often used in colonial scenarios and usually involves women and children.

Like Duras, the fictional character of Eliane Devries defines herself as a hybrid character, an 'Asiate', someone in between – who is not quite French for she was born in Indochina, and never saw France (roughly the equivalent of the French North African 'pied-noir'). She is part of the ruling class with the Mandarins and controls a large rubber plantation. All the elements of the maternal melodrama are present in a story that initially revolves around the mother/daughter relation as an inseparable couple. The most revealing scene pairs them as a couple when Eliane dances a tango with Camille, a scene which is repeated later under a less auspicious light and which signals their ruptured relation.

Eliane's maternal function, outlined at the beginning of the film, is essential. She raises her daughter alone, protecting her from her Indochinese heritage, and alienating her from her ancestral culture. Race thus far does not seem to matter. The dominant theory articulated throughout the narrative lies in the belief that what matters is inside the person, and bears no relation with colour. In an early scene with Camille, Eliane expounds her notion on race by using the mango metaphor: 'The difference among people is not the skin colour, it's this!' She bit into the mango. 'It's this! The flavour, the fruit. Someone who has bitten into an apple cannot be like me. I am an "Asiate". I am a mango' (Montella 1992: 13). The metaphoric association of Asian fruit and Western fruit surfaces elsewhere with Duras, who could not eat the apples her mother would try to feed her. Lebelley, one of Duras' biographers, reports these incidents where the mother would force her children to eat apples, bread and meat – or the equivalent of French food: 'French children must eat apples. They grin and spit them out. They say that they are smothered by the fruit: it has no juice, and tastes like cotton' (Lebelley 1994: 17).[20] Duras, as a child, would steal her favourite mangoes.

Eliane acts as surrogate father to Camille since there is no father, and no husband in the household, although Eliane's father occupies a dominant position in the French film (and script) version.[21] Eliane maintains a stronger colonial position than a sexual one and, along the lines of the maternal melodrama, subordinates her sexual desires to 'protect' her daughter. Her sexual life is repressed to spare her daughter, but her father – who offers to bribe Jean-Baptiste – also, constrains it, unbeknownst to her. At first glance, Western women occupy a relatively powerful position in these colonial narratives. However, this is mostly a misleading script, turning them into the bearers of a gaze which is more colonial than sexual: 'The contradictions between racial and sexual hierarchies become accentuated in the recent liberal nostalgia for empire films featuring venturesome female protagonists and thus presumably appealing to a feminist audience, while still reproducing colonialist narrative and cinematic conventions' (Shohat & Stam 1994: 166–7).

The film invites a psychoanalytical reading, for there is a deeper but unexplored level that concerns a classical Oedipal scenario. Eliane is herself motherless as we learn from the novel that her mother died while giving birth to her. Her father, a self-made land speculator, raised Eliane. The script insists on Eliane's male qualities and her role as a strong working woman (with a whip) at the head of a rubber plantation. Eliane's father, now older, is an acknowledged womaniser, who has relations with younger Indochinese female servants, condoned by Eliane. While her father's sexual role is recognised as part of the patriarchal system she helps preserve, Eliane's own sexual desires are suppressed by her father, who wants to spare his daughter from further humiliation.

Christian de Montella's novel, *Indochine* – published after the film's release – elaborates on or, rather, romanticises Eliane's unsuccessful love life. The reader learns that a former fiancé left her to return to France, and vanished while pretending a suicide. Eliane, ignorant of the facts, has mourned her fiancé for years. The novel follows the script written by four established writers; Catherine Cohen, Louis Gardel, Erik Orsenna and Régis Wargnier. Orsenna, Gardel and Wargnier have shown a close interest in colonial fictions and what qualifies as 'the return of the Romanesque'. Gardel's trajectory is interesting as he co-wrote *Fort Saganne* (1984) and *Nocturne Indien* (1989), both directed by Alain Corneau. *Fort Saganne* was a television mini-series before it was turned into a feature film. It is 'an epic adventure story following the career of Charles

Saganne (Gérard Depardieu), an army officer stationed in the Sahara' (Austin 1996: 148). This film is part of the nostalgia for empire films that Guy Austin calls 'heritage films'. Incidentally, Catherine Deneuve acts in *Fort Saganne*, and comes to 'function as an icon of France' (Ibid.). *Indochine* was written with Deneuve in mind.

Eric Orsenna is best known for writing François Mitterrand's presidential speeches. He also wrote novels, one of them entitled *L'Exposition coloniale* (1988), which won the Goncourt prize. Wargnier heavily borrows from the colonial matrix and reworks it in his films. The film garnered 12 nominations for the César in 1993, and won the Academy Award for best foreign film. Released on 15 April 1992 the film sold 136,141 tickets in one week, and after 35 weeks at the cinema, it made 586,115 entries. It made over 3 million entries in its first-run career. The amount of tickets sold is fairly substantial in view of France's box office in 1993, where only American blockbusters *Basic Instincts*, *Lethal Weapon III,* and *Beauty and the Beast* surpassed it. When *Indochine* was nominated 12 times, its career was revived in movie theatres. However, the film made fewer entries than *L'Amant*, which led the French film market in 1992 with 3,147,000 seats in 41 weeks.

Indochine delivers an awkward presentation of a woman's sexual identity. Eliane is stronger when she happens to establish her position as a colonialist and mother. Although melodramatic scenarios are usually composed of (sexual) sacrifice and suffering, as well as a loss of social status for the mother, both female protagonists, mother and daughter, sacrifice something personal to survive. Eliane loses her daughter, her plantation and 'her country' at the end of the story, whereas besides losing her mother, her son and lover, Camille has sacrificed her personal life to the political cause of her country's independence. As in all melodramas, 'the mother, as a mother, represents a fullness, a presence, a wholeness and harmony that must ultimately be broken' (Pratt 1992: 97). The severed bond between mother and daughter does not survive the story, but a newly-established relation is forged at the end, with a mother-son relationship, and the possibility of a new immaculate birth.

In the second part of the film Eliane becomes the invisible, omnipresent spectator and narrator of her daughter's political emancipation told to her grandson Etienne, played by photographer Jean-Baptiste Huynh. The romantic scenario gives way to the epic narrative of Camille who sheds her mother's (mango) theory about people's racial and cultural difference (or lack thereof) and through her cross-country trek joins and adopts the cause of starving Indochinese workers and peasants. She is initiated into a national struggle from which she had been sheltered all her life. The camera adopts the powerful gaze of Camille in the second part, and focuses on poverty and injustice. The voice-over narration that frames the film takes place years later; here again the use of the flashback structures the scenario. Eliane recounts the story of her daughter Camille, her murder of a French officer responsible for the killing of the family of Indochinese farmers who 'adopted' her, whom she eventually followed, and her subsequent escape with Jean-Baptiste, played by Vincent Pérez.

Parallel to a maternal melodrama turned colonial emerges a story of political and personal abnegation for the sake of one's country, that leaves no room for Camille's love-object, who in turn becomes the involuntary auxiliary to be sacrificed to her quest. Camille's character becomes larger than life, and eventually achieves mythic proportions. In one instance, she is compared to an Indochinese Joan of Ark, a term which is deeply embedded in the colonialist rhetoric and can only equal and reflect the irony of classroom situations when French teachers would teach 'Our ancestors the Gauls' to the colonised children of the empire. The film dramatises the transitional period of the old Indochina into the new one. Camille has to reject the assimilationist scenario proposed by her mother (France) in order for her (Vietnam) to gain independence. A total break takes place, and the colonised must reject his/her parents, or what is called mère-patrie. Albert Memmi suggested the solution of a total break in the colonial conflict: 'The colonial situation ... brings on revolt ... the colonised's liberation must be carried out through a recovery of self and of autonomous dignity' (1965: 128).

Following the Oedipal scenario, Camille's break with her mother to enter adulthood is necessary, although at first, Camille turns to a man, Jean-Baptiste, who was previously her mother's secret lover. All the existing tropes of the Oedipal drama are present but the conformist closure of a daughter turning away from her mother, and 'discovering her identity through marriage ... and subordination to the male' is subverted by the geopolitical reality of the time (Kaplan 1987: 133–4).

Camille represents the march toward the country's independence. The plot follows the evolution of the various moments that led to independence and the struggle of the nationalists. She survives several ordeals and ultimately sacrifices the personal for the political. Clear references are made to various moments in the nationalist struggle for independence and the ensuing French repression. The interracial love-story of Camille and Jean-Baptiste is a model to be appropriated and enacted by popular traveling theatres around the country, as an example of defiance against French rule.

Beyond the extreme nostalgia and pathos that permeate the film, the script offers tools for empowerment and resistance: a popular Vietnamese theatre show travels the countryside and rearticulates the history of resistance to French rule. Both Camille and Jean-Baptiste become performers in that troupe. Performance is seen as a front for the nationalist struggle and a way of getting information to the country people. Jean-Baptiste, a young French naval officer, becomes the instrument of Camille's political cause against the colonial regime and is sacrificed by the French authorities for his involvement with Camille – seen as an act of treason. Etienne, the child born from her brief union with Jean-Baptiste, is taken with his father after his arrest. The child owes his survival to Indochinese women, and in an epic scene is seen being breast-fed by Indochinese women – another melodramatic device whereby native women suddenly gain access to the plot, only to be discarded immediately.

Eliane, whose role as the eternal (but never biological) mother, controls the story, and is eventually able to rescue and adopt Etienne as her son, a role she readily embraces, and a role he assigns her at the end of the film: 'You are my mother' ('Ma mère c'est toi'). Camille, once arrested, spends years in the Poulo-Condor penitentiary, one of the worst sites of repression by the French colonial police. She becomes a communist and, despite obvious ideological contradictions, she is reverently called the red princess. When briefly reunited with Eliane in a climactic and surreal scene set during the Popular Front's release of the Poulo-Condor prisoners, Camille tells her mother that to live she has to forget the past. Camille cannot afford to revel in the colonial dream of the past and land-exploiting schemes of her adoptive mother. Eliane's ambition, exposed in the opening scenes, was to combine land and agricultural resources to the benefit of her adopted daughter and to perpetuate the colonial heritage.

The bond between France and Indochina is severed. It is up to people like Camille, and her former fiancé Than, free from the conservatism of their upbringing thanks to a French education and the formation of a European-educated elite encouraged by the likes of Eliane and Guy Asselin (the police inspector) to inject life into their country. It is inferred that Camille will take a leading role in the forthcoming independence of Vietnam. Eliane's situation as a plantation owner and French coloniser, a position she inherited and maintained all her life, is thus brought to an end by the rise of nationalist struggle. Initially a forceful mother and father figure to her Indochinese workers, Eliane is forced to 'go back' to France where she has never set foot before. Eliane's exile from the paradisical plantation and her return to an imaginary France for a 'better future' with her adopted grandson, who now considers her his 'true mother', is left out, as the film never relocates in France.

The potential moment of reunion between Eliane and Camille, and Camille and Etienne, never takes place. Eliane decides to remain on the periphery of this potential meeting and dispatches Etienne to meet his mother. She becomes the outsider, a silent spectator, sacrificing herself for her daughter's future. Camille accompanies the Vietnamese delegation for the signature of the Geneva agreements that were to lead to the short-lived independence of Vietnam and cut the country in half in July 1954. The spectator does not see Camille again but may imagine seeing her in what amounts to five seconds of a documentary-style news sequence. The film thus concludes with the end of the French colonisation of Indochina, given as a final note, in the neutral zone of Switzerland.

There are some evident shortcomings in *Indochine*, which cannot function as a model for a colonial film, assuming that there is one. Such a model ideally would reconcile both sides of colonial history, and speak in two voices: that of the colonised and that of the coloniser. So far, the films only represent the perspective of the coloniser. Here the authoritative voice behind the voice-over narration belongs to Eliane. She is telling the story of her daughter and her native country. The attempt to merge the two sides of Indochina and France is both Manichean and simple. The vision is thoroughly nostalgic of the ties between the two countries, presented as a maternal love affair. Ginette Vincendeau (1993) suggests that the film is successful only because of the choice of Catherine Deneuve for the female lead, and the use of the Vietnamese landscape, not because of its recreation of the past.

L'Amant and *Indochine* explore the colonial ties between France and Indochina under the primarily erotic and sexual components of a nubile order, leading to a surface exploration of interracial intimacy between a Chinese man and a French girl, or its reversal that falls into the more classical trope of intimacy between a Vietnamese girl and a French man. The denouement of both colonial stories shows the European reabsorption of the coloniser, his/her fear of being cannibalised, whereas the native reintegrates the colonial space assigned to him/her. The Chinese lover marries his Chinese bride; the young white girl leaves for France. Camille fights for her country's right to independence. Respectful of linear history, *Indochine* stops short at the Geneva conference and leaves out room for further development. It imposes a giant ellipsis in time past and future, like Camille's story, and Eliane's return to France, as well as Etienne's potential adaptation in France as a Eurasian child, not to mention the fate of Vietnam as a nation. It flushes the representation of extensive wartime conflicts, Vichy times and the Japanese occupation, or the final defeat at Diên Biên Phû, and leaves out the names of political leaders on both sides.

The end of colonial Indochina suggests a loss for France, amounting to a dismemberment, visually emphasised by the incision made on rubber trees, which are said to be bleeding: 'Tomorrow France loses Indochina.' Marina Heung perceives *Indochine* to be a departure from 'colonialism as a male enterprise' (1997: 175). A European and an Asian woman are playing out the East/West relation. The running metaphor throughout the film is displaced onto the rubber trees, whose sap is running like milk or semen.

A celebration of mourning and memory structures the film from the credit opening sequence which shows Eliane sporting black clothes, which in the West denote mourning, holding younger Camille's hand, surrounded by a crowd of Indochinese people dressed in their white mourning attires. The crossing of a river (the Mekong) has deeper symbolic meaning, especially looking at Durassian plots. Eliane is attending the funeral of her closest friends, the parents of her adoptive daughter. The mourning anticipates the final sequence which closes with Eliane again dressed in black. She stands out as the orientalising practitioner, now the adoptive mother of her grandson, mourning the loss of her native country and resigned to the loss of her daughter. The camera lingers and the landscape next to the musical score becomes grandiose and colourful.

The picturesque landscape blends opposite views that are presented throughout the narrative, emblematic of France and Indochina: one is the marine painting of the coast of Brittany and the second is the aerial (bird's-eye) point of view of the bays in Vietnam, a recurrent motif. It is interesting that the young French officer is of Breton origins, close to some Schoendoerffer characters. Brittany traditionally designated the departure point for sailors and other nationals on the lookout for other/better horizons and colonial ventures. The closing scene presents the now-familiarised spectator with the shot of the Vietnam bays craftily and surreptitiously transposed onto Swiss mountains surrounding a lake; the shot produces a feeling of disorientation. The final frame reinforces the travel motif reminiscent of 1930s films, which it re-enacts here, ending with the protagonist's (failed) escape on ocean liners. Annaud and Wargnier have carefully crafted 1930s imagery into their scenes; *L'Amant* concludes with a false impression, with the female lead as a ship's bow figure on board one of these old-time liners, on her way to France.

Both films were blockbuster productions, at least in terms of French film production. *Indochine*, produced by Eric Heuman (Renn films), had an estimated budget of 118,600,000 French Francs, or enough to finance the making of five films (Ferenczi 1992). It grossed an estimated record of $5,734,000 in the United States, with *L'Amant* following close behind with $4,899,000. Both films also made it to the French top sellers list for 1992–93, on the heels of *Bodyguard, Hook, Basic Instinct, Aladdin*, and *Jurassic Park*. The most successful film of this period was *Les Visiteurs* (*The Visitors*, Jean-Marie Poiré, 1993) a typical French farce centred on a group of medieval knights who find themselves transported to twentieth century France. The comedic satire of contemporary French society is far removed from the world of *Indochine* and *L'Amant*, the tone of which is dramatic and frequently gloomy. Both films emerge from the French tradition of literary adaptation and also of orientalist narratives. *Indochine* is an effective mix of prior fictions and chromos (or visual images) repackaged into a sweeping Romanesque saga. It borrows from earlier essays like Roland Dorgelès' *La Route Mandarine*, accounts of missionaries and travelers and pulp literature that was popular in the 1930s, as *Une canonnière en embuscade sur le Mékong* as well as Claude Farrère's opium narratives. *Indochine* resulted in the rewriting of the script for publication, while *L'Amant* is the product of a best-selling novel.[22] The use of voice-over in both films reinforces the literary aspects and at times waxes poetic. It sets a lyrical tone from the beginning, when Eliane evokes her belief system in incredibly nostalgic and reactionary prose, which resonates earlier colonial formulas: 'Maybe this is what youth was about. The belief that the world is made of inseparable things: men and women, mountains and plains, humans and gods, Indochina and France'.

The myth of colonialism as eternal and the humanist trend to blend differences infuse the story of colonialism. Its discourse is faithfully adopted in *Indochine*. In a similar vein, *L'Amant* closes with the voice-over narration of the now older heroine (what better voice-over to use than Jeanne Moreau's?) who recalls the telephone call that she – the girl, now relocated in Paris – receives years later from the older Chinese lover, when he reiterated his eternal love for her. A linguistic difference separates both films: Wargnier made his film in French and sometimes mixed in Vietnamese, but Annaud made his film in English, using a Franco-British cast, dubbing and subtitling it in French for the French spectator, and allowing the two versions to be distributed in France, transferring Duras' discourse into a more international language by using two English-speaking actors – Jane March and Tony Leung. This difference instills a necessary distance with the French colonial past for a French spectator, while at the same time it internationalises this aspect of colonisation, as well as making the film more marketable to a foreign audience. Ultimately, the linguistic preference for English reconciles us with the fact that French is scarcely the dominant language now spoken in Vietnam where English has replaced French. In addition to this, French is losing ground in national and international cinema, with more and more films that speak 'English'.

Poetic moments in film veil the events that happened before the end of the colonisation, and lead the spectator astray from the problematic appropriations taking place in these narratives. We can discern several of these instances: when Eliane Devries in an omniscient perspective narrates her daughter's escape and life with Jean-Baptiste, almost to the point of becoming one with her, and borrowing her gaze. When Eliane and Guy, the police inspector, discuss the future of Indochina as belonging to the young generation of intellectuals sent to Paris for their education, like Than. These instances demonstrate that the colonial representatives can be omnipresent, even when absent from the picture, and decide what is best for people under their rule, even under the cover of liberalism that becomes paternalism (for example, Eliane telling her daughter's story).

One can ponder the renewal of interest in Vietnam as evidenced in filmic production. Echoing or preceding the renewal of the diplomatic and commercial links among Europe, the US and Vietnam, the emergence of the Orient as the focal point of these films displaces some problems in the domestic scene – some of them being the direct legacy of colonialism. Ultimately these films tackle the vision that French people have of themselves and the divorce created by the end of the colonial era – a nostalgic vision that is definitely not shared by Vietnamese people now.

The films discussed above do not evoke the decolonisation process and its aftermath. Instead they court the past and present harmony between France and Vietnam and have another agenda. *Indochine*'s discourse is emphatic in its attempt to authenticate colonialism, and the influence of 'good' colonisers like Eliane. In 1992 three films of epic proportions returned to Indochina, but primarily to the Vietnamese country.[23] Only one of them, a war film constructed as an opera, tackled the military battle of Diên Biên

Phû. Schoendoerffer's film proposes a 'visual and auditory symphony' and a sober look at the long battle that decided the fate of Vietnam.[24] Composed by George Delerue, the violin concerto entitled 'Le concerto de l'Adieu' played by the Hanoi orchestra 'succeeds in evoking a sentimental war yet is 'the soul of the film' (Schoendoerffer 1992: 127).

Unlike the films previously discussed, *Diên Biên Phû* retraces the final months of the French military battle which figures as the significantly absent moment in *Indochine*. For two hours, Schoendoerffer exploits in a stylised and operatic manner visions of shelling and the absurd butchery that war is. Schoendoerffer's involvement with the past differs radically from other film-makers. Despite conservative political views, he can objectively and lucidly present his transformation as he personally witnessed the French army's defeat. However, *Diên Biên Phû* is unable to give the Indochinese side of the war. A Vietnamese documentary version of the Diên Biên Phû battle has been put together and is now showing at the Ho Chi Minh City War Remnants Museum.

Most films discussed in this chapter were initiated in the late 1980s, right after the turning point of 1989. Never before had so many films faced France's colonial past in Asia, even during the 1930s – a moment of French colonial splendor par excellence – a moment that French historian Charles-Robert Ageron describes as the apotheosis of the French empire and its ideal.[25] In general, France has remained closer to her former colonies in North Africa, at least in their filmic transposition.[26] However, Indochina still generates and exerts an uncanny fascination in France, more than North Africa or West Africa, especially in recent French fiction. As Panivong Norindr observes, this fascination has constructed 'Indochina as a phantasmatic object while commodifying its aura' (1996: 13). *L'Amant* and *Indochine* elaborate on what I have called the colonial maternal melodrama to explore the historical moment that marked the end of the colonial era. The representation of Indochina on film is a displacement and interlude for problems at home. At a time France was approaching the unification of Europe in 1992, a move supported by President Mitterrand, but disapproved by 49 per cent of the electorate, the image of former colonies or empire celebrates a moment of splendour necessary to maintain the myth of France. Such an image was perceived as a unifying gesture for the French nation and its citizens, who are still increasingly concerned with an ongoing economic crisis and the influx of immigrant workers. The focalisation of the gaze toward the past of what was once the jewel of the empire suggests the desire to escape from problems at home. The colonial past is embraced with nostalgia, in a gesture oblivious of, or indifferent to, the native struggles that marked the pre-war times and whose legacy is still lingering. This colonial nostalgia seems heavily targeted at the young generations born in the postcolonial period, or roughly after the 1960s, in an oversimplified pedagogical attempt to educate them about the past.

CHAPTER TWO

Where Clouds and Dragon Meet

In the 1990s, dozens of critics claimed that French cinema only returned to Indochina in 1992, yet Lam Lê's film debut in 1979, along with his orientation toward Vietnam, contradicts these claims. Lê is in fact a precursor who first reproduced Vietnam in France, in a Parisian studio. His film production, albeit quantitatively limited since – he has only made two commercially released films – tackles crucial emerging issues in postcolonial praxis, such as Vietnamese identity and its position in France and abroad, and auteurism.[1] After *Rencontre des nuages et du dragon* (*Meeting of Clouds and Dragon*, 1979), he returned to Vietnam to make *Poussière d'empire* (*Dust of Empire*, 1983), a film which was praised as an anomaly, the 'strange work of a Vietnamese man who disappeared without leaving any traces'.[2]

Lê is generally considered the first Franco-Vietnamese film-maker to make a film in France, with *Rencontre des nuages et du dragon*: 'I was the first Vietnamese to be in the profession, the first film-maker with basic training.'[3] Although the claim might need revision, Lê wrote, produced and directed the medium-length film. It was part of the Cannes official selection that year, and its critical recognition secured him funding for *Poussière d'empire* (Uranium films, FR3), which was partly shot in Vietnam. The second film was released in 1983 but its career was cut short when the production company collapsed immediately after its release. The film eventually aired on FR3 (a French television channel). Both films have become cult, mythical films that placed Lê on the map of French cinema. Since then, he has accrued a following. He participates in film conferences on Vietnamese cinema and screens the sole copy of the film.

In the context of Franco-Vietnamese history and relations, Lê made his films when nobody wanted to hear about Vietnam, especially during the making of *Poussière d'empire*. Vietnam by then had invaded Cambodia and had become an aggressive force. After his career was launched, Lê never compromised to the demands of several controlling ideologies, be they government and/or film industry or film community, and turned down many projects. His next project, after a 15-year hiatus, comes after the renewal of relations between France and Vietnam and after a new generation of Vietnamese artists had emerged in France and abroad – some of them directly inspired by or indebted to him.

Positioning: France or Vietnam?

Lê's films reflect his quest for an identity in France. He is positioned as an in-between, a crossover between two distant nations and cultures – a *'passeur'* or transmitter between two cultures, to borrow a term coined by Serge Daney (1986: 178). Lê's creative sources are inspired by an interest in mathematics and astrophysics, as well as Buddhist and Taoist beliefs, which he does not faithfully practice but which are an intrinsic part of his culture and life. As an exile in France and a French citizen, his identity in French society is constantly in flux, a double position that draws a bridge between France and Vietnam. Through training and life, he has acquired a Western identity and by birth, culture and 'inherited' beliefs, he has a Vietnamese identity. His exilic and artistic condition leads him to link these two worlds through his work. Recently, a 1999 documentary film made by two Belgian film-makers on Vietnamese artists living in the diaspora, *Là où vont les nuages: Art et identité de la diaspora vietnamienne (Where the Clouds Go: Art and Identity of the Vietnamese Diaspora)* featured him among a spectrum of Vietnamese artists living in Europe.[4]

A latecomer to the film industry, which he entered when he was 29, Lê left Vietnam for France in 1966 when he was 18. He was born in 1948, in Haiphong, a North Vietnamese port city. Trained as a mathematician, he was expected to attend the Grandes Ecoles in Paris, but once he had obtained a Masters degree in mathematics and prepared for the concours des grandes écoles (entrance exam), he followed another course in fine art and theatre. Instead of becoming a Polytechnician according to his father's wish, Lê started painting and acting, pausing only briefly to teach mathematics. He first ventured into the film world as an art director, and witnessed the process of film-making for the first time on the set of Joël Santoni's comedy *Les Oeufs brouillés* (*Scrambled Eggs*, 1976). He also worked for Jean-Pierre Mocky.[5] His passionate cinephilia, evinced by his regular attendance at the cinémathèque de Paris (Chaillot and rue d'Ulm) is essential in understanding his development as a film-maker. Lê learned his art from watching films. Though having never attended a film school, he now teaches at the FEMIS, formerly IDHEC (National Film School), and is part of the jury for each year's exams. Based on his experience, a film-maker does not have to follow a special training to make a film, yet should have, like him, an artistic eye.

Lê belongs to the generation of francophone Vietnamese intellectuals who were born during the final stages of the French colonial era and migrated to France in the 1960s. In her detailed work on Vietnamese culture and identity, Hung Agustoni-Phan (1997) defines this generation, starting with the war of liberation of Vietnam, as the last generation of francophone intellectuals, ending in 1975 with the closing of French schools. Lê grew up in Vietnam during the French presence and witnessed the American arrival and take-over. His childhood years were thus marked by French colonialism and the transition to American 'imperialism'. By comparison, Tran Anh Hung belongs to the younger generation, born after the French had left Vietnam, who were forced to emigrate from their home, to France or other countries as boat people.[6] The different experiences of these generations are significant, especially in the context of France's immigration waves and on a semantic and linguistic level.

Poussière d'empire is one of the first films made in France by a member of the former colony that addresses the fallout of colonialism and calls for Vietnamese national unity and resistance, but it is ironically also one of the last films of its genre. It is the first film made by a Franco-Vietnamese artist to physically return to Vietnam. The film was subsequently highly debated in several milieus – for example by the Vietnamese government that tried to embrace Lê as one of their own; it has raised several critical and polemical responses in France, depending on the ideological tendency of the discussants.

Coming from a francophone background, Lê was educated in the French lycée of Saigon and only spoke French at school. His father encouraged him to attend French schools and was himself a product of the French colonial system. That system promoted integration with France and, by learning the master's language, he would acquire the tools to ascend the social ladder. The familial origins were located in North Vietnam but when they migrated South, his family was divided by politics, as was the plight of many Vietnamese families. One uncle stayed in the North and as a VCP member fought against the South, and therefore against his family, during the war. This uncle, an artist, is the model that Lê used later *Rencontre des nuages et du dragon*, for the artist-calligrapher, Uncle Xuan.

Lê is extremely critical of the renewal of interest in 'Indochina' and those who package commercially exotic products. His native country has been turned into an exotic commodity: 'The selling of close-ups, as seen in *Indochine*, it's impossible, it's not my style.'[7] This critical and lucid stand has forced him to refuse projects, or cancel them whenever they became part of the selling of Asia. Lê sees this current trend reflected in fiction films made not just by French (of the majority) but also by Franco-Vietnamese directors.

Lê recently worked on Eric Heuman's *Port Djema* (1997) and storyboarded the entire film.[8] He applied his painting and drawing skills to the film as he did for other films and *Poussière d'empire*. To 'storyboard' means to write a text and illustrate an entire film with ink sketches for every scene, in print form before the shooting. This in turn constitutes a path for each film take and *mise-en-scène*. It resembles a cartoon form. One of Lê's formative models comes from *Tintin* (Hergé), a comic-strip character that fascinated him in his youth. His interest in Tintin is rooted in the image-making process that stands at the core of film-making:

> I have just reread *The Blue Lotus* by Hergé – an author who left a mark on my entire childhood in Vietnam. I was struck by its perfection. For example, in an image that covers a full page, you see Tintin on a cyclo in Shangai. What interests me is the reason Hergé decided, at that moment, to draw a large box instead of four or five small ones.[9]

The attraction to Tintin, who is and has been a questionable character over the years, especially when considering ideology in the years of World War Two, is doubly interesting. Hergé's creativity and artistic orientation were influenced by his meeting with Chinese painter Tchang Tchong Jen, who became his 'mentor'. Tchang had travelled to Europe on a scholarship in the 1930s to perfect his watercolour skills and there met Hergé, a Belgian cartoonist. Both artists prepared the adventures of *Tintin in China*. Tchang initiated Hergé in the art of brush and ink painting. The sudden transformation of Tintin, a nationalist xenophobic and anti-Semitic hero, into an international human rights advocate in China, is largely due to Tchang. The latter was influential in *Le Lotus bleu* and signed his name in some of its calligraphy work.

Lê is passionate about the North-South dialogue and the way that the West tries to have a clear conscience by doing humanitarian work. At this level, he shares with Cambodian film-maker Rithy Panh some of the same concerns (Panh's work will be discussed in chapter 6). The script of *Port Djema*, written by Jacques Lebas, a doctor who belonged to the humanitarian association Médecins Sans Frontières, gives an incisive portrait of French humanitarian action conducted in Africa: 'Jacques Lebas thought that humanitarian work is an illusion of Western governments, which think that they can solve Third World problems.'[10] *Port Djema* is a direct heir to *Poussière d'empire* in its message. It is a blend of Duras, Depardon and Antonioni. There is more of Antonioni in *Port Djema*, especially when considering *Profession Reporter* (1975).

Rencontre des nuages et du dragon[11]

This early film has not been written about, probably owing to its limited release, although recently, it was screened again at festivals and conferences.[12] This first medium-length film requires several viewings; the director claims that it took him years to analyse and comprehend in retrospect what he had put into the film. The narrative is set in colonial Vietnam. The presence of French soldiers is immediately visually ushered in after the credit sequence as they arrive abruptly in a jeep and search a house. Military-uniformed men barge into a small modest house where a photographer is quietly busy touching up pictures of dead people. The French soldiers brutally arrest Uncle Xuan, the photographer. A child, his assistant, witnesses his arrest. When the soldiers arrive, the child warns that 'Westerners' are coming. Simultaneously, a voice-over commentary, coming from the photographer's client, ascertains the exact year of this incident as 1952, with the subtitle: 'Sending Général de Tassigny to Tonkin starts the Indochinese war again.' Actor Thang Long played the principal character Uncle Xuan, also called Magical Brush, who is most likely arrested because of his profession. The French soldiers perceive him as a resistance fighter. When he is removed off-screen, the camera – in a left to right slow panning shot – focuses instead on a wooden palisade behind which the soldiers are taking the photographer away. The point of view stems from the child who witnesses the tragic moment. The shot of the palisade opens the next sequence, located in a prisoners' camp seen behind its railing. The passage of time is formally noted on the soundtrack with the sound of thunder and wind, as well as the visual drifting of a smoke cloud.

A madman, played by Lam Lê, is looking out from his cell. This man, called Uncle Vengeance, tries to hire Magical Brush to kill another man, convinced that his artistic skills enable him to transform people's destiny, potentially killing them. He sings his praise in a poetic form: 'Divine harvest fell the day you were taken away, your skilful hands know how to change faces, you refuse to eat lizards, Uncle Springtime, you are a powerful man. Magical Brush, you must help me.'[13]

Magical Brush refuses the job; instead the madman steals his tool kit and tries to use them as the artist would. These tools were introduced in the opening sequence, in a close-up of a photograph, next to a brush and butterfly-shaped pencil. In a fantastic sequence whose lighting is close to German expressionism, a large white butterfly brushes against Uncle Vengeance's face and attacks a train conductor at night. A close-up of his face reveals extreme fear, as well as the physical airbrushing of black strokes on his face, done by an invisible brush. This compels him to pull the lever and stop the train. The man steps out and walks onto the railroad tracks, in front of the headlights, and realises that the track ahead has actually collapsed in a deep ravine.

The next shot opens on a stone quarry and shows prisoners labouring. Radio-Vietnam is heard in the background, while an American GI is repeating Vietnamese words he has just learned and discusses the meaning of the words *Long* – dragon in Vietnamese – and *Karma*, with a Vietnamese colonel as a tutor. The latter patiently explains that the dragon is the symbol of Vietnam. A close-up shot of a newspaper page later presents the surrealist headline 'A train conductor saved by a butterfly'. The South Vietnamese officer in charge of the camp that reunites Magical Brush and Uncle Vengeance jokes about torture devices with the American GI. He hires Magical Brush, reiterating the earlier praise sung in verses by Uncle Vengeance, and asks him to touch up a negative. The officer recognises the artist's power but flexes his militaristic power. Magical Brush, who has practically never said a word, requests him to send Hoang, the madman, to the hospital, in exchange for his services. He is then given an enlarger and from the negative emerges the live image of a bald person sleeping on a veiled bed. A chrysalis-like form is shown in front of a mirror. Her sexual identity is not established right away in terms of gender and appears androgynous; it turns out that it is a bald, disfigured woman whose white made-up face looks more like a mask in Japanese Nô theatre.[14]

Transformations are exteriorised, as the woman's wig becomes suddenly real. She is the wife of the South Vietnamese colonel who just ordered a make-over. Her scarred face becomes spotless – a transformation performed while facing the mirror – or the camera. While she faces the camera – a forbidden gaze in cinema – and witnesses this uncanny transformation, she becomes crazed, crawls on all fours and walks out on rooftops and new construction sites. A crane is shown accidentally dumping dirt on her, hastening an off-screen death that one guesses after hearing agonising screams.

Rencontre des nuages et du dragon concludes with Magical Brush, now free, entering the frame and collecting his cane and tools. He is a free man but he is blind. He fumbles his way back to his village with his cane. The last remarkable sequence features a child's singsong and a child doing a headstand, feet reaching the sky. In a tilt, the camera shows the sky upside down next to a smiling Magical Brush. Calligraphy plays a major role in Lê's films, with the final credit sequence rolling on I-Ching hexagrams.

A tentative analysis

> One wonders about one's self: If these objects that we so absolutely want to question were only historical and geographic particularities, idiotisms of our civilisation? We want things to be impenetrable so we can penetrate them: by ideological atavism, we are creatures of decipherment, hermeneutic subjects: We believe that our intellectual task is always to search for a meaning. (Barthes 1974: 1)[15]

Since we are, fortunately or unfortunately, human beings on a mission to decipher and analyse, *Rencontre des nuages et du dragon* stands at a crossroad but should probably, like the submerged iceberg, lie dormant and unmoved by questioning. However, it contains a system of codes that beg to be deciphered. Inspired by Christian Metz's argument in *The Imaginary Signifier* (1982), my approach anchors itself in the necessity for some interpretation, within the classroom or outside, and attempts to tease out some of the issues that are at stake in this project.

The film recounts one segment of the history of Vietnam and its people: 'It is the first time that a Vietnamese is making a film on Vietnam, speaking about the entire history of Vietnam, starting with its French colonisation until

Figure 3 *Poussière d'empire* (© Lam Lê)

now.'[16] It is an allegorical but cryptic representation. The myth of the origins of Vietnam recounts the mating of a sea dragon king, Lac Long, with an Earth fairy, Au Co. From this union, one hundred sons were born. The couple separated and fifty sons followed the king father toward the lower aquatic regions, while the other fifty sons followed their mother into the mountainous regions. One of these sons became King Hung, founder of the Vietnamese nation, then called Van Lang. Van Lang always evokes the country of origins and is the name invoked by Vietnamese people living in the diaspora: 'In their solemn declarations, Vietnamese people always designate themselves the sons of the dragon and the fairy.'[17]

When the clouds meet the dragon, the literal translation of the title, such an occasion brings felicity. However, felicity in this otherwise dark film surfaces at the end, when Magical Brush is reunited with his child on top of a hill and both are seen facing the sky, in an upside-down image. Happiness is adjourned to a distant future in a narrative constructed otherwise around the concepts of imprisonment, madness and control. Several factions are in control and change over time. The French soldiers, who arrest Pinceau Magique, are the first jailers. Yet these jailers are interchangeable with time. Temporal transitions are subtle and more pronounced, ultimately, with a smiling chubby South Vietnamese colonel exchanging information with an American soldier in an apparently friendly manner. The ellipsis in time occurs in language such as the transition from French to American English, interspersed with Vietnamese. The colonel explains (for us, the spectators) the symbolic meaning of the dragon, or the people of Vietnam. However, the South Vietnamese colonel has a more personal scheme in mind and forces the artist to touch up his wife's negative – most likely to better her ailing (leprosy-like) condition.

The presence of an image or image-making process shapes the film. This image-making process is about writing. Both systems, writing and photography, are perceptual registers. The artist whose primary function is to embellish images of people who are now dead, on the threshold to the next world, could well represent the film-maker, whose task is, figuratively speaking, not that different, but maybe more in a 'star system'. The presence of still images, paintbrush and enlarger forms a *mise-en-abîme* of the cinematic apparatus. The function of the photographer instills the importance of ancestors and the cult of the dead in Vietnamese culture as well as the belief that 'dead' people are still living among their families, be they Catholic, Buddhist or Taoist. The cult of ancestors held by Vietnamese and other Asian cultures comes under the form of altars adorned with pictures, incense and bowls of fruit. The shot of Uncle Xuan touching up a picture discloses the transmutation of the person – from old to young, a metamorphosis that cinema and moving images can magically achieve under the spectator's eyes.

Death motifs permeate the text owing to the presence of Xuan, who throughout the film is acclaimed and respected for his artistic talent, but will be condemned by the madman, for being a sorcerer who betrayed him by not killing the train conductor. Death registers on the soundtrack with a female voice singing Uncle Xuan's praises, as in a panegyric or ode to his memory. Xuan's role is ambiguous, as he does not always embellish people. The function and position of the photographic image in Vietnamese culture is explored with pictures of dead people adorning the family altar.

Uncle Xuan's 'sacred' work is to touch up images that will forever attest to the permanence of people's souls. In his essay on Asian signs and faces, 'Le visage écrit', in *L'Empire des signes*, Barthes establishes a difference between Eastern and Western representations: 'The face is the only thing to write about; but its future is already written by the hand that whitened the eyebrows, the nose, the cheeks and gave its page of flesh the dark limit of a hair as compact as stone' (1970: 120).[18] The mixture of signs and impassability, which Barthes sees reflected in Asian theatre ultimately, loses some of its meaning. For it relates to one's attitude toward death: 'To imagine and make a face, not impassible or insensitive, but as if it came out of water, washed of meaning, it is a way to answer to death' (1970: 123).[19] Barthes has extensively explored the link between photography and death in *Camera Lucida*; *L'Empire des signes* anticipated his meditation on death, representation and zen. The work of *Magical Brush* is to touch up dead people's pictures, inscribing and airbrushing their good qualities for posterity.

Playing with a multiplicity of layers, the film celebrates the power and resilience of the artist under various political climates. Xuan effectively survives under several regimes, be it the French colonial presence or the American presence. Several parallel readings occur as the temporality may designate an immortal Xuan or his double. Similarly, the position of the artist in the film is understood in its generic terms, serving under various political regimes where in each instance, the artist is interned and jailed. Artistic skills are exploited for the personal gain of others. Instead of touching up pictures of dead people, Xuan is made to alter living people's blueprints. He walks free at the end but in the process, or in exchange for his freedom, he has lost his eyesight. His blindness is a blessing as it prevents him from repeating this type of compromising work in the future. We will not venture into a psychoanalytical interpretation, but variations according to an Oedipal script may be read here. In a rare interview with journalist Hervé Guibert, Lê interprets the film as: 'The story of a photographer who has the power to make people's desires come true … [but] the story is nothing but an excuse. I wanted to propose a metaphor on the future of Vietnam and possibly the Third World. How could I help Vietnam? At first, I believed in making it [the country] better known.'[20]

Rencontre des nuages et du dragon, in a quiet and unequivocal way, denounces the colonial regimes that have oppressed, separated and alienated the Vietnamese people. French soldiers appear like overgrown boy-scouts in their ridiculous outfits of shorts, black socks and boots – different from the navy officers' portrayal in their shining outfits in the more recent *Indochine*. The gum-chewing American GI appears childlike in his questions. The entire film duration (45 minutes) is spatially confined to a jail whose actual site was located in a former slaughterhouse at the Porte de Versailles, in Paris. The parallel between a colonial-made Vietnamese jail and an animal slaughterhouse is not fortuitous. Following the argument that French colonisers had reproduced their habitat and urbanism overseas, Lê in turn felt legitimate to reciprocate and reproduce Vietnam in Paris. In many ways, the director could find and duplicate 'French Indochina' in Paris and, by so doing, expresses the possibility that France still contains signs of its former empire within. Although such a discussion is rarely evoked, there are visible signs of fortunes made by the former colonisers in France. For example, the fountain where his family would buy water was French-built and its replica discovered in Montreuil (a neighbourhood at the edge of Paris). Guided by this precept, Lê scouted Paris and its environs to find locations for his movie.

The film is a poetic incantation achieved through language and black and white cinematography. Even if one is unfamiliar with the Vietnamese language, one can hear the way the text is recited at several moments. Adopting the system of repetition, poetic form is used deferentially when addressed to Magical Brush. Understandably, Lê – living in exile since 1966 – is interested in not merely revisiting a form – a set, an interior – but a signifier, here Vietnamese language and words, as well as legends, to get closer to his roots. The story reclaims the Vietnamese myth of origins in the figure of the dragon and the mountain. The final sequence offers a cosmological interpretation by uniting man, sky and earth in a single frame; Lê sketches the relation between nature, sky and earth. Harmony manifests itself at the end, with the final shot of Xuan's ecstatic face. Traditional Western spatial notions are disrupted when the sky appears not in the traditional Western vertical line, at the top of the screen, but instead, is tilted and reversed in the frame. The sky acquires a new meaning, and in Vietnamese cosmology:

> The Sky or Trò'i is not only a vault above our head; considered under the principal of natural forces, the sky is transcendent and personified. One says in Vietnamese: Mister Sky … for in the mind of people, the sky is a respectable spirit, master of atmospheric phenomena … the sky is a powerful spirit that sees, brings justice, helps, punishes and knows everything that goes on earth.[21]

Lê, in one frame, has ushered a new vision that borrows directly from Vietnamese Taoist beliefs and traditions, departing from the traditional geometry used in Western frames and its logic of vertical or horizontal lines. Initiated in the opening sequence with the calligrapher's brush, the angle of framing and the optic separate two universes and bear the (calligraphic) signature of the film-maker (Lê will sign or author both films he made with calligraphic signs).

The final sequence is organised around the cosmological representation of man, as a small entity, in front of the vastness of the cosmos. The latter can be found in paintings and sketches: 'The Asian human being has often been represented in Chinese or Japanese prints as an infinite element lost in the vastness of nature. This signifies that man is totally dominated by cosmos, inside which he is alone to meditate on his own state of mind and on mankind.'[22]

Uncle Xuan's final position, holding the child's legs, facing the tilted sky, brings in the figure of the triangle, a geometric symbol of importance. The final shot merges heaven and earth, two elements adding a third entity, that of man. The connection of man with heaven and earth is reasserted here and shows the gaze of the artist now blinded as a strength – a perspective writer and art critic François Cheng develops in his book on Chinese painting and the void:

> A traditional rule says, 'In a picture, a third fullness-emptiness.' … The philosophical thought that lies behind it must be emphasised. Since the third of fullness actually corresponds to the earth and the two-thirds of emptiness to heaven (celestial elements and emptiness), the harmonious proportion established between heaven and earth is the same as the one man attempts to establish in himself, since he is endowed with the virtues of heaven-earth. The picture thus gives concrete expression to the desire of man, who, having taken the earth upon himself, reaches toward heaven in order to attain emptiness, which draws the whole into the life-giving movement of the Tao. (Cheng 1994: 89)

That connection between man and the universe is further explored in astrophysics, a domain that Lê continually draws from in his films.

Poussière d'empire[23]

Poussière d'empire was released the same year as Euzhan Palcy's *Rue Case-nègres* (*Sugar Cane Alley*, 1983) and for that and many reasons both films remain connected. Both were shown at the Venice Mostra and featured in opposite pages of the daily *Le Monde*. Whereas Palcy's film takes place in Martinique, Lê's goes to Vietnam. The similarity between the two film-makers is located in their identity and position in France, but at its margins. Both address postcolonial issues that were still rarely discussed in early-1980s French cinema: 'They were speaking about her from a position at her borders, at the border of "France", since a colonised territory is, in essence, destined to break away, to be separated, or at least, to be on the outside' (Ménil 1992: 158). *Poussière d'empire* takes us back to French colonialism and 'the dirty war' (la sale guerre), jumping back from 1983 to 1954, on the eve of the battle of Diên Biên Phû. Jean-François Stevenin and Dominique Sanda, who received top billing, play the role of two clashing representatives of French colonial history; one is a soldier, the other is a former socialite/fashion model, who has now become a missionary in Tonkin. Lê stresses the Christic figure of the nun in the first part.[24]

   Poussière d'empire sketches out the itinerary of a return. Lê returns to his native country and to the history of Vietnam already drafted in *Rencontre des nuages et du dragon*. In this attempt at reversed anthropology, a term borrowed from Jean Rouch's ethnographic film work in Africa, Lê reproduces

Figure 4   *Poussière d'empire* (© Lam Lê)

the itinerary of a Eurocentric film-maker who goes to film other cultures in the world. Here a Franco-Vietnamese film-maker goes back to Vietnam to shoot European others' interactions with Vietnamese. The film appropriates an out-of-place odd couple: the soldier and the nun, two pillars of early French colonisation of Indochina. The French couple in turn become the objects of reversed exoticism and stand as 'displaced' and 'exotic' through the gaze of a Vietnamese director.

The Catholic religion exported to Vietnam was the first power to occupy and evangelise the country. Jesuit missionaries started in the seventeenth century and settled at first in the Tonkin region (North Vietnam). The Tonkinese people were, according to members of the Church, predisposed to embrace Catholicism and were, in that, different from the Chinese. Father Tisanier, in his *Relation de voyage* (1663), claims that 'Tonkinese people are very far from the Chinese people's pride and are marvelously disposed to follow reason and to believe in the truths of another life.'25 Philippe Franchini explains that the success of conversions might be accounted for by the similarities between Buddhism, Confucianism and Catholicism and the belief in the immortality of the soul. The French government sent the army later to protect the missions, which were by then under attack.

The nun carries the ideological and evangelical baggage of the Catholic missions on her shoulders and is set to indoctrinate the natives whom she senses are ready for the word. Her intention to teach the Bible is mediated through the cinematic medium – a Western-imported technology. She carries along a copy of an early silent film, *La Vie du Christ* (*The Life of Christ*, Alice Guy & Victorin Jasset, 1906) and a Pathé Baby camera. Lê's first childhood filmic experience was through an itinerant barrel, where images were projected, and of the same Christian film he would use again, years later. An example of the early medium is featured in Raoul Coutard's film *Hoa Binh*, 1970.

Poussière d'empire includes semiotic markers: it has its own grammar and codes. The elaborate plot revolves around a message, a messenger, a message recipient, and a translator. Not unlike his previous film, *Poussière d'empire* resists any attempt to summarise its plot (see Norindr 2001). Because of the nature of the message and its recipients, we will examine the structural elements of the plot, whose central message is issued in five installments. However, there may be a series of messages deriving from the first one, like the message addressed to the spectator. Vladimir Propp's (1965) structural grid for tales illustrates best the inner workings of *Poussière d'empire*, a tale that borrows from Vietnamese mythology and the marvelous.

Message #1

The hero, a soldier who survived the battle of Binh Gia, issues the message. The Vietnamese soldier, Dao, played by Lam Lê, trained in the 'living theatre' method, approaches a young deaf-mute boy and asks him to deliver a message for his wife. He glues the message onto the child's kite. The boy is later captured by the French soldier/nun couple and brought to the hut. He escapes but the kite remains, preserved by the nun. It nearly sinks as the river floods the hut at night when all the occupants are trapped by guerilla warfare. The message, detached from the kite, floats on the water; the nun tries to comprehend its meaning. She can barely decipher 'villa des roses' and asks the village translator to explain the meaning. Villa des Roses is the name of a French colonial mansion in Saigon where the wife of the Vietnamese soldier, a nanny, works. He translates the following: 'Stone of the waiting, faithfulness and transformation.' The nun has an inner understanding of the legend and screams the tale in a moment of delirium during the downpour: it is the tale of the married couple that discovers they are brother and sister.

Message #2

Dao, now a prisoner in a camp, transmits his message for the second time. This time, he orally communicates its text to escapees at night. At the same time, a shot of the first message delivered to the child is inserted, with a man writing it in flashback. The message is now heard in its entirety for the first time: 'How can I with a magical stick shorten distances/or like the immortal one change a shawl into a bridge/must I wait to be transformed into a stone/or to no longer have any tears while going up the tower.'[26]

The intended recipient of the message, sent unsuccessfully twice thus far, is the wife of the prisoner who works in the colonial quarters of Saigon. The husband wants her to know that he is alive. This message is chanted as a poem whose lines are excerpts from an eighteenth-century work, the Chinh Phu Ngâm, or the 'Chant of the Warrior's Wife'.

Message #3

The film shows the second carrier of the message – a man who escapes from the camp and reaches a hut, where a young boy lives with his blind grandmother. She is told the message and instantly memorises it. This instance evokes precisely the saying that with older generations, entire books disappeared, as old people from all classes knew entire tales by heart. The grandmother teaches her grandson to memorise its lines. He is to carry it to Saigon and travels with nuns on a Red Cross truck. On the way to Saigon, the truck makes a stop, at the location of the 'stone of waiting' shot in wide frame – a location that attracts pilgrims. The young boy will be unable to deliver the message orally to the woman; he manages to copy it on paper in a romanised version of Vietnamese characters (or ngoc ngu). As he arrives at Villa des Roses, the French occupiers are departing for France. In an episode that concluded the first part of the film, the French army was defeated. The final days of French settlers are counted. The message almost reaches its destination. The young Vietnamese woman is leaving with the French family on board a sea-liner. A long gaze is exchanged between her and the child, but nothing is said, or given. The camera follows her closely, as she is 'mourning' her loss after leaving her country and going into exile. The written note is given instead to the last person available, a French female pop singer who is boarding the sea-liner. She has no idea that the message is supposed to reach another woman and in fact is unable to decipher the message, or understand that it is indeed a message as such.

Message #4

A sea-liner slowly crosses the ocean separating Vietnam from France, as shown on an awkward animated map. Entertainment is offered and the female singer sings a 'colonial' tune: 'Somewhere on the South China Sea.' The note/message falls off her fan and a little girl picks it up and keeps it. The daughter of the French family who left Villa des Roses now holds the message. It is the first circular movement where a message reaches someone close to the recipient. She folds the paper into a fan and looks at the singer. However, it will take another 21 years for the message to be read, roughly from 1954 to 1975.

The family arrives in France and travels to Paris by train. The single shot of Paris is of the Eiffel Tower, standing tall at the end of a street. Once they settle in their apartment, the news broadcast is heard and the camera stays on the apparatus. Indochina is now independent and free. The camera is fixated in a long take on the radio while the broadcasting subsequently evokes the passage of time and objects surrounding the old transistor. The narrative crosses over decades with the announcement of Ben Barka's death, the death of André Breton, the voice of De Gaulle, words about what is now 'the Vietnam war', the Saigon uprising, the Paris peace conference. The sequence segues from 1954 to 1975, moment of the Paris conference and fall of Saigon to bridge colonial history with postcolonial history. After thirty years of war, peace in Vietnam is finally declared. In the large sunny Parisian apartment, children playing 'cowboys and indians' break the radio where a written note is discovered. The camera takes us to the thirteenth district – the location of Chinatown – in search of the governess. The message reaches its recipient while a young Vietnamese woman sings an opera in front of the audience. The now-older Vietnamese woman collapses silently after deciphering the message. The camera respectfully focuses on her back and shoulders. The woman has never uttered a word throughout the film. In view of this, the singer stops her song.

Message #5

The last part of the film returns to Vietnam in a circular structure. A young woman of the new generation, the Têt singer, a foreigner to Vietnam or a Vietnamese living abroad, arrives by plane and asks her way around. All modes of modern and traditional transportation are explored: from sea-liner, to train, car, airplane, cyclo, bus and bicycle. After a long journey, she eventually rides a bicycle and arrives at the 'stone of the waiting' erected in a large field. Approaching the stone, she caresses it and hugs it. The meaning of the stone has evolved over the years, depending on colonial times. During French colonial times, the stone was the place where resistance fighters would meet. Under the American presence, the stone was more or less abandoned.

Incidentally, the stone looks like a woman's back. According to the legend, as the singer bitterly remarks, it is about a woman who waited so long for her husband that she metamorphosed into a stone. The young Vietkieu (Vietnamese person living abroad who returns) knows the woman who waited so long for her husband's return. Her mother waited for her husband's message of hope all her life. The message has now reached its recipient or repository, albeit years later, as the young woman inserts the message into the cavity of the stone. Apparently a sacred circularity has been respected and the message has come home. In response to the delivery of the message, a shining comet falls in the sky at dusk as a final image.

Stones elicit many things in Vietnamese lore. They can appropriate magical properties, and embody a spiritual entity. The cult of stones is common, along with the cult of trees. It is primordial to respect these, along their geological position, be it for a village, or its inhabitants. A stone can acquire magical powers over the years, depending on people's reverence for it. Léopold Cadière from the Ecole Française d'Extrême-Orient devoted a long study to the Vietnamese cult of trees and stones (1992). Stones are venerated in Vietnam and contain magical and religious elements. Stones house spirits and have a personality that needs to be respected. The geological formation found in the Bay of Halong, represented in *Indochine* when the protagonists are shown drifting in the junk, invokes the presence of spirits and the impossibility of travelers to ever return alive from that maze. These stone formations were/ are the objects of popular cults because of the dangers that they represent to sailors. Their importance parallels Celtic rituals found in England, Ireland and Brittany. Lê has linked the Vietnamese cult and legend with the West by inserting a line from Breton poet Guillevic 'Si un jour tu vois / Qu'une pierre te sourit / Iras-tu le dire?'(Were you, one day, to see a stone smiling at you, will you go and tell?') in his prologue to *Poussière d'empire*.

The central character of the film is a stone. Initially a young soldier is the anonymous hero of the tale. Following the Proppian grid, the hero is a soldier who personifies the Vietnamese nation as a whole. It is not so much his personal story that unravels here, as one can tell, especially since the young man quickly disappears from the plot, but the story of countless families that were separated. The message about the stone is the sole link to his family. The 'evil' role is assigned to the French colonisers who disturb the peace.

According to the Proppian scenario, transformation in tales is essential.[27] Magical properties and transformation occur on many levels. The stone formation opens the movie with an out-of-space shot of a meteorite exploding and landing on earth. The actual geological formation in Vietnam, at the centre of the country, is material for legends; it has spawned a certain form of music, the Vong Phu: 'The Vong Phu, a very melancholy musical mode that came to enrich popular music.'[28] We hear this type of music through the voice of a woman, several times during the film, as a lament. Lê designed a stone and contracted a sculptor in France and transported the sculpture to Vietnam. It has the shape of a woman's back, holding a child.

The film is built according to an extremely precise two-part mathematical scheme, with each containing its own temporality. According to Jean Blot, who wrote an extensive review and programme of the film, which Lê was invited to present in Blanc-Mesnil, a suburb of Paris, the 'meaning of the first part of the film (35 minutes) is based on the "square" that constitutes with the "circle", the Chinese symbol for the universe. (The square representing the sky, the circle, the earth)'.[29] Four protagonists, or three and a pillar, continually play during the first part centred on the European couple, once they are in the house. Any additional person is eliminated from the narrative and either disappears or dies.

The first shot of the film shows a meteorite landing on earth. The subsequent sequence opens on the two French protagonists who have literally landed in Vietnam, representing the two foremost colonial powers at the origins of the conquest of Indochina: the French army and the Catholic Church. Their first appearance plays out in a western-like landscape, with large rock formations surrounding them. Their presence retraces the beginning of French colonisation of Indochina. This first part closes with their death after a long drawn out sequence in a mud-filled hut, or the literal transposition of the quagmire of the French in Vietnam (and their dirty war).

The first part is performed theatrically in a sacred hut where dead people are honoured in mysterious cabinet drawers. This segment does not even cover a twenty-four-hour cycle, yet it compiles years of French presence. The message sent in the first part never reaches its destination. The nun discovers it but is unable to understand its meaning, except in fragments. She is aware of the legend and recites some of its lines during the hysterical moment when the river floods the hut.

The second part is based on the figure of the circle, symbol of the earth. This number represents fertility and reproduction. Women and the child are the dominant vessels for the transmission of the message. Men have sporadically intervened and more at the beginning of the message transmission. Space opens after the death of the colonial protagonists on the battlefield. The ocean liner allows for large sky views and the film closes on the stone and the sky of Vietnam. The message goes home to the stone through the intervention of the woman, a singer, presumably the daughter of the governess and soldier, though it is never said. The presence of a female singer and the importance of the voice here, oppose to other forms of communication. There is a large part of unspoken words and unexplained occurrences in the film. Through time, it reaches its destination through another generation, but at a high cost.

The geometric figure of the circle is launched at the opening of the film, with the figure of the meteorite exploding on earth. Landing in a thousand pieces, its visible signs take the shape of pamphlets dropped from an aeroplane. The full circle is accomplished at the end with the fall of the comet.

Screen memories

The image-making process shapes the narrative with the opening sequence that paint brushes a golden calligraphy. The nun uses a silent film as a prop for the natives' education, *La Vie du Christ*, thereby including the notion of reflexivity and the apparatus of a film within the film. Incidentally, the film juxtaposes Christian imagery to film-related objects. Screens, an intrinsic part of the film apparatus, are at the receiving end of the projected moving images. Hauling the earliest form of the cinematographer – a device invented by the Lumière brothers that could both record and project films, the nun reinvents the screen which she improvises with a sacerdotal white sheet embroidered with a cross. Lê introduces the figure of the primitive within the frame. The nun hangs the cloth on a flat and square surface inside the hut helped by Sergeant Tamisier (or Sergeant Tam-Tam). In so doing, her profile shows behind the cloth. Unfortunately, in her wish to use a flat surface, she places the screen in front of the funerary cabinet and commits a sacrilegious act. In an earlier scene, after entering the hut, the nun had approached the cabinet, next to which the funerary cabinet-maker was at work; her body was then seen through a veil. At the beginning of the projection of *La Vie du Christ*, the nun's body is superimposed onto the screen, as she walks in front of it. There is a play between veiling and unveiling, seeped in Christian imagery and the notion of the shroud. The first shot of the Vietnamese funerary artist (listed as cabinet-maker in the credits and played by the same actor who played Magical Brush in *Rencontre des nuages et du dragon*) was behind a thin cloth. When he later approaches the nun, he stares at her 'forbidden' body through the veil/screen that separates the cabinet from the central room. This highly charged moment is broken by her screams for Sergeant Tamisier. The cloth that can be called 'film' adds texture and grain to the celluloid. Of course, this motif duplicates the apparatus, in another *mise-en-abîme*, as it reinforces the presence of the projection screen, onto which the spectator is watching the film.

Death imagery ties *Poussière d'empire* and *Rencontre des nuages et du dragon*. Both scripts interconnect and communicate with each other. The actual death of the two Westerners – a simulacrum of the death of the colonial regime – is a muted non-event. Similarly, the death of the hero is rendered by his absence and the chant. These deaths are not a macabre event. The nun and soldier have initially entered a sacred space (Vietnam) by crossing over a ford and inviting themselves into a hut that houses the ashes and tablets (records) of dead

Figure 5   *Poussière d'empire* (© Lam Lê)

people. They refuse to acknowledge the sacrilegious nature of their (colonial) act. Their death is foretold by their entering/breaking into that sacred space. One of the first lines uttered by the nun is: 'You know sometimes in life, there are signs one has to read.' Does it mean that she intuitively knew that this mission was going to be her last one? The first part strongly conveys the notion of Christian sacrifice, pronouncing the word 'martyr' once. The nun, a former wealthy socialite, dropped out of that life and became poor when she joined the order ('je me suis faite pauvre').

The space they inhabit for several hours houses the remains of dead souls, termed 'silk souls' by experts and that are fixed in calligraphy by the attendant. Léopold Cadière, a priest and lifelong researcher and scholar of Vietnamese culture and traditions who belonged to the illustrious Ecole des Langues Orientales, wrote extensively about the funerary rites and symbols that he observed in Vietnamese villages. The silk soul, or a piece of silk that is used as transference when the person is dying, takes the actual place of the dead person. Once the body is buried, a tablet then replaces the silk soul. *Poussière d'empire* enacts rituals that are unknown to a Western spectator and involves the presence of a writer, or calligrapher: 'When the burial is half complete … this silk soul is replaced by a tablet. At that moment, the designated writer with a light brush traces a small dot that will complete the last character of the inscription, whose other strokes had been traced previously' (Cadière 1992: 36).[30] Once the body has left, the soul mysteriously resides in the tablet after the ceremony has been performed. The French soldier and nun take the artist as hostage and have no idea, at first, that they are trespassing a sanctuary for dead (and live) fighters, nor do they care. However, the nun ultimately is able to see a ghost or spirit at night in the hut, while they are besieged by guerilla warfare. She does not reveal this to the Sergeant, as sometimes things between them remain unspoken. Along with its interest in the Catholic faith, the film sows doubt and raises questions about perception and visibility. The nun becomes the ideal vehicle for these questions. Did the nun see a ghost/spirit of a fighter? Did she bury a man in a coffin that night, just to find an empty coffin the next day? Invisible forces participate in the traditional (animist) beliefs in two worlds. Man is said to move in two worlds, the world he sees, the natural world, and the one he does not see, the supernatural world: 'Cultivated classes, artisans who handle heavy modern machines and students initiated to Western disciplines, do not escape from this supernatural hold, to experiences that prove that the ancestral belief can lie dormant in their heart, to be awakened … at the first occasion' (Cadière 1992: 7).[31]

My reading of *Poussière d'empire* started with the claim that the film was a journey back to Vietnam. This travel performs a double movement, from Vietnam to France back to Vietnam. The return engages in border crossing and reclaiming one's personal or parental past. It activates a circular pattern that is strong in Buddhism and Taoism. Lê's cinema has been characterised as a cosmogonic cinema. The relation among people and space as explored throughout the film adds a fascinating dimension that I wish to explore further.

> I still want to create a cinema of verticality, of the sacred, of magic. Western film-making is losing ground, by its absence of the sacred and lack of verticality. *Poussière d'empire* is definitely placed under this dimension. (Lê cited in Séguret 1983)

A certain poetics of space informs Lê's films. Geomancy – the use of space, or the disposition of places, the East-West, North-South orientation and the importance of numbers – all this is carefully laid out. Lê shot a segment of *Poussière d'empire* in Vietnam and then reconstituted it in a small 22m² French studio for the remaining 55 minutes. A Vietnamese hut was reconstructed in a Parisian warehouse, a former dairy, located in the Porte de la Villette that was transformed into a studio (see Ostria 1983). It follows a precise geomantic Vietnamese map: the facade faces West, emblematic of iron; the back part of the house faces East, the wood; the North, the right, symbolises water; the Red River and South symbolises fire: 'These four elements form a magical square, the same one that represents a turtle on its four legs: the part image of the Vietnamese universe, founded on a total stability' (Séguret 1983: 27). *Poussière d'empire* is ultimately a hymn to the strength of love, faithfulness and transformation of the Vietnamese people. The legend at the root of the film is a war legend and a myth. The myth has given in turn many legends and poems, one is *The Married Woman of Nam Xuong*, the tale of a wife who is waiting for her husband to return from war with the Champa – the same legend discussed in chapter three. Lê adapts the legend of the Stone of the Waiting but his intentions are different. He shows fidelity towards one's spouse, one's country, separated by time and space, encapsulated in a message. The incestuous connection is never evoked. The wait ultimately embodies the plight of Vietnamese people in the diaspora, their resilience while waiting for their country to be whole again, at peace and independent.

'The first shot of my film … shows a paintbrush that draws an ancient Vietnamese ideogram that stands for sky. The film ends with the child who writes in modern Vietnamese' (Lê cited in Guibert 1983). Lê touched on some personal motifs behind the making of the film and his career as a film-maker. The film opens on a brush painting a Chinese ideogram in gold. The ideogram, once formed, explodes in the dark sky. The inscription of ideograms, writing and lettering, the cult to the dead and ashes of dead people are carried over from *Rencontre des nuages et du dragon* to *Poussière d'empire*, with the transposition of the same actor who played Uncle Xuan, who is again in charge of dead people's ashes this time. One of the common denominators is the child used as a vehicle for carrying primary messages, a bridge between past and future.

It is an essay about the film-maker's own hopes for his native country and symbolically a wait: 'The hectic political visible fate of Indochina matters less to Lam Lê than the secret unfolding of time, below the surface. Bombs make people blind. The message whose flight he has followed from the fifties to the eighties makes one lucid' (Lebrun 1983: 20).

The Vietnamese reception to his film was mixed. It was not exactly a co-production, although it did involve Vietnamese technicians. After his first film, Lê was asked to make films in his native country, where he projected *Rencontre des nuages et du dragon* in private screenings. The reasons for this are that his films did not project the party's official line and were considered as 'non-socialist cinema that could not be understood by people' (Séguret 1983: 34). Lê wanted to shoot in impoverished areas, not just in colonial neighbourhoods. This was forbidden to him. He would have preferred a reconstitution of Vietnam in France, instead of shooting in Thailand or the Philippines as Coppola or Cimino did. For these countries are diverse and do not look familiar. For example, a Vietnamese field is not configured like a Thai field. Space and architecture in Asia are not a monolithic block. *Poussière d'empire* is the last film he made, in what had started as a trilogy on Vietnam. Lê moved on to other projects that involved film-making, but thus far has devoted his time to advertising and teaching. His next project will see him back after a long hiatus.

The French reception was extremely positive from all sides, drawing praises from *Cahiers du cinéma* to *L'Humanité*. The critical response refers to the Eastern symbolism at work in the film, like the lines and the notion of the sacred: 'The film takes us from the Orient's sacredness, treated in a theatrical way, to the futility of the Occident.'[32] Lê's position has remained that of an Asian film-maker living in France.

CHAPTER THREE

Scented Papaya

Tran Anh Hung's films are deeply influenced by the very fabric of Vietnam. The corpus of films he directed in the 1990s exhibit the unmistakable signature of an auteur. Their narratives and thematic concerns, *mise-en-scène* and techniques, all interconnect, displaying the director's mastery of the medium. His beautifully crafted work has also reached out to an international audience with a significant degree of success. Tran's first feature-length film, *L'Odeur de la papaye verte* (*The Scent of Green Papaya*, 1993), was produced and distributed by Les Productions Lazennec, MKL and co-produced by SFP cinema and La Sept Cinema in Paris.[1] In the first section of this chapter, 'Take one', I will embark on an initiatory approach to the film by contextualising its making and proposing a reading of a text that was produced, written and directed by a Franco-Vietnamese film-maker about Vietnam. The second part of this chapter, or 'Take two', engages in a more critical and sometimes personal assessment of the film while acknowledging the debates it has generated in media and academic circles and, whenever possible, within Franco-Asian or Asian American communities.

Take one

Early shorts

Born in 1962 in My-Tho, located in the Mekong delta (South Vietnam), Tran left his native country for a temporary stay in Laos then resettled in France with his parents in 1975. The family lived in Villeneuve le Roi, a suburb of

Paris. Tran was a student majoring in philosophy when he screened a film by a Vietnamese film-maker living in France that aired on French television. This film was Lam Lê's *Poussière d'empire* and this moment decided his orientation toward film-making. His first short film was his final project for the Louis Lumière film school in 1987; Tran is one of the few film-makers trained at this film school, since its primary orientation is to train film technicians, not directors.[2] *La femme mariée de Nam Xuong* (*The Married Woman of Nam Xuong*, 1987) is an adaptation of a Vietnamese tale, 'Histoire de la femme de Nam-Xuong' written by Nguyen-Du in the sixteenth century, now published and translated in French in a collection of tales entitled *Vaste Recueil de Légendes merveilleuses* (Nguyên-Du 1962).

The cinematic tale reconstituted on a set at the Lumière film school recounts the story of a woman whose husband has left for war. When night comes, she pretends to her child that the shadow projected on a sheet is his father. When the father returns, two years later, the child rejects him, telling him that his father only returns at night. The wife subsequently commits suicide. The original sixteenth-century tale sets the story at a time of war against the Champa. A husband left his then-pregnant wife to fight the war, and she waited for him for three years. When he returned, suspecting that she has been unfaithful, she throws herself into the river to preserve her honour:

> If I confided to you, it is for the peace of the household. I did not expect calumnies to be as high as mountains and your goodness as thin as a leaf. Now the vase is full, the pin is broken, the clouds are swept away and the rain is gone. I can no longer climb to the mountain of 'the waiting for the husband'. (Nguyên-Du 1962: 210)

The allusion to the mountain of 'waiting for one's husband' is a reference to the Stone of Waiting and the concept of fidelity. The legend applies to wartime situations – the Champa, the Franco-Vietnamese war, and the American/Vietnamese war – and involves a faithful wait and subsequent transformation. Here, a wife will wait for her husband for such a long time that she is transfigured into a stone statue. This legend was adapted at different times by Lam Lê, Tran Anh Hung and Raoul Coutard. As is traditional in French cinema and especially since the 1960s, film-makers have first to prove themselves by making short films. Christopher Rossignon, from the production house *Lazennec tout court,* produced Tran's second short, *La Pierre de L'attente* (*The Stone of the Waiting*, 1991). The plot borrows its title and inspiration directly from *Poussière d'empire* and bears the same Vietnamese title.

Tran Anh Hung's version of *La Pierre de l'attente* is the tale of a man and a woman, both boat people, who meet in a transit refugee camp in Indonesia. Years later, they live in Paris, married with a child. One day, the husband discovers that his wife happens to be his younger sister, whom he thought had died during the war. He subsequently leaves home. The story draws on the theme and fear of incest between brother and sister. The narrative has few words, a fundamental principle governing Tran's writing. Lê, a model and mentor to the director, agreed to act in the film. Tran's companion Tran Nu Yên Khê played the sister, who lost her entire family at sea.

Tran's work is characteristic of many exile directors whose first project, be it writing or directing, finds its source of inspiration at 'home'. Such a phase, defined by Teshome Gabriel as the 'remembrance phase' or a 'return of the exile to the Third World's source of strength, i.e. culture and history' (1989: 32) is particularly fitting in this case. Although I do not want to categorise the director as a Third World director, Gabriel's methodology for a critical inquiry into Third World cinema appropriately corresponds to that particular phase when it comes to Tran Anh Hung and the return to one's roots.

The theme of waiting runs deep in many Vietnamese (and Chinese) legends, some of which have been adapted for cinema. In the previous chapter we examined *Poussière d'empire*, where the stone of waiting resurfaces in the form of an encapsulated message that takes years and different continents to reach its destination. Originating in Vietnam, it crosses over oceans to reach its intended recipient in France then returns to Vietnam. More recently, the same theme, albeit in a modified form, is played out in Wong Kar-wai's *In the Mood for Love* in a sequence geographically located in 1960s Cambodia, when the male protagonist leaves a paper (his secret) in a stone-cavity of the Angkor Vat temple.

L'Odeur de la papaye verte

Tran Anh Hung's first feature film, *L'Odeur de la papaye verte*, was awarded the Caméra d'Or for best feature film for a first-time director at the 1993 Cannes Film Festival. He received the Academy Award for best foreign film in the US in 1994, representing Vietnam and gratifying the country's recent opening to the West. After 1986 and the sixth congress of the Vietnamese Communist Party that took place that year, Vietnam eagerly re-opened trade with the West and prioritised exports of goods in its *do moi* policy: 'The sixth PCV congress, postponed until December 1986 because of the crisis, initiated the movement of socio-economical renovation, the Vietnamese equivalent to the Soviet perestroika' (Fourniau 1989: 328).

The lack of treatment or absence of meaningful roles given to Vietnamese actors in French cinema should not be surprising as such films are produced by the neo-colonial powers themselves, which continue to perpetrate the myth, or what has been called the 'tendentiously flawed mimesis of many films dealing with the third world' (Stam & Spence 1985: 637). We have now reached a moment when former colonies, or their children, living sometimes in the diaspora – such is the case for Tran Anh Hung, Rithy Panh, Karim Dridi and others – can make films and speak in their own terms about their past, their parents' past and country. Such films reinscribe the country of origins' own history and voice. Tran's decision to become a film-maker is not an easy route to take in the Vietnamese community, where film-making and acting have traditionally not been recognised as profitable and respectable careers. His father accepted his decision, realising that after all, a need to discuss Vietnam from a Vietnamese perspective would arise in France and thus going against the long-time precept that Vietnamese immigrants of the last wave have to worry first about settling down economically and making a living.

Trinh T. Minh-ha, a female Vietnamese film-maker and cultural critic based in the US, underlines the way that representations of Vietnam on film have turned the country into either a nostalgic object or a revolutionary model. In either instance, these representations have shaped an 'invisible' Vietnam. Spectators go to see films 'about' Vietnam and are met with images of a war-torn country; such spectacles are part of the expectations of many spectators when they go to see a film about Vietnam. Tran Anh Hung was committed to go against the trend with this film; his subsequent project, *Cyclo*, takes him even further. Yet the extremely critical and divergent responses to Tran and his film(s) betray the precarious and divergent positions to be found in the Franco-Asian community.

Roland Barthes, Christian Metz and Jean-Louis Baudry have all analysed the position of the spectator at the movies. The intrinsic mechanisms of cinema and its apparatus force a viewer to a certain immobility that may equate passivity (see Baudry 1975). I believe that certain films do not promote entertainment for its own sake, but rather jolt the spectator, and send him/her home with questions. A spectator in the West may feel at odds when watching a non-Western film, where pace and language might be different. Some themes are cross-cultural, though, and reach us across borders. I do not claim to fully understand *L'Odeur de la papaye verte* and certainly the film's language, its gestures and details, may not translate well as our cultural background and education may be entirely different. The film was originally shot in Vietnamese with French subtitles and destined for a French audience. A dubbed French version was also released. However, to solely apply a Western grid of interpretation would not be appropriate, yet we can learn from the story once we set aside our Eurocentric preoccupations.

Perfumed immigrant memories

Tran gives us some clues, about time and space, at the beginning of the film: we are told that the story takes place in Saigon, circa 1951. It is set during the French occupation of the country, three years before the battle of Diên Biên Phû and the subsequent withdrawal of the French army. An audience that did not grow up in Vietnam will not be familiar with a green papaya, except from maybe seeing one at the supermarket in the 'exotic produce' section. Tran introduces the spectator to the different facets of the fruit and explains it as an ethnographer on a mission to investigate his people for a Western audience.

The title reinforces a certain type of synesthesia, or the mixing of two senses, the smell and vision, a practice found in Baudelaire or Rimbaud's poetry as well as in Proust. The visual imagery of the papaya is explored: green on the outside, growing in the courtyard of a house, it is cut, shredded, then split in half by Mui, the young servant recently hired by a middle-class family. Extreme close-ups suggest Mui's fascination for the papaya. The camera follows the papaya when it is picked and drops of a milk-like white liquid bleed from the incision when cut in half. What the spectator, ignorant of the language does not know, is that Mui, the name of the young ten-year-old girl, means 'scent'.

Tran's notes on the film contain an elaborate description of the fruit:

> The papaya is a fruit when it is ripe. When green, it is a vegetable. This is why the papaya tree is always planted behind the kitchen, in the vegetable garden with vegetables and herbs … The green papaya reaches man on his plate, ready to be consumed. On the other hand, it is picked, washed, peeled and prepared by the woman. This is why the evocation of a green papaya reminds me of an entire world of motions and attitudes by woman in her domestic chores. The smell of the green papaya is for me a childhood memory of maternal gestures.[3]

This descriptive quote was recycled and repackaged by film critics and historians into an instant explanation for the film and many critics suddenly became experts in Vietnamese culture and its culinary traditions.

The film could best be summed up as the tale of Mui, who is displaced from the countryside and comes to town to work for a merchant family as a servant. However, such a history of displacement is not shown on screen and the film has been criticised for leaving out socio-historical events. The naming and dating of Saigon in 1951 points otherwise; the narrative takes place after Ho Chi Minh declared the independence of Vietnam in 1946, and after the final withdrawal of the French. The year 1951 is crucial when considering the history of Vietnam: Mui's microcosmic tale of displacement reflects her countrymen's tale of migration and diaspora and her story is located within the larger context of Vietnamese national history. She left her family because of economic reasons and probably because her father is dead. The soundtrack bridges the inner intimate household world where 'nothing happens' with the outside world using extra-diegetic sounds of curfew sirens, airplanes and jets. The narrative spans a ten-year period from 1951 to 1961, incidentally the year when the Americans started to intervene directly, under Kennedy's presidency.[4]

The space is limited to the inner world of a merchant family. It is confined to the perimeters of the Vietnamese house, an agency of several one-level buildings assembled in a square, surrounding a courtyard, flanked by the main thoroughfare, or alley, where commercial exchanges take place. The mistress sells fabric from a small shop attached to the main house near the alleyway. The entire structure is physically and spiritually controlled by the mother-in-law's quarters, the only room located on a first floor, accessible by a steep staircase. The room at the top houses the altar to the ancestors where incense constantly burns next to pictures of the dead daughter and grandfather and various offerings.

Tran shot the film in the (SFP television) studios of Bry-sur-Marne, unable to do so in Vietnam because of certain budgetary and logistical reasons. As discussed earlier, his first shorts were studio-based films made in Paris suburbs recreating Vietnam on film. The director had previously evoked the impossibility of 'framing' in France. For Tran, the ideal filmic space is located in Vietnam. The frame, defined as a constraint, constantly tries to erase:

> The process confusing the frame of the image and the border of the support has important consequences on the spectator's imagination. The cutting attributed to the dimension of the support more than to a choice of framing, pushes the spectator to imaginarily construct what one does not see in the visual field of representation, but what completes it: the outside field. (Quoted in Joly 1993: 82)

The composition of the frame, analysed elsewhere by Gilles Deleuze as a relatively closed system, has remained a major obstacle for him. Mostly understood as a very precise geometry, Deleuze examined the vertical or

Figure 6   *L'Odeur de la papaye verte* (© Les Productions Lazennec – Laurence Trémolet)

horizontal lines that enter the structure of the frame and may for some limit it.

> It is for me a huge handicap to shoot in France, because I don't see how I can take a frame in an apartment. By this I mean, that it is an entire interrogation linked to the writing of a film. In addition, it is entirely related to cinema. Vietnam gives me this freedom, this range of frames, and allows me to make everything believable ... people won't say, but what is the position of the camera, why such an awkward angle, this will not seem strange because of space. (1995, interview with W. M. Makki)

Consequently, the space covered is extremely theatrical and intimate. The smooth, sweeping camera movements, or tracking shots moving from right to left and left to right (that Tran calls plan-séquence), follow the open interior geography of the house where the drama of its participants unfolds but follow more closely Mui's passage and chores. The households change, as Mui, a young woman, is sent away from her 'home' ten years later to become Khuyen's servant. The transition occurs over a water bowl that mirrors her reflection. Khuyen, a close friend of the family's son, who appears earlier under Mui's ten-year-old point of view, is now a composer and seems untouched by time. The spatial organisation is extremely different, even if her work and movements through space contribute to tone down this transition, suturing Mui's domestic gestures to the gliding movements of the camera and the sound of crickets and frogs. Khuyen's house is more partitioned, with a larger number of doors, hallways and mirrors than the former household. Alain Nègre's set design of Khuyen's house together with Benoît Delhomme's cinematography filter Eastern and Western influences in an unusual way. A few spectators left the screening convinced that they had just watched a film shot in Vietnam, whereas others, who knew better, felt that the film was Japanese-like. The *Mekong* review, a short-lived francophone newspaper that came out of Cambodia in the mid-1990s, insisted on that authentic feeling: 'Even if the theatre on the Champs-Elysées is air-conditioned, nothing can change it: as soon as the first images roll, one feels the humidity and mugginess of the extreme Orient, the softness of its lights, the bicycle of the merchant, the house with its many rooms, waxed floors, everything seems more real than nature.'[5]

The film-maker has coded an entire world of sensations or sense memories that concur to give the illusion, the verisimilitude, of a small corner of a Vietnamese neighborhood, with its scents, sounds and music. Something paradoxically made possible by the reconstitution of a 'mental Asia' in a Parisian suburban studio. Going against the theory previously advocated and the impossible task of 'framing' in France, the film forced a reconstituted return home, in France. The process is not atypical, as many first-time exilic films or novels and short stories return to the country of origins, or the parents'

Figure 7   *L'Odeur de la papaye verte* (© Les Productions Lazennec – Laurence Trémolet)

country in the host countries. This artificial return would in turn enable the director to negotiate a return to Vietnam with *Cyclo*, his second feature film.

The household embodies a matriarchal world, 'an inherent structure of Vietnamese society that predated the Chinese and French colonisation experiences' or a strong female (yin) presence (Thúy Dinh 1994: 81). The memories of such a world dominate the first part of the film. In the mind of the mistress, Mui (Lu Man San) replaces Tô, her dead daughter, as she is the same age as Tô, had she lived. The domestic chores of the female servants and of the wife who runs her fabric shop are interrelated. However, the spectator can only enter the psyche of the two female servants, Mui and the older one Thi (Nguyen Anh Hoa). Mistress and female servants work in unison at keeping the household alive with food and together when the father absconds with the entire savings (which he presumably gambles and loses) in a Durassian scenario. The death of the father, after he returns from his escapade, brings a blow to the family and will have repercussions years later, when the family's daughter-in-law decides to let go of Mui to reduce the household expenses.

In the second part of the film, Mui is transferred to the world of Khuyen, who was Western-educated in France, as evidenced by the Conservatoire National de Musique diploma displayed on the bookshelves. He composes music for the piano while she peacefully goes about her chores. This portrait is certainly at the root of conflicting impressions for the female spectator, for it is about the submission of woman to the male master. Love and submission merge in the scenario. Tran claims to give the portrait of a traditional Vietnamese woman in a traditional society:

When I wrote *The Scent of Green Papaya*, I wanted to address the problem of servitude, at the heart of the Vietnamese woman's condition. I chose to construct a narrative in two movements, the first one describes the way that this submission works, since its start until its full acceptation, that has been constituted as a tradition, all the way until the aged or abandoned wife continues to serve her husband. (Press kit)[6]

The transposition of one form of slavery for another one takes place, as now Mui becomes Khuyen's mistress and servant.

Tran's homage to his mother and Vietnamese women shows in the different sequences on food preparations, rituals and prayers to the ancestors; yet it contains a certain form of oppression or conservatism or at least points to the role of women and especially domestic workers, in their task of preserving the dignity of the household even in times of poverty. For instance, the use of nuoc-mam (fish sauce) is required so that salt will hide the lack of meat. Tran honours the traditions and rituals maintained by women in Vietnam and that are acknowledged by many who attribute the preservation of the Vietnamese identity, language and culture to women:

It is a permanence in our history: women have always less accepted the occupier's customs than men did. It is true in their way of dressing. It is true in familial customs. It is flagrant in the linguistic field. Who else preserves language if it is not woman? (Hoang Xuan Han in Ruscio 1989: 61)[7]

The rhythm of green papaya

The film choreographs the repetition of certain gestures and the harmony that subsists between Mui and nature – in an essentialist treatment if one considers that women are usually paired with nature in essentialist narratives. The director uses animal symbolism to coach his actors in their roles. Mui apparently was to follow the lemur and Thi, the older female servant, the cat (Cross 1994).

Tran's soundtracks are carefully elaborate and show that he is not just interested in visual elements. The second part of the film's invisible but growing Western influence registers both visually and on the soundtrack. It is filtered by the relations between Khuyen and his fiancée. Both are influenced by the West and it is through them that Mui and the spectator come into contact with 'it' (the West) through their rather free relation and the trail of various objects they leave like lipsticks and high-heel shoes. Khuyen stands at the interstice of two worlds and two cultures: East and West. The fiancée he abandons later in the film fills the same position.[8] The artwork displayed on the walls further accentuates these tensions.

The first part of the film brings in traditional instruments and beat and inserts them into the diegesis during the first sequence with the master and older son's duo recital. Music soothes the mind during the early curfew hours when father and son play together. The ceremony or ritual for the dying master rushes a group of traditional musicians to his bedside, to place acupuncture needles (*moxas*) in a healing attempt. We must presume that it is a Vietnamese custom. The second part of the film, at the juncture of the father's death, confronts two musical traditions. The musical score shifts from an earlier traditional rhythmic Buddhist beat, originating from the mother-in-law's *mo gia tri* and traditional instrumentation, to the overpowering and sometimes strident violin cords found in the original musical score by Vietnamese composer Tôn-Thât Tiêt and piano pieces by Chopin and Debussy as well as a jazz tune.[9] Tôn Thât Tiêt, who lives in France, has composed original scores for each one of Tran's films; his music is evocative of Vietnam, and he has composed operas about the war. Buddhist philosophy directly inspires his musical works (see Durney 1998). The use of music underscores the psychological conflicts that erupt between the Westernised fiancée and the more traditional woman represented by Mui. Khuyen's music and the traditional instruments work together at expressing emotions and what is not articulated between people, better than language. Khuyen's minimalist use of dialogue becomes evident by the end of the film. The economy of language is further restated in the economy of shots. Without heavy-handed camera movements or extensive melodramatic dialogue, the narrative accentuates body gestures, rhythms, and attention to details and exchanges of gazes throughout the film until the final sequence. One sequence is a silent, erotically charged pursuit between Khuyen and Mui, who has just tried the red lipstick. The camera chases Mui in the maze-like house. This seduction scene was picked up in the film trailer shown at the movie theatres in France. The trailer is a fast montage of different takes of the film carefully spliced by the rhythmic beat of the *mo gia tri* that in retrospect seems to dictate the gestures of the inhabitants. Tran's passion for Japanese film-maker Ozu is translated by the way communication is established between people on screen – a rapport that definitely corresponds to a certain Vietnamese sensibility.

Khuyen's piano-playing and inspiration dominate the last part of the film, next to his sketches of Mui, whose features are compared to a Buddhist idol. Tran pays homage to his mother and his wife, actress Tran Nu Yên Khê in this portrait. Finally, Khuyen chooses Mui, the traditional woman, as his partner and teaches her how to read. This act empowers Mui for the first time in her life and gives her the tools for a future transgression from her role as a servant.

Tran selected this intimate and sensuous portrait of the growth of a young woman, resisting the action-packed spectacles shown in film houses to chronicle a moment in the life of a family in Vietnam. However, there are ellipses to this growth, like the important moment of Mui's teenage years and her transformation into womanhood. The flash-forward sequence that jumps ten years ahead is an ellipsis in time, occurring during Mui's contemplation of her face in a water basin. *L'Odeur de la papaye verte* has been compared to a cinematic equivalent of a haiku: 'Green Papaya marries nature and artifice, taking the graceful shape of an Oriental character that grows, like a cherry tree, into ever larger meaning as pen-strokes are added' (Murphy 1993: 66–7).

The first text that Mui learns how to read is about a papaya tree; it is structured around a caller's response. When Mui reads, Khuyen responds:

> In my garden, there is a papaya tree
> The papayas hang in bunches
> The ripe papayas have a pale, yellow colour
> The ripe papayas are sweet with a sugary taste

Khuyen responds by dictating to her. It is the first time he has uttered several sentences together:

> We have been raising a black dog
> For three years now
> His body is long. He has big feet and big ears

Mui opens a papaya again and plants one seed. The next scene shows a pregnant Mui reciting a poem written by Japanese prose poet, Soseki, 'The Grass Pillow', sitting on a chair. Time has passed imperceptibly:

> The spring water nestled in a hole in a rock
> Shimmers softly when disturbed
> The vibrations of the ground
> Have given birth to strong waves
> Which crash together in an irregular swell
> On the surface without cresting
> If there is a verb meaning
> 'To move harmoniously'
> It must be used here
> The cherry trees gripped in shadows
> Spread out and curl
> Sway and twist to the rhythm of the war
> However, the interesting thing is
> However much they change
> They keep the shape of a cherry tree

Upon reciting these lines, Mui looks ahead straight into the camera. The camera moves up to the Buddha standing tall above and behind her. Mui's face merges with the face of a Buddhist statue in the second part of the film. A Western spectator might feel frustrated by the general stylised appeal achieved by the film and the supposed lack of a historical perspective. However, the rhythm of the film is intentionally different and measured. The passage of time is virtually glossed over; life and its changes, like the passing of people, are really seen as a continuum and as a flow. Tran points to the spiritual and philosophical permanence of things evacuating the need for an explanatory rational Western discourse. What better choice could have been made when a film produced in France, entirely shot in Vietnamese, with a French crew, resorts to obliterate the French Western presence out of Indochina, at a time, where they were still present, but slowly evacuated from the synopsis of history.

Take two

The large critical response to *L'Odeur de la papaye verte* in France and the United States deserves some attention. I would like to propose that scented (immigrant) memories could suddenly become a 'perfumed nightmare'. Do memories have a scent? By avoiding a representation of a country that is usually portrayed in most Western films as a country at war, Tran was going against the grain. However, by 1993, the mere evocation of 1950s Vietnam is 'contaminated' by colonial and post-colonial history, not to mention its earlier filmic representations. Tran states that he wanted to evoke 'the soul of Vietnam' in the film. 'What was important for me was to create a specific rhythm, to find the very movement of the Vietnamese soul' (quoted in Cross 1994: 35). This rather ambitious aim formulates an almost Barthesian project. It has had its detractors but garnered many praises and prizes at film festivals. As I will attempt to show, the film elicited a wide range of responses, some of them contradicting one another.

L'Odeur de la papaye verte has been accused of being neither French, nor Vietnamese, but … Japanese. It attempts to capture a 'mental Vietnam', therefore echoing the director's intentions that are reiterated in a 1995 interview (Jeancolas 1993). Tran, a profound admirer of Japanese art and culture, takes Japanese film-maker Ozu as one of his cinematic models for whom 'nothing is precise – things float, they don't find a precise conclusion. I feel that life truly is that way' (Cross 1994: 36).[10] Most reviews have condemned the absence of history. However, if history enters the film, it is in an oblique way, not necessarily head-on. There are signs begging to be deciphered. The soundtrack and set design are filters to the outside world, with the curfew sirens, the sound of jets or warplanes, the death and vanishing of fathers, not to mention the increasingly impoverished middle-class merchant family trying to preserve a semblance of high-class status. The spiritual breath of the film prevents the spectator from fully grasping its socio-political nature. The exploration of the passing of time, devoid of chronological markers and Western paraphernalia, associated with Vietnam in the movies, may seem startling.

The Oriental theme park

Carrie Tarr has compiled a taxonomy of fiction films involved with minorities in France and has focused specifically on 'beur' cinema, or films made by the first-generation of Arabs born in France. She approaches Tran Anh Hung and Rithy Panh as film-makers exemplary of their minority status in France, since they are respectively Vietnamese and Cambodian. However, she criticises them as they 'sidestep a critique of the effects of empire in their films, concentrating instead on the lived experience of their indigenous subjects' (1997: 64). I assume that Tarr did not take account of Rithy Panh's films *Site 2*, or *Bophana, une tragédie cambodgienne* in her essay. Tran stated that he did not want to make a documentary film, or another film about the war, a position he shares with Minh-ha: 'As soon as one speaks of Vietnam at the movies, one sees images of the war. Violence has masked for years the humanity of my people.'[11] However, as a hyphenated French citizen, Tran somehow is the designated film-maker to carry the burden of speaking for the others and addressing a historical situation. He is not alone in that task.

Richard Gott's *Guardian* article attacks the French treatment of its former empire showing countries 'unrecognisably transmogrified into an oriental theme-park of the imagination' (1996: 10). The strongest and most outspoken response based in the Franco-Vietnamese community comes from Lam Lê, his mentor. Lê accuses Tran of being the perfect product of integration politics in France: '*The Scent of Green Papaya* is the perfect example and product of French integration politics toward new French citizens of foreign origins.'[12] Tran and Lê were both born in Vietnam and arrived in France at different moments. Lê describes Tran as part of the 'tronci' generation ('citron' meaning the 'lemon' generation – a *verlan* French term). Verlan is a back slang used by French youth that plays with inverting syllables –'citron' here is a term used by beurs to designate their Asian counterparts, or those who are the first generation of immigrants growing in France. The political agenda behind the film arguably results from a thorough French upbringing and conveniently evacuates history from the narrative. However, Lê's heated response, written for and published the day after the film was released by the leftist daily *Libération*, shows that history, the repressed factor in the film, somehow returns forcefully through other means: 'To evacuate History from his smaller story, in order not to pain some spectators, the auteur has ushered history into his film, despite himself' (1993: 42). Through the lens of this critique, the script increases in complexity. For instance, Mui's origins are to be traced in South Vietnam yet she comes to work for a wealthy North Vietnamese family (re)located in South Vietnam. More than the film translation can ever transpose for the non-native speaker, accents play a large part and betray a different agenda for the author whose origins are South Vietnamese. Lê similarly reflects on the year 1951 as a crucial year in Vietnam history, the same year that he used previously in *Rencontre des nuages et du dragon*. That year, the General de Lattre de

Tassigny was sent to North Vietnam to quell the rebellion against the French colonial authorities in the aftermath of the Cao Bang defeat, or in short, the mobilising forces leading to Diên Biên Phû's defeat for the French army. It is the first time that Vietnamese troops were recruited to form the first corps of Vietnamese paratroopers. This is relayed in the film by the sound of airplanes. The Vietminh did not yet have planes in their defensive strategies. In the casting, the members of the master's family located in Saigon speak with a Northern accent, whereas the domestics, Mui and the street people speak with a Southern accent. Since Tran recruited and selected actors within the Franco-Vietnamese community, except for the older female servant who comes from Vietnam, the film incorporates a larger implicit agenda – one that cannot be known to an outsider to the culture, language and history.

Identity in question

By and large, the range of critiques is astonishing, from accusations of not being French enough, or being too French, to borrowing from the New Wave, borrowing from the tradition of quality, from being Proustian, opportunistic and sentimentalist. These critiques have not ceased and were projected onto *Cyclo*, his second feature film. How can I, a Western feminist, analyse the film and conclude with a concern over the extreme sexism of the film, without being attacked for misunderstanding the point that a Franco-Vietnamese film-maker is trying to make about his own culture, traditions and the place of women in his society? Tran may be deeply aware of women's positions in Vietnamese society, but the contrary could be and has been said about him. However, his response to such an analysis is predictably weary of Western feminist grids:

> One must not apply a Western point of view on this situation. The relations between men and women over there are 'soft', slow, far from European or American confrontations. In my country, man is not considered superior to woman, far from that. He is by ancient tradition a cultivated and idle man who depends on his wife's trade. (Tran Anh Hung, television interview with Mona Makki, 1995)

The struggles of Vietnamese women throughout the history of Vietnam have a long reputation documented for example by both Arlene Eisen-Bergman's study *Femmes du Viêt-Nam* (1975) and Trinh T. Minh-ha's film and script *Surname Viet, Given Name Nam* (1989). Minh-ha recounts and details the many years of battles and sacrifices women made. She in turn borrows from Mai Thu Vân's (1983) narrative and account of her own return to Vietnam and interviews with Vietnamese women under socialism.

Lam Lê's influential essay, written on the spur of the moment, is critical of the lack of a political agenda and of the 'miserabilist' treatment of women à la Victor Hugo that he finds in the film. It strongly evokes Vietnamese women's servitude in a patriarchal society and as such was programmed in a film festival devoted to 'Masters and Servants' organised by the vidéothèque de Paris in 1997. In Vietnam, Confucian principles have relegated women to 'nothingness'. Philippe Franchini, in his autobiographical essay on a childhood in Vietnam, underlines the birth of male children as a celebration, whereas the birth of a girl is deemed less interesting:

> They were educated under the precepts of the venerable book of Chinese poetry: 'Boys will be born to the emperor, they will be laid on beds, dressed in beautiful clothes and will have jade tablets for toys … girls will be born to the Emperor, they will be placed on the ground, wrapped in diapers and given a brick for a toy.'[13]

While the space allotted to Western criticism is extremely narrow and slippery, since according to Tran, Westerners cannot understand Vietnam, I am left on the periphery of a project to observe the iconography used in the film. Yet as an avid observer and spectator (and researcher), I see that Mui's body language and gestures constantly frame her in subservient poses that I previously recall observing in documentary pictograms taken by early ethnographic expeditions. The rare moments when her body is erect and still occur at the end of the film when she sits facing the camera in an *Emmanuelle*-like bamboo armchair and pose – the armchair being the epitome of the Orientalist object and trend that dominated the 1970s. The visual Emmanuellian antecedent lurks behind the screen, almost signaling to the spectator.

My reading of the film is informed by Pierre Bourdieu's notion of Habitus. The habitus is explained as a life-style, an 'ensemble of tastes, creeds, systematic practices that are characteristic of a class, or a fraction of a given class' (cited in Bonnewitz 1997: 63). The mode of habitation found in *L'Odeur de la papaye verte* ranges among the 'gestuelle' that is sometimes linked to a sexual but also cultural and racial identity. All these markers of a *habitus* sustain the film's creative process and accompany Tran's other films. It informs the way his actors speak, walk and stand. To evoke his past and his mother's past, the director becomes a teacher and translator, and teaches an entire (seemingly forgotten) 'gestuelle' to his actors, mostly Vietnamese people living in France for his first feature film. They had to be taught how to hold their body in a special way because 'one moves differently in France than in Vietnam'. Indeed, Western film-makers are unable to emulate this practice whenever they want to film in Asia or shoot Asia in France.

Conscious of the plight of women in Vietnamese society, the film-maker refuses to propose a solution to the submission of women in his film. However, he claims to have given Mui the tool to empower herself, in the act of learning how to read. As a spectator, I cannot positively answer how far Mui will go with her book-reading practices and unfortunately the film ends with that glorifying moment in sight, while showing a nine-month pregnancy. Tran has explained that if he had made the film five years earlier, it would have been a film of revolt, adopting the 'Western model'. Also, that film, according to him, would have been simple and not fair to all these women, whom behind their servitude and sacrifice, Tran perceives as endowed with a magnificent 'spiritual life'.

This 1993 film was made in the aftermath of the three blockbusters previously discussed – *L'Amant*, *Indochine* and *Diên Biên Phû* – yet subsequently suffers from it. Ironically, these earlier dramas paved the way for a Franco-Vietnamese film-maker's project. These films are worlds apart from Tran's own experimental film-making project. 'What they said about Vietnam … is uninteresting to me. The stories could have taken place in Kenya. The humanity of the Vietnamese people is not visible through those films. All they have is a setting' (quoted in Cross 1994: 36). At the same time, the epic films have trivialised the way that the French audience looks at Vietnam. The normalisation of the links between France and Vietnam prepared the terrain for such a film, as in the late 1980s, Vietnam's economic policies opened to the West. The culmination of this ten-year cycle and opening was celebrated at the Francophone Summit, hosted by Hanoi in autumn 1997.

French cinema's return to Vietnam has not gone unnoticed. *Indochine*, *L'Odeur de la papaye verte*, and then *Cyclo*, appear as French cinema's latest 'absurdities' according to Richard Gott's take on this trend: 'All three films typify the continuing degeneration of French cinema. They purposely pay no attention to war or to empire, indeed almost all political references have been airbrushed out. This is escapist cinema suitable for our times' (1996: 10). Ranking Tran next to the British Merchant and Ivory heritage films located in colonial India, or television Masterpiece theatre series' venture in British colonial India with *The Jewel in the Crown*, Gott considers Tran Anh Hung's films more ambitious but also deceitful. The essential attack on Tran is his assimilation or the fact that he is more French than Vietnamese 'with Vietnamese origins, although since he has lived in France since he was 12 (since 1975) it would be more reasonable to consider him to be French' (*Ibid.*).

The identity and position of the film-maker comes under attack. As a product of French (post-)colonial history, Tran is difficult to situate. Is he French or is he Vietnamese? Is he francophone? The identity of film-makers of Franco-Vietnamese origins is under question and their positioning is crucial since it enters the larger historical and socio-cultural frame of French politics and is now part of what is called Vietnamitude. Vietnamitude corresponds with the West Indians' and Africans' return to and reclaiming of their roots and heritage as part of the larger movement that took place in the 1930s French artistic and political scene with the Negritude movement. In that hybrid location, Tran now stands alone and without any role model, or national cinema model – 'when I decide to make a movie, I have no national mirror for myself. I'm alone. That's hard' (quoted in Cross 1994: 37).

Tran has been denounced as representing the 'tradition of quality' – a term that applied to 1950s studio-made films in France that was criticised by

François Truffaut's famous 1954 *Cahiers du Cinéma* essay 'A Certain Tendency of the French Cinema' (see Sterritt 1994). Tran's excellent craftsmanship is attacked for being 'too French' in his creativity and thus deriving from the former colonial powers his own style and substance.

> The irony of *The Scent of Green Papaya* is that it looks and sounds more like a French art movie – reflecting the cautious 'tradition of quality' in French film-making – than a product of Vietnam's own national cinema which barely exists as an industry ... Vietnam is free of French rule in political affairs, but French influence clearly lingers in the style and substance of some Vietnamese cultural products. (Sterritt 1994: 16)

This criticism stands in opposition to the earlier commentaries pairing Tran Anh Hung's film with Japanese products.

The response to *L'Odeur de la papaye verte* originating from the American *Viet-Kieu*, or the Vietnamese living abroad, is different and definitely shaped by conflicting ideologies. Tran showed his film in California, where a large segment of Vietnamese-Americans live. Resistance to the film before it was screened was considerable since the audience had only heard of a film made by a Vietnamese director about Vietnam. Invited to a reception after the screening, Tran had to face a barrage of ideological questions coming from Vietnamese-American journalists asking him to explain certain sentences: 'In the film, the father tells his wife about the dead young daughter, that she is perhaps better off where she is now. Do you imply by this sentence that it is better to be dead in Viet Nam today?'[30] Apparently, the film did well in Japan, where it stayed for three months in a row and gave the director its warmest reception.

Present-day Vietnam as Principal Character of the Story

In Japan, modern dance has stopped being what it was after Hiroshima. For me, cinema can no longer be what it was after the Vietnam War. – Tran Anh Hung[1]

This chapter analyses Tran Anh Hung's second feature film, *Cyclo*,[2] shot in 1995, and closes with his latest release to date, *A la verticale de l'été* (*The Vertical Ray of the Sun*, 2000). Tran weaves recurrent motifs into his films and navigates between apparently radically opposed themes, ranging from male/female relations, to urban violence and everyday life and poetry. The director plays on several registers and sensibilities, especially through original music and 'native' sounds.

My attempt to examine *Cyclo* is through a reading and interpretive strategy extracted after multiple screenings. However, the film is not self-explanatory, as its dialogue is sparse. If the conclusion shows a resolution of the conflict, it does not elucidate anything. My reading argues that the position of the spectator is crucial in deciphering a text, especially one whose meaning is not necessarily fully exposed. This interpretation of *Cyclo* borrows from spectator-response theory but also functions as a Marxist and feminist reading that is particularly interested in issues of language and culture.

First, the term 'cyclo' immediately ushers in the rhetoric of a colonial world. It is linked to colonial legacy. Besides the immediate tourist connotations associated with the word, the cyclo remains a commonly used means of transportation alongside scooters and motorcycles. The cyclo metonymically designates the person who drives the machine. *Cyclo*, the film, ascribes a bad image to the cyclo operator by converting him into a thug. Over the years, limitations have been given to the use of cyclists and access to some streets has been forbidden to them. Official communist policy has restrained their use. In Hanoi, cyclos are used as 'decoy' for luxury hotels like Hotel Metropole, which has its own team. A cyclo belongs to urban landscape; it is the recurrent object shown on most documentaries on Vietnam. You cannot walk on the streets without cyclists soliciting you. In his promotion of the film, the director demonstrates the use of a cyclo: 'The Cyclo designates man whose work instrument has imposed itself naturally as the best-moving vehicle. Through him, I could speak of the working world, of exhaustion, perspiration, food and money.'[3] Tran Anh Hung omits the colonial fabric link to the term.

Film theoretician Christian Metz places the position of the film spectator in a good object/bad object relation along a psychoanalytical and Marxist analytical grid. Read under that lens, films belong to a market economy that valorises a love relation between its object and spectators, to keep generating a return and profit from its products. Most commercial films exploit the good object relation to please audiences and generate a profit. Other films distance themselves from this pleasurable experience and stir diverse emotions and questions in the spectator.

Almost following this design, Tran celebrates a sort of communion between film-maker and spectator. Close to the Metzian proposition, a film does not just provide entertainment but constitutes an experience, if possible one that will transform the spectator. In a radical way, Tran Anh Hung claims that when he goes to the movie theatre, he expects to experience the equivalent of a rebirth. Accordingly, films will or should bring new feelings, new sensations and not feed old feelings.

As a film-maker and thinker, Tran finds himself in the uncomfortable position of an 'in between', neither Vietnamese nor French, but rather an impure hybrid product at the intersection of two cultures. As such, he identifies with the character of Khuyen (the composer) from *L'Odeur de la papaye verte*. This feeling is echoed by his own producer, Rossignon, who said after the making of *Cyclo*, that the director is 'an apatrid' (without a country) (1995: 11). This positioning makes him the easy target of criticisms not only in France but also in Vietnam.

The Western spectatorial space assigned by his films projects one at the heart of Vietnamese culture and 'soul'. However without a code, Western spectators struggle to watch the extreme violence and sentimentality that underlies *Cyclo*. These two poles play out and, according to the film-maker, they constitute the 'very essence of the Vietnamese soul'. Without a code, spectators who are not familiar with Vietnam might perceive the violence as a sign of the new Vietnam. One should suspect that this extreme violence is a transposition of Western violence onto an Asian space. Either way, questions about on screen violence arise and the film-maker argues for a difference between an American and Asian *mise-en-scène* of violence (1995d: 141–42).

 Cyclo's descent into hell takes place in modern Saigon, now Ho Chi Minh City and Cholon. Violence clashes with innocence off and on screen. Tran Nû Yên Khê, who has selected to play only in her husband's films, reports, 'French people only offer me stereotypical roles of Asian women that men fantasise about.'[4] According to her and Tran, these roles, if she were to accept them, would perpetrate the notion that Asian women can only be cast as prostitutes in film. However puzzling this may be, *Cyclo* engages the very notion by forcing prostitution onto an innocent young woman, played by Tran Nû Yên Khê, whose brother has fallen into the criminal underworld. Some of the violent actions displayed on screen includes execution-style killings, torture, self-mutilation, self-immolation, suicide and beatings. If sexual acts (of an implicitly violent form here) mostly remain off-screen, sexual violence is strongly evoked while sexual intimacy is carefully avoided or displaced. One erotic sequence does occur when the Poet washes the Sister's hair. However, it is examples of sexual perversions that abound, which will be discussed later.

 The film, scripted by Tran, presents an essay on the evils of capitalism and globalisation in Hô Chi Minh City.[5] The giant and ever-present machinery of consumerism crushes most characters. After years of war and occupation, and although located in the *doi moi* period, the national economy has now shifted to an aggressive market-driven economy. 'Cyclo focuses on the "working poor" who are caught in the maelstrom of rampant economic expansion' (Narkunas 2001: 149). American dollars – part of the accepted shadow economy in Vietnam – surface frequently throughout the film and eventually some of them are burned. Although the practice of burning money is common in rituals to the ancestors, the burning of the most common currency in Vietnam – the dollar – acquires another connotation. Unlike Linda Lê's novel *Les Trois Parques* (1997), which negotiates a return to 'Saigon' and her childhood country through fiction, Tran does not mention that this capitalist nightmare comes after years of repression and re-education under the communist regime. *Cyclo* was critically perceived as a bold film since it gives no explanations as to its violence and pairs radically unusual film styles. All characters are nameless, only referred to by their activities, a practice shared by Linda Lê. The Boss of the gang, a woman, played by Nguyen Nhu Quynh (who appeared earlier in Lam Lê's feature film) runs a cyclo company and commissions the young Cyclo (Le Van Loc) into a circuit of terror and extortion. The Cyclo is unaware that the gang-related activities, which he ultimately accepts, are prearranged. It forces his sister into a web of prostitution that the film-maker sees as part of modern Vietnam. 'I made *Cyclo* to show distress and misery in today's Vietnam. It is ravaged by wild capitalism and bled by years of American embargo. There is no more morality. When one meets a beautiful woman in Ho Chi Minh City, one can be sure that she sells her body' (quoted in Pantel 1995).

Gangster Poetry

The character of the Poet, played by Wong Kar-Wai's favourite actor Tony Leung Chiu-Wai (not to be confused with Jean-Jacques Annaud's actor in *L'Amant*), adds a dramatic and poetic note to the film. Yet the narrative crushes him against the corruption and violence that he helps foster, since he belongs to the Boss's gangster crew. The Gangster-Poet recites poetry at four separate intervals in the film. It is through a voiceover effect that we hear the lines that the Poet himself is not reciting on screen. This creates a distanciation effect. First poem:

Nameless River. I was born sobbing
Blue sky. Vast earth. Black stream water.
I grow with the months, the years
With no one to watch over me
Nameless is man
Nameless is the river
Colourless the flower
Perfume
Without a voice
O river, O passersby
In the closed cycle
Of the months, the years
I cannot forget my debt to my roots
And I wander through worlds
Toward my land

These lines speak of displacement and exile; they are pronounced when the Poet is sitting with the Sister. The camera frames them together as she leans over his shoulder; he turns toward her. Facing the camera, their eyes are shut. A fast montage of faces of children, in front of the camera, is superimposed onto their first image, in the same camera angle. The montage represents the two grown-ups as children and innocent.

The second poetic instance occurs with the Sister again, in the countryside. This scene is not scripted. Instead, the synopsis 'shows' them together on top of a bridge. The Poet tells her about his childhood by the 'black river'. This note does not figure in the film, but could refer to the Mekong River familiar to Tran during his childhood. The director instead asks the reader to look at the script as an unfinished product and to 'imagine' them. It is the only escape that the film allows from the claustrophobic city. The Poet rinses her long hair, with a bowl of water, while the verses are pronounced:

Dawn in my soul
A bit of sun from each home

A bit of light for everyone
Under the canopy, a leaf trembles
And the dew remembers the clouds
And the earth exhales a huge wind
And life shivers
Kite of my childhood
Fragile hope landing in the sky
Hearts open, human abodes
In a world where no one is excluded

There is a large tree and a temple-like structure behind them. The Poet walks over to the tree and breaks off a flower. The washing of the woman's hair is a recurrent motif in Tran Anh Hung's films, from *L'Odeur de la papaye verte* to *A la verticale de l'été*.

The third poetic instance immediately follows the erotic moment of a man washing a woman's hair. The Poet and Sister are at a nightclub; adorned with handcuffs, she dances for him seductively, but progressively through the editing, it appears that she is dancing for a client, a businessman. All the characters listed in the credits appear nameless or rather are named according to their function or relation; here the businessman appears as the Handcuff Man. The Poet seems in pain, yet fascinated by the seductive image of the woman he loves. The song that plays in English constitutes the only moment in the film where a foreign language is heard on the soundtrack; it expresses intense personal pain. Radiohead's 'Creep' lyrics cover the dance, stressing the lines 'I'm a creep ... I don't belong here' and bridge the next sequence as the Poet walks away after his business deal. Here music is entirely diegetic and becomes subjective. Not unlike poetry, one of Tran Anh Hung's signatures, music plays a major role in his films. For this, he relied heavily on composer Tôn Thât Tiêt, whose classical style both embellishes upon and contrasts with the scenes in which it appears. Tran's latest film score combines American songs by Lou Reed and the Velvet Underground and a popular song by Trinh Côn Son.

The poetic moments described above, found in the lyrics and poetic lines, precede scenes of intense pain and violence. As such, poetry suspends the infernal cycle, but never for long. It provides a momentary release in the violence and tension. The Sister is raped off-camera in what one can imagine as a bondage scene, confirmed by the next sequence, after an ellipsis, where she reappears with bleeding wounded wrists. The Poet will subsequently go and kill the client in an act of revenge – a long scene that will be performed in front of the camera, in what André Bazin would qualify as real time. Before that moment, the Poet used to sell the Sister's body to clients who only asked her to perform and submit to their less dangerous sexual perversions.

That the young woman is still a virgin then comes as a surprise after the various trials she has been through. One client asks her to urinate while standing in front of him and another client has a foot fetish in a sequence scripted as 'The apartment of the foot obsessed man' ('l'appartement de l'obsédé des pieds'). In all these mild sado-masochistic fantasy scenes, the Poet becomes the outsider, and a voyeur – a position that the uncomfortable spectator shares with him. All these scenes entertain an element of sado-masochism, directed at the female character and Poet and the audience. Fetishism, or what Freud has analysed as a penis-substitute, represents the woman's phallus or what the 'little boy once believed in and does not wish to forego'. (1963: 215). The male customer dresses the woman's legs in black silk stockings then lacerates them with scissors around the toes. He bathes her feet and powders them, and paints each toe. She is made to carefully step on some bread dough while he watches in a trance. According to Freud, velvet, fur or hair reproduce the scene of undressing, 'the last moment in which the woman could still be regarded as phallic'. In his essay on fetishism, Freud aptly refers to the Chinese custom of foot binding and closes with a brief discussion of that custom – an instance that surfaces when watching the scene, owing to the inscription of feet and toes and the manipulation of the camera in an extreme close-up: 'Another variety of this, which might be regarded as a race-psychological parallel to fetishism, is the Chinese custom of first mutilating a woman's foot then revering it. The Chinese man seems to want to thank the woman for having submitted to castration' (1963: 219).

The Cyclo, hiding out in the apartment across the plaza, never suspects the Poet's pimping activities, despite the direct 360-degree camera angles, bridging both places and connecting them in time and space. Instead, the Cyclo is symbolically blinded throughout the film. The narrative puts us closer to male characters, at the antipodes of the fundamentally feminised perspective of *L'Odeur de la papaye verte*. *Cyclo* at first ushers the point of view of the 18-year-old cyclo driver, but ultimately the Poet seems to develop the dominant conscience. He lives in a certain luxury. His death by fire, an action of self-immolation, appears like the ultimate sacrificial death, yet a muted event that takes place during the noisy Têt (New Year) street celebrations. It is reminiscent of the 1960s acts of resistance by Vietnamese Buddhist monks, during the Vietnam War, or what the Vietnamese refer as 'the American war', and designates martyrdom and suicide as the only escape. As the fire burns and purifies, characters come together and intersect, unknowingly. For instance, the female Boss enters the same frame as the Sister when her mentally-impaired son (the Crazy Son) has been accidentally killed in a collision with an army truck. Through fire and death, the Poet and the innocent child connect; the Boss loses a lover and a son, at once. The drama will be unexplainably resolved and the Cyclo will regain his freedom thanks to 'higher' intervention.

Eventually, the pedicab driver is released from gang activities. The nuclear family, consisting of the older sister, younger sister, grandfather and cyclo driver, is miraculously reunited and seen traveling through the city in a crane shot. The end steps away from the realist genre, and becomes idealistic.

Innocence has been corrupted, people have been killed, raped and prostituted and a return to the family unit is necessarily tainted by history. The celebratory moment takes place during the Têt festival, one of the holiest days in the Vietnamese calendar, announcing the year of the pig. The camera performs a fascinating panoramic shot of modern high rises next to empty lots, then roof tops and pans to a hotel tennis court and pool for tourists, stuck between buildings to close on the city traffic.

Most readings of the film take into account an ideological positioning. I wish to look first at the unusual mode of production of this film. Tran, a Franco-Vietnamese film-maker residing in France returned to Vietnam to win the support of Vietnamese authorities, the Giai Phong Film Studio and Salon Films (Hong Kong). The Lazennec French production company that has now bankrolled four of his films, including his latest film, *A la verticale de l'été*, is supportive of his work and vision. Producer Rossignon does not consider *Cyclo* to be a French product.[6] To secure Vietnamese support, Tran had to undergo the daily visit of the censorship police commonly called Madame la censure. The censor was on location every day to prevent 'damaging images of Vietnam'. The intention to make a film about modern Vietnam had to follow party lines. For obvious reasons, communism is not under attack here, but neither is French colonialism. Instead, American-style capitalism becomes the evil of a society corrupted by its own internal violence and by consumerism. This portrayal of Vietnam cannot please everyone, even if dollar banknotes materialise throughout the film as the flagrant evil force, paired with the repeated significant shot of a damaged American helicopter, no one can actually be duped. The film was blocked from being released in Vietnam. Once more, the Franco-Vietnamese production shows an entirely French-subsidised film with a budget of 35,004,000 francs. Producers who shared the venture include SFP Cinema, Lazennec, la Sept Cinéma (Arte), Lumière and Canal+.[7] Vietnamese support is not listed in the published budget. The film screened in Paris in 13 theatres for 14 weeks. Its total first-run figures amounted to 167,298 entries in France. This reflects a drop in comparison with *L'Odeur de la papaye verte*'s success, amounting to 29 weeks in Paris in only 8 theatres (first run) and a total of 340,958 entries in France after its first run.

Male characters in Tran Anh Hung's films persevere at understanding both the events of their childhood and the nature of their relationship with their father. The Cyclo speaks to his dead father, who died in a traffic accident the previous year. The beginning of the film opens with the dead father's voiceover. The Cyclo subsequently dreams of his father's death, believing that his father has saved him from trouble and died twice to help him. The Cyclo thanks his father again at the end of the movie, when order is restored. On the other side, the dominant character of the Poet whom the Cyclo reveres is clearly estranged from his father. When he takes the Sister to visit his parents, the father comes out of his room to violently attack and beat him since he brought 'his whore' with him. He chases him away from the house as he would an animal. The mother accepts her son and shows a picture of him as a five-year-old boy to the sister. The mother resembles the Boss; this uncanny resemblance at first suggested is reinforced through continuity editing when the film cuts to the next scene showing the Boss in bed with the Poet. His poetry alludes in a figurative way to paternal abuse, as can be construed from lines such as 'punished in secret at night'.

The feelings of the Poet and the constant nosebleed that affects him at various stages throughout the movie suggest psychological trouble and trauma. His virility or emotional maturity is questionable. This questioning works for the Cyclo who is at the transitional stage from a child to an adult. Although by playing the pimp figure, the Poet surrounds himself with women, there is no explicit sexual relation among them. He chooses to sell them and receives payment in return for their services. The persistent nosebleed occurs when people are tortured, when the Sister is sold and raped and when the Cyclo goes into a drugged frenzy. Sexual perversions as a recurrent motif carry a discomforting statement about violence directed at women in general, yet they seem to affect him and provoke his anger.

The internal violence transforms all the protagonists and indirectly speaks of the state of (South) Vietnam after years of corruption and conflicts. Tran claims that he wants to show violence with an extreme softness. Each moment of intimacy and tenderness is followed by violent actions that reinforce one another. The postface to the published script explains *Cyclo* as:

> The portrait of a town, with a social and identity questioning in the background. *Cyclo* interrogates the meaning of the economic opening, the possible loss of innocence and the loss of values of those whose poverty only equals their desire to step out of their condition and who find themselves confronted to the seduction of money. (1995: 141)

When screened at the Rotterdam Film Festival in 1996, the film was attacked for 'being violent, unrealistic', and perhaps the cruelest cut – 'a French movie that has nothing to do with Vietnam' (Dupont 1996). As I have previously commented, a constant in Tran's cinematic oeuvre (thus far) is the creation of a 'mental Vietnam', a dreamlike version of his native country.

Franco-Vietnamese Collaborative Work

In 1991, after a 16-year absence, Tran returned to Vietnam for the making of *L'Odeur de la papaye verte*. While the location of this project was abandoned owing to certain conditions, the first seeds of his return to the country to make a film, were sown. Tran rediscovered people, the familiar smells/scents of his childhood and the names of trees and flowers – names he had not used in years. Though unable to shoot his first feature film there, Tran returned to Vietnam in 1995 to make *Cyclo*, strengthened by the favorable international reception of *L'Odeur de la papaye verte*. In a country that was and still is heavily rebuilding and opening its economy, film production was almost non-existent in 1994, with only one film shot in that year and none in 1995. The arrival of a foreign film crew was viewed as a fortunate occasion to bring in new hard currency. Such was the case with *L'Amant*, *Indochine* and *Diên Biên Phû*, all shot in Vietnam (not all of them entirely) and more recently with Tony Bui's film *Three Seasons* (1999), made in Vietnam but subsidised by an American producer. Before *Cyclo* was made, distributors worldwide had already bought the rights to distribute the film.

Cyclo is the second film about Vietnam, made by a film-maker living in France, who privileges the site for his films: 'There's nothing much of interest for me in this country [France]. What happens now in Vietnam is much more interesting and intense.'[8] Our reading of his first feature film, *L'Odeur de la papaye verte*, reconsidered Tran's place in France in view of his films. This second film clearly positions him as the 'cinéaste de la vietnamité' or the spokesperson of Vietnamitude in France. Despite himself, he may have become the spokesperson for a (new) Franco-Vietnamese cinema in France. This view seems to prevail, especially more recently with the Printemps Vietnamien festival held at the vidéothèque de Paris (24–26 April 1998) whose programme included films by Vietnamese film-makers presently living in Vietnam next to Tran's early shorts made in France. *Cyclo* speaks of contemporary Vietnam:

> Cyclo speaks of today's Vietnam, of work, food, money and the temptation of evil, innocence, ancestors' spiritual heritage, but above all, it is an interior trip inside a country that is made of the concrete substance of my dreams.[9]

No matter how poetic Tran's explanations may be, a code is required to read his films – I am using this term as I take films as mostly (visual) texts. Tran's metaphors remain only understandable by Vietnamese and/or specialists and/or travelers. For instance, the Betel nut and its connotation of marriage or the Areca flowers could be lost. In *Cyclo*, the betel nuts – always cut in half – are meant to represent the relations between men and women. When Tran uses fruit, he breaks away from its primary symbolic function and turns it into something purely artistic. An outsider to the culture may not understand the Poet who expresses himself in verses only and practices 'oriental cruelty' (Baignères 1995: 22). Translation may be the important element here, when trying to interpret his films; they may speak Vietnamese and carry Vietnamese legends and traditions, but the sum of it might not be accessible to the larger Western audience despite its subtitles. Walter Benjamin stressed the importance of and dependence on original texts and the intent of the writer, here film-maker: 'In all language and linguistic creations there remains in addition to what can be conveyed, something that cannot be communicated' (1969: 79). Language and positioning is at the core of the criticisms addressed to Tran, who feels sometimes overwhelmed by these attacks. For instance, Tran's most virulent critic denounces his films' characters that speak Vietnamese but 'their body language remains unmistakably French' (Gott 1996:10).

The films that we have discussed in this and the previous chapter draw from a large reservoir of Vietnamese legends and traditions. Tran considers his cultural background as acquired by most people except for Westerners: 'It does not matter if this dimension escapes Westerners. I am addressing myself to the Vietnamese. I do not give the "how to use".'[10] Producer Rossignon's task was to make sure that the film would be understandable to a Western audience.

The collaborative work between Tran Anh Hung, a French crew and multinational crew as well as the Vietnamese authorities, resulted in the training of technicians encouraged by Lazennec Productions. This training took place in a three-step process over nine months: at first, language acquisition, and the use of French language to work on the film for three and a half months. The multinational crew was composed of French, Vietnamese, Hong Kong and Filipino technicians. Their common goal was to work together and to teach people how to operate the equipment.

The presence of chief operator/cinematographer Benoît Delhomme on both *Cyclo* and *L'Odeur de la papaye verte* is important for the aesthetic qualities achieved by the film in its use of colours. *Cyclo* has been termed a social '*polar*' – a French slang term for detective films, or films noirs. This disturbing postmodern gaze into modern Vietnam cast from the outside and inside ties to the director's double identity. Fredric Jameson locates postmodernism in France after the establishment of the Fifth Republic. The concept of postmodernism is difficult to pinpoint except through some of its by-products:

> The erosion of the older distinction between high culture and so-called mass or popular culture ... [But] many of the newer postmodernisms have been fascinated precisely by that whole landscape of advertising and motels, of the Las Vegas strip, of the late show and Grade-B Hollywood film, of so-called paraliterature, with its airport paperback categories of the gothic and romance, the popular biography, the murder mystery and the science fiction or fantasy novel. (1983: 112)

The 1980s French *cinéma du look* was strongly rejected by French film critics. Guy Austin best sums up some of the critical attacks: 'Lack of plot and of psychological realism ... Comparisons to "inferior" cultural forms like television, music video, advertising and the comic strip also abound' (1996: 119). These objections targeted the lack of ideology in films. *Cyclo* unquestionably fits the label. The film-maker uses stylistic escapes from the sordid reality into poetry, with flowers of a tree, blue paint clearly quoting Jean-Luc Godard's *Pierrot le fou* (1965), and with audio-clip-like moments. The *cinéma du look* (with Jean-Jacques Beineix for instance) used images, akin to advertising, to arouse feelings of nostalgia.

The spectacle offered has been termed in slang 'crado chic', or dirty chic, and has been seen as a compilation of images borrowed from several film-makers from Vittorio de Sica, to John Woo and Jean-Luc Godard. Most critics agree that it offers a rarely seen but terrifying portrayal of Vietnam, a country in mutation which Tran Anh Hung does not understand himself. As in his other films, dialogue is minimal yet people seem to understand one another without words – a practice that is intrinsic to the Vietnamese soul, where people do not have to talk to one another to communicate, according to Tran.[11]

The violence of the film stands in total opposition to the softness and 'femininity' encountered in *L'Odeur de la papaye verte*, that attempted to link every object through the 'plan-séquence' and to show seduction, Asian-style. *Cyclo* here seems to perpetrate a cycle of violence yet contrasts it with soft moments.[12] It was released the same year as Mathieu Kassovitz's *La Haine*. Rossignon and Lazennec produced both films that were screened at the New York Film Festival on the same day. *La Haine* portrays a day in the life of three suburban youths of various ethnic backgrounds (African, Beur and Jewish) whose destiny is sealed tragically and violently at its conclusion, resulting in violence by all means necessary despite the status quo.

Accused of being outside history in his earlier film, Tran claims to carry the consciousness and memory of the Vietnam War in this film. Confronting the reality of the war and meeting older people who would narrate their tragic memories of the war, the film-maker's response is one of a listener: 'The strangest thing was they were discussing it with a smile of extraordinary serenity and sweetness. One of them even listed the menu of tortures she had gone through during the wars – and she has known both wars, the French war and the American war. It's that sweetness that inspired me to make the film with the same serenity.'[13]

Refusing war film spectacles, yet 'contaminated' and traumatised by war and its conscience, most Vietnamese artists are forced to situate themselves ideologically in the conflict that has plagued their country of origin.[14] It is now impossible to speak of Vietnam without being historically positioned. When Tran was asked if he would consider shooting a film in France, after all his country of citizenship, to borrow from television journalist Mona Makki's question, he replied in an evasive way. However, his answer is symbolically fundamental in understanding his position. Shooting in France is a handicap for him, owing to certain limitations of a technical but formal nature as discussed previously: 'Vietnam gives me this freedom, this variety of shots permits to make a credible story, so that one will not ask, but why this position, this bizarre angle, because it will not seem odd, because of the decor, whereas here, it is always horizontal and vertical lines.'[15] The second part of his answer is evident. Showing a beautiful old Vietnamese man's face is more interesting than showing a beautiful old Frenchman's face. The answer is not necessarily a question of frame/shot but of calling. Tran writes from what he knows and bases his script on his cultural experiences. As clearly said, nothing calls him yet in France. Based on his dual positioning, between France and Vietnam, Tran has been able to negotiate a travel cycle and bridges both countries with his films.

Hanoi On My Mind

A la verticale de l'été explores a sensuous world of emotions and visual aesthetics.[16] Mark Lee, a Taiwanese cinematographer, had previously worked on Wong Kar-Wai's *In the Mood for Love* (2000). Tran dedicated the film once more to his childhood memories and the peaceful family life of three sisters, who live next to one another and once a year honour their mother's death at a large feast. It is a painterly film recalling, for example, paintings by Nguyen Anh – 'Trois Soeurs' – and Tran Van Cau – 'La petite Thuy se lavant les cheveux' (1943).[17] The luscious scenes take place in Hanoi during the summer, a season that suffuses every shot with rich tones and colours, varying from blue to green and yellow. It could prove difficult to explain the haiku-like title here, as it might be a direct translation of a Vietnamese poetic line but such is not the case.[18] Hanoi, considered by many tour guides as a 'sleepy and quaint northern city', seems the embodiment of calm. The soundtrack registers few outdoor sounds, with horns of several motorcycles here and there in total discrepancy with the actual sound heard on small streets in Hanoi. Instead, the picture shows a more intimate, and again, mental meditation on family life, mostly centered in the home and garden and sometimes allows for an escapade into the charming shaded or sometimes rainy streets of Hanoi.

The plot stages the celebration of an important traditional family ritual in Vietnam as its central event and opens on the day of the mother's funeral celebration to close on the father's own funeral celebration, a month later. The cherished parents died a month apart. This significant event gives a rhythm to that special day as it is the occasion for a festive meal, prepared by the three sisters and blessed at the family altar. Again, people are brought together by culinary preparations that are the focus of discussion among men and women. Associations with, and fantasies about, food recall an earlier film about food preparations and family relations with three sisters (and their father) by Taiwanese director Ang Lee – *Eat Man, Drink Woman* (1995).

Beneath the apparent calm and soft exterior surface lies an undercurrent of tensions, desires and frustrations. Each sister has her struggle, be it with her husband or boyfriend, not to mention the hint of a joyful incestuous-like relation between the younger sister and brother. The concept of verticality could explain each sister's life as a vertical line that each would attempt to weave to reverse the geometric tendency of her life. According to Marine Landrot, each dreams of weaving horizontal lines among themselves and their men.[19]

Repetitions of the same (primal) scene structure the film contributing to its ritual-like dance and tone. The humorous first scene is the wake up episode

ā la verticale de l'ētē
un film de trān anh hūng

avec trān nū yēn khē | nguyēn nhū quỳnh | lē khanh

Figure 8 *A la verticale de l'été* (© Les Productions Lazennec – Guy Ferrandis)

occurring each morning, with young brother Hai and sister Lien, played by Tran Nû Yên Khê. Both sleep in the same one-room flat, each in a bed that is separated by a veil. A gentle electronic alarm clock signals the wake in a performance that will be reenacted five times. Each morning sees them waking to the voice of Lou Reed's 1969 song 'Pale Blue Eyes' ('Sometimes I feel so happy, sometimes I feel so sad') either gently stretching, or doing tai-chi exercises. The soundtrack at that point flirts with modernism, including other groups, such as The Velvet Underground, Arab Strap and the French group The Married Monk. The musical choice of Tôn Thât Tiêt comments on the constant actions and emotions of characters while the use of Vietnamese and

Anglo-Saxon songs achieves another state and helps develop a specific rhythm to the film in an attempt to slow down time almost to its stillness (Tran Anh Hung, *A la verticale de l'été* press kit). The young sister is provocative in her approach to her brother and they seductively flirt with one another as a couple in their dialogue and body language, although the sister is without doubt the more aggressive partner.

Each male member of the family is an artist. The older sister is married to a botanical photographer who has a problem with taking people's portraits; the middle sister is married to an aspiring writer now writing his first novel and who has writer's block. The younger brother is an actor surrounded by La Quy Tung's paintings that seem to multiply over the course of the movie and crowd the small flat he shares with his sister.[20] Each man's trade connects to the film-maker himself, who is a writer, a photographer and possibly an actor. The photographer's predicament during the film is rendered in spatial terms. He is attracted by two places and cannot resolve his inner conflict over these. There is a definite sadness in the man, torn between two women (or two places) and who cannot be in harmony with himself, as he puts it. However, the women have control over their men, despite momentary lapses, and escapades, they sometimes decide for them. They seem to perform all the domestic chores.

The older sister runs a café (Café Thuy Duong) with the other sisters. There are many parallels among these sisters and their activity centers on food. Mario Battistel connects them temporally, especially during the rain sequences, in a parallel montage. The camera allows few exterior scenes of Hanoi and travels to the picturesque Bay of Halong once. The steep cliffs of the bay represent verticality, as far as an explanation of the title goes and as shown by the camera movement tilted toward the sky.

The carefully constructed film returns to the feminine realm of *L'Odeur de la papaye verte* that was so acclaimed. The narrative retreats once more to the intimate spatial agency of the household, as most interactions take place inside or within its perimeters.

The film was reviewed under its specifically and singularly Asian treatment of time:

> What makes the specificity of Asian cinema and more particularly *A la verticale de l'été* is a concept and cinematographic treatment of time that is very different from that of Westerners. For T.A. Hung, time is not a fatality, on the contrary; he participates in the joy of being in the world. Instead of reinventing time, the narrative's time, the director prefers to juxtapose scenes with the least possible ellipses, to preserve it (time) fully.[21]

All Tran Anh Hung's films bear a certain philosophy and sensitivity and a signature. I have more than once defined the delicate position that the director finds himself in, in terms of identity and discourse. In the earlier discussion of

L'Odeur de la papaye verte, I teased out the possible consequences of filming Asia for a Western audience. I intimated that the films manipulated our Western fantasies with, for instance, Asian culinary traditions, the otherness of a Vietnamese household and erotic fantasies. Despite many criticisms of *Cyclo*, I will now suggest that the film extends a message of hope despite its violence. The message is encapsulated in several sequences, one with the superimposition of children's faces and poetic lines, that takes place not even half-way into the film with the poem discussed previously that begins, 'Nameless River, I was born sobbing/Blue sky. Vast earth. Black stream water/I grow with the months, the years/With no one to watch over me.' In alluding to the position of a wanderer, it is the first time that the director, albeit indirectly, points to his own exilic condition on film. In *A la verticale de l'été*, the director includes a brief fragment about the two places that divide the photographer. The poetic lines bridge past and present and pay homage to one's 'roots'. When *Cyclo*'s credit sequence rolls, a documentary montage segment features a classroom of Vietnamese children playing a cord instrument in a classroom setting. Then, in the postface that accompanies the film (in its French video format), Tran inserted another classroom sequence with children singing to the camera. With this he offers a view into the future of Vietnam and its new generation.[22]

CHAPTER FIVE

Documentary Approach in Films and Texts

This chapter samples documentary films mostly made about Vietnam that sometimes aired on national television. We will limit our scope to films that are still available and that offer either voices of resistance, or an interrogation on ways to document reality; this chapter does not cover the entire history of documentary films about Vietnam. Films and novels returned to Vietnam before the 1990s, however: some films made in France skirted the Vietnamese/Indochinese region; others entered a dialogist situation with Vietnam from a diasporic position. An important corpus of films/texts flirts with the notion yet does not venture to go directly there. I alluded to this earlier in the Introduction and mentioned Duras' narratives, located for some in India, yet in reality a reworking of colonial Indochina.

Louis Malle

Financed by British funds, Louis Malle's personal journey East finds shape in seminal documentary footage taken in India that, altogether combined, produced *Calcutta* (1969) and *L'Inde fantôme: Réflexions sur un voyage* (*Phantom India*, 1969).[1] The trip to India marks a departure point in his career as a film-maker, a deliberate move away from the auteur tradition and an attempt to get closer to reality, even if that reality escapes him. '*Calcutta* constitutes the departing point of a reflection; my trip to India is the beginning of a movement that is going to take me in a direction that I do not know.'[2] Malle travelled to a former British colony, explaining that *the* French should feel concerned by the colonial enterprise that took place. According to Malle, Calcutta did not exist before the English arrived, and the town developed because of colonialism. The profits made from the colonial economy sustained the industrial revolution and capitalist boom that took place in England. *Calcutta* awakens a memory and consciousness by its inclusion of images of misery and poverty.

Calcutta avoids romanticising exoticism. It borders the documentary, reportage, or travel diary, leaving out any commentary, whereas *L'Inde fantôme* contains Malle's post-editing voiceover commentary in English. The gaze on India, at the gate of Indochina, constitutes an approach to, and discovery of, the self – not too distant from the Barthesian and Malrucian encounter with the Orient. Malle's reasons for leaving France in 1968 were to break loose with society, for a detour. India was indeed a privileged location for many during these years. He returned to France in the midst of the May 1968 events. However, in the meantime the trip to India had become a 'quest'. For he soon became aware that 'a Westerner with a camera is twice a Westerner'(*L'Inde fantôme*). His travel through India contains many stops to shoot ceremonies; scavenger birds eating the decomposed body of a buffalo, women painting, beatniks on their quest for an imaginary India. The trip attests to the influence that India has had on him, the discovery of a culture that he self-consciously approaches with his Westernised schemas, or modes of thinking. It becomes an introspection on time and memory, as well as the meaning of images.

During the filming, the team was confronted with the gaze of people everywhere they went. This cinema-direct type of film-making incorporates the gaze, not just that of the Westerner, but the gaze of filmed people who return the look by looking directly into the camera or the spectator. Malle is aware of the effect of the camera that can be construed as a weapon: 'Why should I tell them not to look at us since we're intruders. First, I don't speak their language … we're the intruders, disturbing them … To tell them not to look at us, it's the beginning of *mise-en-scène*' (French 1993: 71). There is a distance between documentary film-making and people pretending that 'they are not there' – a form that Malle considers a lie, or a distortion of truth. His decision to let the camera record is a constant of a narrative that has no pre-formed script and does not demonstrate an idea.

The critical reception of the film by Indians in India and abroad denounces the attempt to shoot misery in India from a Westerner's privileged position of control. However, his camera does not just stay on poverty but deciphers religious rituals and the caste system. More than once, Malle deconstructs the first opinion Western spectators could form of his images, by helping *us* with the codes. Years later, Malle, himself an expatriate, made films about the Vietnamese diaspora in Texas (*Alamo Bay*, 1985) and about the immigrant condition (*And the Pursuit of Happiness*, 1986).

Some films documenting Vietnam testify to a situation that has largely been unverified by other lenses from the inside. I want to show that while some of their territory has been unmapped, some of its images stand out as models in the history of film-making, yet may not appear in film history books. I will start with Dzu le lieu's report on Indochinese forced labour in France during Vichy times, then move to Raoul Coutard's experiment with fiction to document a conflict and the more recent foray into modern Vietnam by American-born Robert Kramer. Some of these untold resistance stories are inextricably linked to contemporary writing on Vietnam by dissident voices. The segment on writer Duong Thu Huong brings these articulations to the fore.

Dzu le lieu: *Les Hommes des trois ky*

Les Hommes des trois ky (*The Men of the three Ky*, 1996), directed by Dzu le lieu, records the previously uncharted history of forced migration of Vietnamese young men to France between 1939 and 1950 through their oral testimonies.[3] These men are now in their seventies and for the first time testify to their forced colonial labour and deportation to France to help with the 'war effort' in 1939. Most of them have never spoken of this episode in history and the first man interviewed specifies that 'Vietnamese people do not like to tell these things', especially when these are stories that they did not tell their children. Another fragment of French history that applied to Chinese immigrants this time was reported in another documentary film, *140,000 Chinois pour la Grande Guerre* (*140,000 Chinese for the Great War*), directed by Olivier Guitton, Véronique Izambart and Gilles Sionnet in 1997.[4] The amount of immigrants during World War One and immediately after has been unsurpassed in France, with many foreign workers coming from Europe but also from Africa and Asia, including 37,000 Chinese. The ratio of foreigners reached its peak in 1931 with 7 per cent of the population, or 2,715,000 persons (Ronsin 1997: 36). The French colonial authorities would recruit by force one male child out of families of three children and would send them either to the army or to work camps in France. The governmental intentions were to take 300,000 men out of Vietnam. They shipped them to France and on arrival, first debriefed them at the Marseille prison des Baumettes.

The reportage consists of interviews with these now older men, interspersed with newsreel footage of colonial Indochina and walking through the former barracks of French work camps where Indochinese workers were used in the war effort. The conditions of internment and forced labour are a sinister reminder of other camps of the time. These 'colonial' camps were organised and controlled by ex-colonial forces and pro-colonialist Vietnamese – in a nearly autonomous organisation called Moi: Office for the Indigenous Workforce or Bureau de la Main-d'Oeuvre Indigène. The authorities apparently had full control over these natives transplanted in France. The workers suffered from cold, food and clothing deprivation, as camp directors would steal directly from their dues during Vichy time, including their meager wages. Many of them died. The specialised workers worked in ammunition factories and salt mines during the War, in the south and southwest regions of France. After several years of oppression, they started to organise themselves and went on strike to secure better living conditions. The Indochinese Workers' Movement was born. They opposed colonialism and supported Vietnamese independence. However, after 1946, the French government started its repression against the movement's organisers. In 1950, they were suddenly and secretly arrested and deported back to Vietnam. Solidarity with French workers' trade unions such as the CGT (Confédération générale du travail) was short-lived and, once deported, they could get no help. After their return to Vietnam, they found themselves jailed again. A few of these men stayed on in France and, as we learn, most of them have been repatriated to Vietnam and have organised a campaign to obtain a retirement pension from the French government for their years of labour in France, which sometimes amounted to ten years or more.

The Vietnamese workforce constitutes the first immigré reservoir called to work in France, along with Chinese recruits imported during World War One. Most of these migration histories have never been recounted and some of them are still being made, resorting to archival documents. As such the history of Vietnamese exiles working in France predates North African, African and Portuguese immigrant workers recruited to work in France. The first wave of labour recruits among Vietnamese people, as documented by Mireille Favre's thesis, dates back to World War One: 'The first world war, after 1915, starts the first massive organised migration of Indochinese workforce in a remote country: nearly 90,000 men, recruited among the poorest peasants of the Tonkinese delta and North-Annam, were brought to the metropole between 1915 and 1919.'[5]

The French army was at first reticent to recruit soldiers among Indochinese people. Stereotypical associations would place Indochinese among a 'near-feminised' workforce.[6] Such notions show a persistent ignorance about indigenous people on top of the fact that when needed, their bodies were put to use in Indochina or abroad to help the war effort, regardless of these stereotypes with other 'colonial' forces. These soldiers, called 'les exotiques' (Favre 1986: 335), fought in the trenches of Verdun and were 'good enough to defend France' (Malraux 1992: 131).

Both Clara Malraux and Andrée Viollis denounced in their writing the colonial system and oppression they found in Indochina. Their stay there unveiled the way France would treat its colonies. Until then, Malraux had entertained artistic visions of the place. Loti's travel narratives and the visits to the Guimet museum, well-known for its collection of Asian art, inspired her and her generation. This imaginary Asia permeated her childhood.[7] Similarly, Viollis, a journalist on a mission to accompany a French governmental delegation to Vietnam in 1932, ended by reporting on the conditions of Vietnamese peasants and workers that she witnessed and her rising disgust with French colonial methods in her book *Indochine S.O.S.* Both Viollis and Malraux gained political awareness about the plight of Indochinese people during their travels east.[8]

Paul Carpita

Paul Carpita's *Le Rendez-vous des quais* (*Meeting on the Wharf*, 1953–55) is not a film about Vietnam per se, but 'Indochina' is present, especially in the evocation of French workers' solidarity with the plight of the Vietnamese nation. Shot on location in Marseille in 1953 during the 'dirty war', its dominant image lies in the graffiti inscription of 'Peace in Vietnam'. Marseille had a strategic role in the history of colonisation, as a port of entry. In defiance of the government's continuing war effort, the director clandestinely inserted shots of large ships loading army tanks on their way to war and unloading coffins carrying corpses of French soldiers. Similar shots were taken in an earlier documentary by Robert Menegoz, *Vive les dockers* (1950). The world of the dockers, at the core of Carpita's film financed by the Communist Party, shows them united against the war and at night volunteering to paint the walls of the port with a huge inscription 'Peace in Vietnam'. The film was banned because of its oppositional political discourse shot in a neo-realist mode and its clear link with trade unions. Marcel Pagnol, whose Southern location and regional accents are evoked, helped Carpita by lending him his studios for post-synchronisation work. When released and screened a second time in 1955, the police intervened and seized the reels, threatening to arrest Carpita, whose subsequent career in film-making stopped. Copies of the film, presumed destroyed, were discovered in 1983 and a restored version was released in 1988.

The Ministry of Industry and Trade gave a rational explanation to its confiscation of the film in 1955:

> The film retraces (yet the script does not mention it) a strike started by the Marseille Dockers, under a union pretext, to launch a movement against the war in Indochina. It contains violent scenes of resistance against public forces. Its screening might constitute a threat to public order.[9]

However, by 1955, the Indochinese conflict had ended with the Geneva agreements and France was then engaged in another colonial war in Algeria, where Marseille would again play a strategic role. The colonial area would remain a taboo subject in France for years to come and involved many threatening and violent acts. Françoise Audé contextualised the position of the film made at the height of the cold war, as one that could only be perceived as dangerous 'to be the first audience of a film made during the cold war, in the Fourth colonial Republic, is a high-risk experience.'[10]

Hoa-Binh: a Vietnamese film

Raoul Coutard's *Hoa-Binh* (1970), a rare fiction film to enter this discussion, is an adaptation of Françoise Lorrain's novel 'La Colonne de Cendres' that dared to 'return' to Vietnam in 1970 when no one else would.[11] Coutard, previously a photojournalist in Vietnam, is a renowned New Wave cinematographer who worked on Jean-Luc Godard's *A bout de souffle* (*Breathless*, 1959) and *Le Petit soldat* (*The Little Soldier*, 1960) François Truffaut's *Tirez sur le pianiste* (*Shoot the Piano Player*, 1960), *Jules et Jim* (1961) and Jacques Demy's *Lola* (1961). He was Pierre Schoendoerffer's cinematographer in *The 317ᵗʰ Platoon* (1965). *Hoa-Binh* is the first feature-length film he directed and was partly produced by Warner Bros. and Gilbert de Goldschmidt. It won the Best First Film prize at the Cannes Film Festival as well as an Academy Award nomination for Best Foreign Film.

Hoa-Binh documents the war ravages on civilian populations and more specifically on women and children. The chief protagonist is an 11-year-old boy, Hung, who struggles to take care of his smaller sister Xuan after their mother dies of tuberculosis. The father is at war and returns at the end of the film. *Hoa-Binh* contains many essential elements that would resurface in 1990s films about the colonial past: the emphasis on a child's perspective, the effects of war, the fight to survive in a cruel world and the reference to Vietnamese folk legends – all these circumstances and settings are part of the recent formula found in contemporary scripts. Coutard paints the inhumanity of war through the eyes of children yet the war is only a backdrop as the film-maker insists on its repercussions. Coutard's realistic portrayal of children's exploitation cautiously avoids painting a miserabilist picture à la Victor Hugo's 'les Misérables' or an Asian "Without Family", a melodrama in all its pejorative meaning.'[12]

Assisted by an entirely Vietnamese cast and crew, Coutard made *Hoa-Binh* in South Vietnam during the American occupation. He juggles with nationalist discourses and communist models without seemingly taking a position. His theoretical preoccupation with how Western spectators might not identify with an Asian family and Asian protagonists is rarely observed in French cinema, yet is crucial when it comes to the representation of Vietnamese 'others' on screen in France. Such a concern and sensibility with spectatorial identification needs to be addressed more often in national cinema. Coutard believes that the presence of children will lift the identification problem:

> I think that it is a question of cinematographic form. One difficulty can arise out of the fact that for a Westerner, for whom the film is addressed, identification with the Vietnamese character will not be simple. To overcome this obstacle, we will keep the children always present ... We will show life in Vietnam, without falling into folklore, or the misery of abandoned children, and without falling into the social fantastic genre.[13]

The script refers to two legends based on Vietnamese folk tales. The first briefly alludes to 'the mountain of waiting' when Hung goes to burn incense and paper money. The mountain of waiting is the wait for the absent soldier/father.

The second legend, named the Betel legend, is about fidelity to memory – the sick mother tells her children its legend at bedtime. Two brothers loved one woman. Tan, one of the brothers walked away from his brother and the sister-in-law he loved. He sat by a river and died of pain. He then turned into a stone. His brother, full of remorse, went looking for him. As he reached the river, he sat against the stone, leaned on it and was then transformed into a tree. The wife went looking for him by the river, embracing the tree while crying until she died. She was then transformed into a vine that grew around the trunk. The script stops the legend at that moment and does not explain about the betel leaf. The inscription of these legends may prepare the child and spectator for the death of the mother (foretold) and the wait for the father.

Critics condemned the apparent lack of a political agenda. The use of children instills sympathy in any viewer; a script about an eleven-year-old child struggling to survive with his two-year-old baby sister on the streets of a city, doing odd jobs as a shoe-shine boy, newspaper salesman and coolie, raises some questions. Filming and writing about Vietnam unleashes polemical debates and passion about one's ideological positioning as the critical debates surrounding films by Wargnier, Annaud and Tran have shown. This polemic registers on a semantic level as well with the terms 'return' and 'Indochina', both ideologically loaded terms in Franco-Asian narratives. The title, meaning 'peace', generates an ideological position. Even if the script does not wish to take sides, a South Vietnamese location with the presence of good American soldiers or doctors forces a political subtext. *Télérama* film critic, Claude-Marie Trémois (1970), praises the film for its documentary interest and noble traits.

The film is paved with good intentions, occasionally bordering on the religious, especially at the closing of the narrative when the father returns from war and is reunited with his son and daughter. A prayer and invocation to a god who is responsible for the pain endured in the Asian plains omit any references to Western imperialism and guilt: 'Lord, let these eyes open themselves again one day on a world where men will not add to the pain that you have placed in your creation, especially in your Asian plains.'[14]

A Vietnamese spectator responded in *L'Humanité*, the communist daily, that the rhetoric behind the film 'glorifies the so-called all powerful American army'.

> How can one not be uncomfortable, or even righteously angry, on seeing that far from protesting the presence of half a million American soldiers who day and night kill, pillage, rape and massacre women, old people and children, the film instead celebrates their presence.[15]

The critic underlines the fact that the film does not show a single good Vietnamese person besides the child and his mother and sister. All the Vietnamese characters depicted either exploit, steal or deal, from Hung's relatives to the female boss who exploits children and drives an American car. The implicit message instead turns the American forces occupying South Vietnam into benevolent creatures distributing gum to children.

Claude Mauriac of the *Figaro* (a daily of the right) reviews the film as 'a melodrama that he did not want to see' and expresses his embarrassment with the topic. He reproaches Coutard for not being political for if 'one casts Vietnamese people in Vietnam today it is still a political act'.[16] In a different way, Lucien Bodard, a long-time commentator and writer on Asia, praises *Hoa Binh* for being truthful to Vietnam and for being a Vietnamese film.[17] Once more, the debate is highly sensitive and shows polar oppositions of an ideological nature.

Robert Kramer's Return

Robert Kramer's 1993 film *Point de départ* (*Starting Place*) premiered at the Locarno Film Festival.[18] Kramer, an American-born cineaste had relocated in France in 1980 until his premature death in 1999. His documentary film constitutes a return to the country where he had previously shot *The People's War* in 1969, reporting on the Vietnamese fight. In a 1992 project backed by the French government, he returned to Vietnam on a 'mission' to train Vietnamese professionals in a cinema 'du réel'. His team 'Les Films d'ici' sponsored the making of four short films – all of them documentary films. One of them, *Chi Dung*, directed by Dao Ba Son, records the life of a former ballet dancer, now handicapped, which aired on French television.[19]

Kramer does not cast a nostalgic look on Vietnam. He might be settling his own problematic relation with North America, especially in his critical stance against its imprisonment of anti-war protesters such as Linda Evans, who has been serving a forty-year prison term since 1985 for terrorism. Evans appears several times in a jail interview.

Kramer registers his position toward a country and its people in their opening to the West after a period of closing. Similar to Rithy Panh's work in Cambodia, he helped train technicians and film-makers and cooperated with them. 'The film is not really about Vietnam. It concerns the passage of time and forgetting, as well as the major changes that took place and the way hope became something else … I think that I'm making a film about absence.'[20] Video artist/film-maker Chris Marker's work also addresses memory, mostly of a visual order that precedes the birth of cinema and photography: 'I wonder how people who do not film, who do not take pictures remember … how does humanity remember?'[21] After a 25-year absence, Kramer thus returns to Hanoi (North Vietnam) and meets some of his former film crew and his 1969 camera operator. The montage includes newsreel footage dating from the 1960s and mostly images of present-day Vietnam.

This nostalgic trip for the film-maker is also a reassessment of modern Vietnam – a country that has deeply affected the film-maker's life. Kramer scrutinises images of the new Vietnam without being critical of it. Since he could not speak the language, the reliance on interpretation hindered his questions. He was aware of, and disappointed with, the discrepancy between his questions and the answers given him.[22] Exterior shots abound, briefly cutting to more intimate spaces. Film-makers, actors and workers interviewed all testify to a current situation where the country is finally at peace, but at a high cost. One of the Vietnamese film-makers interviewed is concerned with making films 'to show the contradiction between past and present, between forgetting the past and living in the present. Yesterday's ideals are a comedy today but the most important thing was to liberate a country, a consciousness, a people' (*Point de départ*).

Kramer organises a didactic montage about modern Vietnam, starting with the process of building and rebuilding. His camera accompanies women at a brick factory, carrying bricks, and shows the entire chain of production, starting with mud, to the end product in the factory. Clearly conscious of the choice and effect of images, the 'associative' montage pursues the brick analogy, by introducing a male 'urban planner' in the next segment who explains the year 2010 plan for reconstruction. New buildings arise, while women at the bottom of the chain carry and stack heavy loads of bricks. One woman admits to carrying three tons of bricks a day. The camera shoots her at home with her children and husband in a subsequent scene. These images speak for themselves and the segment concludes with one of his characteristic extreme long-takes, a frame of the factory worker standing against the wall.

The building and rebuilding of a country – literally brick by brick – is one of the guiding lines used here. It is not in any way a 'new' concept applied to the region. Modern Franco-Vietnamese and Vietnamese literature and film develop this problematic with (as seen earlier) *Cyclo*, and in fiction with the work of Linda Lê, Huy Thiep and Duong Thu Huong. The image of a new country in full reconstruction enters Viet Linh's script, *L'Immeuble* (*Chung Cu*, *The Building*, 2000). Her film offers an insider's perspective into the life of a building requisitioned to house a collective of people after the reunification of Vietnam, from 1975 to 1980.

Another metaphor associated with new Vietnam is the recurrent image of the metallic bridge, the Long Bien Bridge, in Hanoi, one of France's accomplishments in Vietnam – the illustrious Pont Doumer. The bridge survived hundreds of bombings and stands out as a 'scarred' resistance signpost against colonialism and imperialism. It is shot from all angles. Scars are present in the story of the ballerina whose legs were cut off in a train accident, a story somehow linked to the bridge in the montage. Kramer visually quotes from this woman's story, now scripted by one of his Vietnamese trainees: 'The train cut her story' or 'The train has remade her story/history.' Train, bridges and bricks are the necessary components used in this musing on time past and present in Vietnam. The ballet dancer does not speak, but juxtaposed close-ups of her intense gaze as she is made to watch earlier footage of her dancing as a young ballerina help to communicate her despair.

The visit to official monuments with the Ho Chi Minh museum forms a long segment when the camera stops in front of the enshrined display of various objects that belonged to the communist leader in North Vietnam. Some of the displayed objects include books, snapshots, a pressed uniform, statues and rubber sandals. Kramer questions a man about the importance of Ho Chi Minh. The interviewee praises the leader who inspired his people and was a formidable teacher. Owing to location shooting in front of the encased shrine dedicated to the memory of Ho Chi Minh, the film-maker pays homage to Ho, who is linked to Kramer (whose daughter was named Kija Ho in respect). Images of the daughter's birth legitimate that point and confirm the long rapport Kramer has had with Vietnam.

France is visually absent from the film except in short vignettes as a picture of the Eiffel Tower shown next to the French-trained translator, or a shot of a tricolour map of France upside down, in a 'formerly French' bakery and an inscription that reads 'Wheat flour for sale' as well as the shot of the bridge, a reminder of France. France is present as Kramer conducts his interviews in French.

Point de départ releases endearing images of the Vietnamese people. These artful portraits instill a human dimension in what could have largely been ignored had it stayed on a purely journalistic level. Starting with the sequence of the woman at the brick factory, to the segment about the circus tightrope walker, the picture echoes Kramer's personal feelings. The film form is close to the photographic album and movement freezes more than once on still photographs, snapshots of people and women.

Linda Evans's interview poses a fundamental debate about history and imperialist politics. Indeed, the spectator is left questioning. Ideological struggles and fight against imperialism have shifted in their form at the end of the twentieth century. Yet, people are still imprisoned and killed for their beliefs and ideologies, everywhere, East and West, or North and South. Vietnam changed Evans's life years ago and her struggle to maintain a clear consciousness has not left her, even behind bars.

Kramer shows, but refrains from comments or critiques. Frames of people and objects express some of what is not explicitly said. He has edited interviews, or selected not to follow up with them, especially the one discussing Thai sexual tourism. He only interviews North Vietnamese people and no dissidents. Yet his notes around *Point de départ* quote three writers, two dissident voices in today's Vietnam: Nguyen Huy Thiep and Duong Thu Huong (see Kramer 1994). Excerpts from dissident writer Duong Thu Huong's texts are read several times in the film. Kramer wanted to meet with her and interview her, but was unable to do so. Huong is a former North Vietnamese soldier whose task was to find and bury corpses along the seventeenth parallel during the war. As a prominent member of the communist party, she was decorated for her dedication. She is now a writer who denounces some of the regime's contradictions and was jailed and assigned to residence in 1991. She has become the voice of Vietnamese dissidence whose cause has been embraced in the West. Before making the film, Kramer wrote her a letter explaining his intentions: 'I am an American but for various reasons, I have lived in Europe since 1980. One can say that the example of Vietnam (or our ideas about Vietnam, our desires) has played an important role in our life.' Kramer expressed how much her writing has inspired him in this project and served as a basis for the film in the making:

> My admiration for your work is at the basis of it. I have read *Paradise of the Blind* and *Novel without a Name*. *Novel* literally engulfed me. It directed my gaze as I was walking in Hanoi, and I would hear the night in my breathing, this suffocating world of people buried alive in their history. It is a magnificent war narrative (*Point de départ*).

Kramer wanted her dissonant voice to resonate in his film and asked her to participate in the shooting in a letter she probably never received.

Writing to Document: Duong Thu Huong's Dissonant Voice(s)

> I've thought a lot … I listen to everything that's said. You see, the people, they do exist from time to time, but they're only a shadow. When they need rice, the people are the buffalo that pulls the plow. When they need soldiers, they cover the people with armour, put guns in the people's hands. When all is said and done, at the festivals, when it comes time for the banquets, they put the people on an altar and feed them incense and ashes. But the real food, that's always for them. (Huong 1995: 275)

Roman sans titre (*Novel without a Name*), written in Hanoi in 1990, was published in French soon after by the feminist press des femmes. Like most of Huong's other novels, it was never officially published or sold in Vietnam. Her books circulate in Vietnam, yet they appear in pirated editions. She is probably the Vietnamese writer most known abroad and is the only Vietnamese writer whose entire works have been published in French. Three of her books were translated and published in France in one year: *Les Paradis aveugles* (1991), *Histoire d'amour racontée avant l'aube* (1991) and *Roman sans titre* (1992). The French Minister of Culture, Jacques Toubon, honoured her with the title of Chevalier des arts et des lettres, an honour that nearly provoked a diplomatic crisis between Paris and Hanoi in 1994.

Roman sans titre weaves the tale of a North-Vietnamese officer who has been fighting for the past ten years in an endless war. Written in the first person (male), the tone varies between sarcastic and poetic. The narrator faces the horror of war, loss of friends, comrades and loved ones. The narrative plunges deep into the minefields of northern forests, in an odorous world of blood, rotting corpses and haunted bodies. Temporary refuge is found in childhood memories, especially the cherished memory of the mother who died when the narrator was eight-years-old, as well as in the multiple dreams and visions he has. After ten years of combat, the soldiers can no longer keep their faith and idealism in the fight. Huong's writing exposes the communist structure throughout. She is the first 'woman combatant present on the front lines to chronicle the conflict'.[23] Instead of euphoric postcard-images of the revolution, images of degenerating bodies abound as well as emphatic anti-revolutionary prose that is to some extent distorted in its translation, between French and English, although the same translator worked on both:

> Look, we were fifteen years old at the time. We were young. The revolution was also young, fresh. We sang our way from one battle to the next. 'The Comrades' Chant' – how did that go again? … Lovely lyrics, eh? Words that flowered and bore fruit. Now they're starting to fade. That's the universal law. Revolution, like love, blooms and then withers. But revolution rots much faster than love, 'comrade'. The less it's true, the more we need to believe in it. That's the art of governing. Spreading the word, now that's you intellectuals' job. We pay you for it.[24]

Quân's hopes and dreams are shattered after a brief return to his village. He discovers that his younger brother, a brilliant student, whose birth he attended and relives in his dreams, has left for the front and died, and that his beloved Hoa, who had been waiting for him for the past ten years, is now pregnant and ostracised by the entire village: 'In the end, the girl I had loved had been cast out, but not for having loved me' (p. 143). The war has destroyed and maimed what was left of his hopes: 'Never. We never forget anything, never lose any-thing, never exchange anything, never undo what has been. There is no way back to the source, to the place where the pure, clear water once gushed forth. The river had cut across the countryside, the towns, dragging refuse and mud in its wake' (p. 148).

Marxism is denounced as the new religion corrupting people and destined to serve an elite. Quân survived ten years of combat and mastered a new self-taught philosophy. It is more about reversed logic: for example, one cannot escape bombs, but they can escape you. 'Bullets may miss people, but no one dodges a bullet' (p. 36). This image is invoked more than once.

Images of sheer natural beauty contrast these moments of danger and horror. These are located around sunset or in dreams, as well as in flashbacks to childhood memories of the mother – offset in the text – and of food prepa-rations. More often than not, these images of beauty and horror contaminate each other: 'Me, my friends, we had lived this war for too long, steeped our-selves for too long in the beauty of all its moments of fire and blood. Would it still be possible, one day, for us to go back, to rediscover our roots, the beauty of creation, the rapture of a peaceful life?' (p. 193)[25]

Time stretches itself and the sense of its passage becomes blurred. Roughly speaking the narrative takes place during the last weeks/months of war, on the North Vietnamese side. It ends in a joyless victory. The narrator is removed from its reality, as if detached and emotionless. 'The battle had unfolded as predictably as if it had been a parade: assault, a rapid conclusion. We had never dreamed of this outcome. Compared to the battles of the last ten years, it almost seemed like a game' (p. 282). The only Westerner in the novel is an American photographer who, while still in Vietnam, is arrested. Instead of accepting his soldiers' revenge scenario, Quân instead focuses on the human dimension of the prisoner:

> I suddenly imagined a green hill, this young man embracing his lover, rolling in the grass. Perhaps this was a city girl, like the woman in the strange nude photos I had seen. Or maybe a country girl, like one of ours … the war is over. We're not in the jungle anymore. (p. 285)[26]

The narrative concludes by painting the tensions intrinsic to the fight and foreshadows the future of a country that will have to rebuild itself. This meditation on war inserts a flashback on earlier times and spaces, in the mode of what Terrence Malick accomplished cinematographically in *The Thin Red Line* (1999), a war film but also a metaphysical journey about evil and life. *Roman sans titre* is a tale rich with visual and sensuous memories; its representation of Vietnam intimately pairs the country with the feminine and mother-side. Some of Duong Thu Huong's novels are currently adapted onto film and she also writes scripts.

Her vision disturbs the main line as it denounces the corruption of a system and the scars left by the war. It does not correspond with the official ideology as she develops the story of a people through an individual ego-centered perspective. She is at the forefront of the literary and artistic Renaissance currently taking place in Vietnam and in its diaspora. Both Tran Anh Hung and Lam Lê have praised her writing. Translator and (Picquier) editor Phan Huy Duong explains the historical literary tradition in Vietnam. Placed in the context of centuries of colonisation first by the Chinese, then by the French, Vietnamese people have managed to find, maintain and refine a literary voice. Between 1925 and 1945, the country underwent a massive literary renaissance, which covered all known genres. Locating his country in the francophone world, Duong asserts that Vietnam is primarily a francophone country in its mental structures:

> Vietnam is a francophone country, not only in the number of people who speak French, but because of the values inherited by the French revolution and the taste for French literature, assimilated perhaps by mental structures that infiltrate themselves in its culture, through the rationalising process of its language by writers and intellectuals seeped in French culture.[27]

Silenced for many years under a dictatorial regime, writers after 1989 decided to express themselves and to re-appropriate their country through language.

Documentary films have turned to the Vietnamese community in France and francophone countries. Interviews show an interrogation and a reclaiming of one's identity and origins. Immigrants have to do a balancing act and negotiate between two positions. It is definitely part of a larger on-going movement as far as ethnic minorities in France (and other countries) are concerned, in view of their position in the dominant culture and the culture of their parents. *Là où vont les nuages: Art et identité de la diaspora vietnamienne* ('Where the Clouds go: Art and Identity in the Vietnamese diaspora', 1999), directed by two Belgian film-makers, interviews Vietnamese artists – film-makers, painters, musicians, actors and performers living in the European diaspora.[28] Each speaks of his/her relation with the country of origins and the differences among generations. Lam Lê recounts that when he returned to Vietnam, he was labeled 'a Russian'. Generation differences are important. The first generation of immigrants wants to retain its Vietnamese identity; whereas the younger generation born abroad does not have the same rapport with traditions, culture and language. To be a *Viet-kieu* or a Vietnamese living abroad is to be 'Vietnamese but not quite'. I will close this chapter by covering a made-for-television documentary film that explores these notions and looks at the future.

The notion of a double-identity is explored in the 1991 reportage filmed by Louise Ernct and Beatrice Ly Cuong entitled *Double-Je*.[29] Both journalists go to the Paris suburb of Bagneux and interview children of the second generation who were born in France. A similar reportage into families was done in *Saigon sur Seine* (1980) and the more recent film by Sylvie Gadmer, *Quand on navigue sur un fleuve* (*When one goes down the River,* 1997).[30] These documentaries investigate the position of Asian immigrants living in France and their nostalgic desire to return to their native country. *Saigon sur Seine* questions the way Cholon or Saigon has reconstituted itself on the banks of the Seine. Similarly, but stemming from the Maghrebian experience, Yamina Benguigui's *Mémoires d'Immigrés* (*Immigrant Memories,* 1997) proposed the narrative of North-African immigration in France, closing with a segment on beur children and their own positioning in France and next to the generation of their parents.

Children are the special focus of *Double-Je*, as it follows the younger generation born and raised in France, which enrolls in special Saturday classes that teach them about Vietnamese culture, language and writing. They are taught Vietnamese dances and performances that they will perform during the Têt ceremony (New Year) at the Mutualité in Paris. The film documents the importance of preserving one's ethnic memories and traditions as the purpose of these classes according to volunteer teacher Mr Hoang, and is such that they do not forget that 'somehow somewhere they are Vietnamese'. Some of the youths reclaim their Vietnamese heritage and may even change their (French) name for a Vietnamese one. The film presents the cleavage between the francophone Vietnamese and those who arrived more recently. There is a gap among the different generations and the chronology of their arrival that is best illustrated by their naming. For example, those who arrived earlier are called the 'Francophones'; they learned French in Vietnam. Then, there is another generation called the 'Vietnamophones'; those who fled a communist Vietnam in 1975, 'the boat people'. Tran Anh Hung belongs to the latter generation. These differences were reported in Le Huu Khoa's sociological queries and are crucial when trying to situate the Franco-Vietnamese community. Ideological differences and divisions come out. Some of the older immigrants have 'idealised' the country while those who fled the country do not have the same rapport. The political cleavage depends on the weight of lived/cultural history.

CHAPTER SIX

Khmer Memories

What else did we know of Cambodia than what Loti had told us, the Inventory and the narratives of the Chinese monks whose experience was far too foreign to be useful to us! It was hot, there were strange diseases, the country was 'protected' by France and we had seen, six months earlier, delicate dancers from that country, who, accompanied by musicians, had made the audience flee, an audience used to Opera productions and who had laughed at them. (Malraux 1992: 88)[1]

This chapter focuses on Rithy Panh, a Cambodian documentary film-maker now living in France as an exile. Cambodia became a French protectorate in the later nineteenth century, around 1863, and remained so until the recognition of its autonomy in 1945 and independence in 1953 (see Ruscio 1987). Many considered it 'the jewel of the empire'. Cambodia participated in the 1931 colonial exhibition that took place in Vincennes, showcasing the reconstitution of the temple of Angkor Vat. A major exhibition on Khmer art took place in Paris in 1997 at the Grand Palais.

Cambodia's status differed from the three Ky, or the three regions of Vietnam. The country regained its independence earlier than its neighbors, with whom they have been fighting for centuries; the Vietnamese army invaded Cambodia in 1979 and fought against the Communist Khmer Rouge faction that had taken power.

Figure 9 Rithy Panh, Paris, September 2000 (© S. Blum-Reid)

Rice Stories

Our study of Rithy Panh's career during the 1990s explores his films and incorporates a discussion of their financing, as French and European production companies subsidise them. His films have been critically acclaimed in France and Europe where they have won many prizes, as well as in Cambodia. They have not yet been distributed in the United States although this might be changing in the very near future. *Les Gens de la rizière* (*Rice People*, 1993) was shown at the Seattle International Film Festival in 1995. His latest production, *La Terre des âmes errantes* (*Land of the Wandering Souls*, 1999) won first prize at the festival of Cinéma du réel in Nyon, Switzerland in 2000 and the Golden Gate Award, in the category of Current Events, at the San Francisco International Film Festival in April 2001.

Initially we will look at several of these films, and more particularly *Les Gens de la rizière*, an ode to his country of birth. Most of his productions weave important womanist material and his work persistently engages the function of memory and history. Alice Walker's use of the term 'womanist' fittingly embraces a practice at the core of his films as they are '"committed to the survival and wholeness of entire people", female and male, as well as to a valorisation of women's works in all their varieties and multitudes' (Sherley Anne Williams 1990: 70). In the second part of this chapter, we will examine the film-maker's recent work and investigate the mode of financing his films – an interest that has grown from studying his work. An appendix to the chapter is composed of the transcription of the first interview that I conducted with him, in the summer of 1997.

Besides writing and making films, Panh has dedicated himself to the training film technicians in Cambodia and help support a national film production
there. In 1994–95, he was in charge of the training of documentary film-
makers under Varan, a film production house created by Jean Rouch that will
be looked at below. [2]

Born in Phnom Penh in 1964, Panh witnessed as a young boy the arrival of
the Khmer Rouge soldiers in 1975. Sent to re-education camps along with an
entire population, he managed to escape in 1979 and made his way to a refugee
camp in Thailand. A year later, in 1980, he resettled in France, learned French,
acquired carpentry skills and subsequently started his studies. In 1985, he
passed the entrance examination for l'IDHEC (now FEMIS, a highly selective
national competition giving access to the film school) and trained to become a
film-maker. As early as 1987, he had written a script entitled 'Aux abords des
frontières' (Near the Borders), which in 1989 he successfully turned into *Site
2*, a film about Cambodian refugees in Thai refugee camps. The documentary
film secured many prizes, among others, the Grand Prix Documentaire of the
Festival International d'Amiens. In 1990, he shot a documentary film on African film-maker Souleymane Cissé.

Les Gens de la rizière, his first fiction feature, was shot in December 1992
and January 1993. In 1996, *Bophana: Une Tragédie cambodgienne* was released.
Co-produced by France 3, CDP, and INA, the documentary film adapts Eliza-
beth Becker's American book *Les Larmes du Cambodge* (*Cambodia's Tears*).
Bophana retrieves the tragedy of the Cambodian people during the Khmer
Rouge era. Throughout his work, Panh attempts to reconcile himself with his
country's past and the massive purges, deportation and genocide of a people.
An estimated 2 million Cambodians died at the hands of the communist
Khmer Rouge in what is termed 'the killing fields'. The impetus to record
images predates his arrival in France and goes back to his childhood in Cambodia: 'Having lived the same trials as many of my compatriots, it was vital
as soon as I arrived in France in 1979, or more exactly, as soon as I managed
to master the language, to make my experience known through images.'[3] He
implicates himself in so doing, by re-enacting the life of a couple, Bophana
and Ly Sitha who resisted the destruction of a people. The film-maker uses an
interrogation mode, letters and confessions endlessly extorted from the couple
once they were arrested, to tell their story. Their personal story is used to tell
the larger one of a people.[4]

Les Gens de la rizière, an authentic European co-production, involved
British, Swiss, German and French agencies. It was co-produced by JBA
productions, created by Jean-Luc Bidou, La Sept/Cinéma, (or Arte), Thelma
films, ZDF, TSR and Canal+. Channel 4 also participated in the production,
together with the Direction du cinéma du Cambodge and the Agence de Coopération culturelle et technique Ecrans du Sud. Panh co-wrote the script with
Eve Deboise and adapted a novel by Malaysian writer Shahnon Ahmad entitled
Le Riz (*Rice*).[5] To do so, both scriptwriters had to recast the narrative in a

Buddhist country, different from Muslim Malaysia. The film is entirely shot in Cambodia, in Cambodian language, with an entirely Cambodian cast and a small French film crew. It made the 1994 official Cannes selection. There was no national film production in Cambodia, besides King Norodom Sihanouk's own ventures into movie-making, that he discussed as presenting the 'only true and now disappeared images of a real Cambodia' ('La Permanence de l'identité khmère', 1986).[6]

Panh took along a small crew of people and trained others. As Cissé did, he selected and trained non-actors – not a small task, since most of them had to be persuaded at first to be in a film: 'For them cinema means action films from Hong Kong, or Indian melodramas. So we had to talk to them, give them the script, convince them of the honesty of our intentions.'[7] Panh, who had refused to return to his country for ten years and had stopped speaking his mother tongue, chose to return and face some of the old 'demons', as he had done earlier for *Site 2*. The distance created by the adaptation of a novel onto film helped him acquire some sort of detachment. *Les Gens de la rizière* chronicles a life entirely absorbed by the culture of rice, its growth, and its rituals, as well as the hardships that can affect any family in the region. Buddhist but also animist practices and beliefs that animate the villagers and the film-maker sweep the film. Really, the chief character is the rice-field that rules the entire village and is part of its life, very much like a person, as the Malaysian text explains: 'The network of rice-paddies, like a single and vast breath of the entire body of the village, started to change its hues.'[8] As soon as the film starts, one realises that the director's vision shuns from war-torn images of a nation.

Nicole Biros, French translator of *Le Riz*, first published in 1966, comments on the importance of rice and the Asian sensibility displayed in the book (Ahmad 1987). The Malaysian sensibility shares a representation of the world with other South-East Asian countries: 'Malaysian sensibility nevertheless has to do with the representation of the world common in South-East Asian countries. Among living beings, the borders are blurred and the passage between the living and the dead takes place. This explains their familiarity with one another.'[9]

The drama of rice-growing labour is eternal and part of the natural cycle of the earth. This is the story of Vong Poeuv and his wife Yim Om and their seven daughters: 'Rice culture is their life's rhythm, joy, creed and survival.'[10] Ahmad concentrates on their life, hardships and misery while growing rice. Many natural calamities threaten the production of rice, from birds (called tiak) to crabs, bad weather as well as 'Amok' – a term that runs through the narrative and refers to a 'Malaysian's sudden murderous access' (*Le Riz*, p. 19). Panh transplanted the story to another country, changed the names of the family members and some of their religious rituals. This last task is important since *Le Riz* was based on an essentially Islamic system of rituals and names.

Rice is life and the survival of people depends on it. A Cambodian mythological tale explains that rice can only grow during the rainy season, after the god of rice became dissatisfied with a quarrel among some villagers. While in the West, bread is the symbol of life (at least in France), rice bears the same symbolism in South-East Asia. It has influenced the spiritual and material life of Cambodians. Cambodian language contains many references to rice and its value. 'To eat is "to eat rice", the peasant is called "the man of the rice paddies" and the kitchen is the "house where rice is cooked"' (*Les Gens de la rizière*). The peasant is thus part of a cycle that is integral to the production of rice.

Panh attributes his first documentary *Site 2*, devoted to camp refugees, to the subsequent adaptation of *Le Riz*. All his films are connected and form a tight body, all the way to the more recent *Un soir après la guerre* (*One Evening after the War*, 1998). While preparing for *Site 2*, a remark made by an older woman in a refugee camp stuck with him when she equated freedom with the opportunity to cultivate a piece of land. Children raised in that camp only knew that rice came from 'the NATO truck', had no notion about its growth and were out of touch with its symbolic religious value and their culture (Halberstadt 1994). One of the new sets of values inculcated by the Khmer Rouge was to do away with family, religion and a sense of identity. Teeda Butt Mam, a camp survivor recalls her struggle as a child, facing the loss of her family and the eradication of a culture: 'We were timid and lost. We had to be silent. We not only lost our identities, but we lost our pride, our senses, our religion, our loved ones, our souls, ourselves' (Mam 1994: 115)

In view of Panh's work, *Site 2* is a formative film and returns to the motherland. The intention to bear testimony to the Cambodian people was made clear already in 1987, when he proposed to collect images of refugee camps in Thailand in a documentary built on the gathering of witnesses and the observation of two camps of Cambodian refugees.[11]

A gynocentric film, *Les Gens de la rizière* follows closely the natural cycle of rice culture, from its planting to its harvesting. The cycle of life and death is threatened by natural cataclysms that abruptly alter the life of a family composed of a father, mother and their seven daughters. After the father dies of an infectious wound, the mother becomes mad and the daughters, led by the eldest, Sokha, are suddenly in charge of their rice paddies and have to battle with various natural disasters out in the fields. The camerawork celebrates the growth and sacredness of rice, but focuses on the trials that the family has to endure. Tragedy is continually present, from the beginning with the shot of the snake threatening the mother Yim Om, and killed by the father Poeuv, that in itself propels the narrative. The action of killing a snake is sacrilegious and bears ramifications with the spirit world. The horrible agony of the father and subsequent madness of the mother underscore this effect as the 'spirits' have taken possession of her mind.

The entire community is affected by the initial action and the village takes up the hunt for the female cobra. The villagers also unite to help the daughters cure their mother, by sending her to a city hospital and helping with the harvest. Dreams and visions enter the narrative occasionally, with

Figure 10 *Un soir apres la guerre* (© Jean de Calan)

the hallucinating father's vision of being beaten by Khmer Rouge soldiers at
night – that perspective is the only direct statement on the historic situation of
Cambodia that Panh most likely experienced in his youth. Solidarity among
the seven daughters is reinforced on Poeuv's deathbed by the lesson of seven
sticks held together that will not break – each stick standing for one daughter.
The older daughter quietly assumes the charge of an elder son – as shown in
the act of shaving her head bald, a Buddhist practice performed at the death
of a parent. She will carry out the celebratory rites of the new rice or new life

by the Mekong River at dawn. The offering shows that purification occurs at the closure of the narrative and emphasises a close connection to the sacred, between people and their god(s), as many myths reveal that rice is a gift from the gods.

As a constant, Panh's work places female identity first and shows consideration toward women by giving them back their voice.[12] Cambodia is essentially a matrilineal society. Penny Edwards' essay on colonialism and Cambodian women notes, 'Cambodian women were far more active in the urban and agricultural economy than their French counterparts. At home they enjoyed financial clout and property rights ... which challenged French colonial and metropole gender ideology' (1998: 118). Unfortunately, male colonial authorities and war(s) destroyed this type of society.

Yim Om loses touch with reality and the fact that Poeuv is dead and always communicates with him. In reality, the border between death and life is very thin. She goes out to the village on an errand and drinks alcohol offered by male villagers, who scornfully propose to her. The blasphemous action of drinking by a married woman is punished. Following this episode, she becomes the target of public humiliation by children chanting that she is 'the mad widow with the many children', following her through the village and rice paddies while casting stones at her. Confronted by her madness, the village leader resolves to lock her up in a bamboo cage. The village acts as a collective in their effort to treat her and help the daughters. Their interest in keeping her prisoner and restraining her 'madness' is animated by a fundamental preservation principle: to save the rice plants. The task to cultivate and gather the harvest has obscured the mother's mind. Ultimately, Sokha, the older daughter, frees the mother from her cage, once the harvest is done. After she returns from the city hospital, in a lethargic state and definitely not cured, she is again imprisoned in her cage. When the daughter leads her out into the fields, the camera gives a long take of the mother, touching plants, jumping up and down while screaming. Her screaming closes the film, with Panh's dedication: 'To my family 1975–1979.' It is understood that the family will have to live and cope with her madness for which there is no immediate cure.

Panh's portrait of Souleymane Cissé, released in 1991, gives an African film-maker's vision on film-making as well as an insight into the situation of a formerly French colony.[13] As such, although the socio-historical problematic of both countries is not on the same level, the situation of a neo-colonial nation and a film-maker's practice is comparatively close to Panh's own position, which my reading attempts to tease out. The film pays homage to the film-maker whom Panh considers one of his models. Cissé, in conversation with compatriot and NYU Film and African Studies professor Manthia Diawara, questions the veracity of images of African people given by French (white) film-makers: 'Those who came here to shoot films never showed human beings. They came to show us as animals to their audience ... white men's cinema shows that Africans do not belong to mankind ... they shoot wild animals with more respect.'[14] These words echo Ho Chi Minh's essay, a pamphlet about cinema discussed in the second chapter and the way that French film-makers in fact filmed Vietnamese people early on.

Cissé claims that the task of the African film-maker is to re-affirm people's values and portray them as human beings, without lying. The camera cannot lie, but the film-maker can if s/he so chooses to embellish a certain reality. Cissé, trained in the former USSR, comes out as a dissident voice in his native Mali, or the one who dares tell of the political situation of his country and people through his films. According to him, his cinema was ' born out of violence' – the violence that his country experiences daily, since according to him, in 1991, nothing had changed in Africa, after independence and 'colonialism'.

Speaking of his scriptwriting experience, Cissé isolates himself to write, most of his stories are inspired by his dreams and intuitions that sometimes uncannily reveal a real-life situation once filmed – as in *Yeelen* (1987), for example. The film-maker insists that he does not create with his films, but 'participates' while making films – a stand that I perceive as a necessary clarification and demystification of the role of the director-king adopted in the West. Borrowing from Bambara language, Cissé talks of 'damu', a word that expresses 'a positive impression that one has of people or things'. A film-maker must show a human being with 'damu' to make lasting films. There is no equivalent in French or English of 'damu' except that it comes close to 'soul' in English.

Les Gens de la rizière devotes a large portion of its frames to nature, rice plants, sunsets, altars to gods and collective work efforts. It also consigns the overall structure to women's work and role in society, by paying tribute to the task of the seven daughters and their mother. The film-maker laments that during Pol Pot's times, young Khmer women lost their status, not to mention their fate when they were interned in refugee camps.

> Khmer women have lost the value, place and respect granted to them by culture and religion. If war and resistance concern men who fight with weapons, women are the ones who have to endure the consequences … They are stripped of everything that made their strength: land, house and a stable family life.[15]

Panh stands out as a 'great landscape' artist, between documentary and ethnographic film-making. *L'Humanité* notes that Third World films aptly remind us that cinema is not always about entertainment: 'Often, third-world made films remind us that the cinematographer is not always a frivolous past-time, but a question of life and death for people who have everything to wait for and to do' (Leonardini 1994: 67). As a first fiction film, far – yet never too far – from his earlier and subsequent documentaries, Panh does not revel in pathos or nostalgia. The film inspires respect for a country and imposes itself in a largely ethnographic genre.

Financing indicates a considerable interest in films made in 'developing countries' by contemporary French producers. The example of Jacques Bidou (the founder of JBA Production), who financed *Site 2*, *Les Gens de la rizière* and *Un soir après la guerre*, is worth signaling. According to Bidou, Cambodia, because of France's colonial past, still elicits a feeling of guilt in France: 'The risk was important, since Cambodia is a martyred land, toward which, because of our colonial past, we have a latent feeling of guilt' (in Dumas 1994: 75).[16]

The film-making itself was risky, since in 1992 the Cambodian political climate was unstable. Yet the crew spent days on rice paddies, while Khmer Rouge soldiers were present and sometimes fighting. The technicians had to rely on villagers for the film and sometimes ran across and against religious practices and beliefs that they did not necessarily fully understand, as Bidou reported:

> An assistant director was convinced that he had the evil eye during the shooting of the film because we had shaved the head of the older daughter, who is in mourning in the film, while, in reality, nobody in her family had died. When people from the Cambodian team, that we know are cultured, schooled and intelligent, come and tell us: 'if we don't burn incense tomorrow we won't be able to shoot the scene', one enters a world of the irrational that only Rithy, as a Cambodian, was able to understand. (in Dumas 1994: 76)[17]

These comments made by the producer point to the permanence of Western cultural notions governing such a project.

Of Land, Ghosts and Spirits

Panh's most recent documentary film, *La Terre des âmes errantes* (*Land of the Wandering Souls*), sets out to document the installation of the first fibre-optic cable to traverse the continent and link Europe to China, financed by the French Alcatel Company.[18] It carries a significant commentary on the concept of 'mondialisation' (the French term) or globalisation as it is implemented in Cambodia. The first image seemingly proposes a reportage on the miracle of Western technology exported to an Asian country. The spectator, with the participants, quickly becomes aware of Western hegemony and of the exploitative nature of globalisation. Entire families of migrant workers left their homes and for lack of any other resources, ended up digging trenches for weeks in the countryside. The crew follows co-ed workers and their children trailing for months in postwar Cambodia. These people, prevented by the war to continue their study, not to mention the deprivation of their childhood and family, are critically aware of their plight. The job they find is to dig trenches to bury the cable that will benefit people connected to a computer and electricity – or a relatively small elite group in a nation where there are 9 television sets and 112 radios for every 1,000 persons (Sothanrith & Amat 2000: 9). If the spectator was unaware of the situation in Cambodia in the 1990s, s/he is taught a historical and political lesson.

Moments of laughter erupt in the film as the outlet in this otherwise extremely exploitative situation. An engineer uses religious terminology to explain to a villager that the cable or 'magical eyes and ears' of the Ramayana legend has come. Thanks to cable, people will be watching CNN and instantly connect with their distant relatives in the USA thanks to the Internet. The irony of the situation is obvious when a pragmatic villager remarks that people do not even have electricity, but a petrol lamp and a generator that they sometimes cannot afford to start. The aftermath of the war is palpable; most soldiers who returned home are left without a cultural or financial base. Upon their return, the land had already been distributed to a few. *La Terre des âmes errantes*, because of its subject, echoes a film directed by one of Panh's trainees, Prôm Mesar, during the Varan Cambodge workshop in 1994–95, *J'ai quitté la guerre* (*I Left the War*).[19]

In *J'ai quitté la guerre*, a former soldier, who fought for 14 years in the war, finally returns home (as a deserter) to be with his wife and children. Haunted by his memories, Mesar offers a strong indictment of the war and the class system it perpetuates, in that it has benefited the wealthy. The soldier tells the camera: 'I've left the war, I'm cultivating my rice paddy, but death is still here.' Traumas are in his heart as he evokes 'his spirit going in all directions.'

Again, in *La Terre des âmes errantes*, women take centre-stage and the film-maker praises the extraordinary courage and strength of women in his country. Shying away from any concerted feminist effort, or any programmatic feminist call, he chooses instead to 'capture' women in their daily struggle. His documentaries never contain any voiceover narration or questions; the participants directly speak in front of the camera, or next to it.

When men dig and go to war, women have to fight to survive, raise their children, worry about their daily nourishment, and their education, not to mention the act of digging as well. Women are the ones to voice disapproval with the system, at least in front of the camera; the boss who has hired them eventually absconds with their wages at the end of the film, in a dramatic twist, leaving them as they came, empty-handed, with children to feed in a desperate situation. The film digs up more than trenches; in the process, bones and mines as well as ghosts are excavated and discussed. The cable becomes secondary to the narrative.

When screened in Cambodia the film generated positive responses. Other than this, it showed a side that Cambodian city dwellers do not even know. Ironically, spectators used to documentary film-makers in the authoritative position of asking questions and with a generic voiceover narration, thought that this was entirely staged. This effect results from a filmic approach that participates in the documentary genre but stays away from a certain form of documentary. It is closer to *cinéma vérité*, urging people to speak with the least intervention. Panh professes to observe Cambodian people and their daily life from the inside. As he did for *Site 2*, he refuses any commentary. The voice is given to people, be they refugees, children, women or soldiers.

His films engage a personal return to the 'terrible, yet unfinished story' of his country and a personal involvement, albeit not overtly.[20] The excavated ghosts are also 'his' ghosts, as he would later acknowledge in our interview. Panh's modus operandi is based on an articulation that 'daily reality cannot be said, or told in its entirety unless it is lived'.[21] The spectatorial response discussed above stems from the fact that the film-maker allowed people to express themselves on camera and never controlled the dialogue. Apparently his trainees were able to address the questions posed by the spectators during a post-screening session and explained the inherent work methods.

Panh's goal is to restore his people's dignity, a task favored by film-maker Cissé. By training an entire generation of technicians, a 'generation … is fighting to recover an entire imaginary … In all modesty, we try to film the soul of the country and put people's dignity first.'[22] This type of filming is also termed 'filming from the inside', as only a person experienced in the customs and culture could do. His past comes out, but remains in the margins since his films track situations that Panh had to endure, such as forced migration, living in camps and losing one's family. Each film propels a return to the self, to one's experiences, yet it shows and tells a collective experience.

His recent fiction film, *Un soir après la guerre*, again takes up some of the same concerns that surface in his previous films. This film however, contrary to the previous ones, was not screened in Cambodia, probably because of its more overt political stance. It did not do well in France and ran for only two weeks in Parisian theatres, grossing 2,564 entries after its first run career. This was not successful compared with *Les Gens de la rizière*, which was released in eight Parisian theatres and stayed 11 weeks, grossing a total 42,509 entries in Paris and 70,405 entries in France. Unlike his earlier film, the fiction is here anchored in Cambodia's most recent past and present. Panh composed 'a simple love story, the story of an attempt to live again, to force destiny' (press kit). It confronts the inner conflicts of the 'lost generation' of young Cambodians whose future or life was sacrificed in the war, the same generation to which Panh belongs. Cambodian soldiers return to town, merely to find that they have no money, no job training, no bearings and no means to start anew, after years at war. The story of Savannah casts Narith Roeun, an actor who became a film-maker through the Atelier Varan Cambodge. A young woman, Srey Poeuv (played by Chea Lyda Chan, a non-professional actor) whose voiceover spans the entire film, tells the story in a flashback. She plays 'a little flower' as they are called in Phnom Penh, or a dance hall girl.

The trauma of war persists in contemporary Cambodia (circa 1992) and clarifies some of the madness encountered. The lives of the characters have been altered so much by the war that they can scarcely start over. Phnom Penh acts as another character in the film, a brutal city opening to the era of free market. In the prologue, the young woman testifies, 'It was a time of upheavals. Fear and misery had corrupted all of us, all the way down to love and friendship' (press kit).[23] The female protagonist wants to leave prostitution, to follow Savannah whom she loves, but unfortunately, she is in the grip of the prostitution world that has 'owned' her since childhood. The postwar era reflects a period of reconstruction that at least one of them will not survive. These extreme social changes parallel *Cyclo* in its vista into an extremely violent and corrupt postwar Saigon (Ho Chi Minh City).

Rithy Panh in the Year 2000

Three years after my first interview, I met again with Rithy Panh, to get a closer perspective on his most recent work. For the past year and a half, he had been preparing a fiction film for the Franco-German television channel (ARTE) – a channel that has helped with three of his projects. The shooting started in the summer of 2000.[24] The film *Que la barque se brise, que la jonque s'entrouve* (*Let the Boat Break*) connects the Vietnamese and Cambodian communities in France, something that has never been done thus far, especially by a film-maker from South-East Asia. Panh looks into the situation of Asian refugees who came to France twenty years ago, in an attempt to address the post-traumatic stress disorders they experience. By so doing, he hopes to reconcile both countries and make peace with the 'racial hatred between them that has been politically exploited'. 'Cannot one see life among neighbours otherwise?' A French psychoanalyst, who has been involved for the past twenty years with refugees, is now assisting him on the project. According to Panh, people who arrived twenty years ago, without anything, are finally settling down in their life, with children going to school, with their own place and car, a precise moment when traumas resurface.[25] The metaphor of the 'boat' suggests a place of rest, compared to the traumas experienced.

Methods

Panh's work advances slowly, as he reportedly takes time to shoot and write. His entire approach to people and the way he engages with them reveals intense and careful preparations in the field that in turn produce strong films. Yet it does not preclude chance encounters and unforeseen events. For example, *La Terre des âmes errantes* took three months to shoot, when regular documentary film crews would usually allow four weeks. The difficulties that he experiences come from the financing of his films and the task of finding producers responsive to his work method and his area of choice. A few of the criticisms that he has received, directly or indirectly, stem from a discussion of the financing of his films that some view as 'problematic' (see Tarr 1997: 60).

Panh maintains a close connection with his 'protagonists' and still visits them, sometimes trying to find some help and projects once the film is completed. This has been the case for *La Terre des âmes errantes*, especially after following workers for three months and sharing their life. I see his need for fiction and documentary as meshing in all his films – something akin to Joris Ivens's call that 'Documentary (is) the conscience of cinema' (1982: 289). Panh effectively admits that 'I need fiction to free myself from documentary and I need documentary to free myself from fiction'.[26]

Panh trains technicians and film-makers in Cambodia and is going to produce some of them. The scope of his work is long-term, especially in the way it relates to the training of the mentality of the people and the way to bring a certain gaze onto one's country, how to look and ask questions. Most producers and film-makers are not interested in this type of formation. His trainees do not subsequently follow him out of technical or financial interest; they come back to him when he shoots in Cambodia, because with him they 'learn to understand men or women, to know where we are going and where we are coming from'. 'To train a film-maker in three months' time is impossible, except on paper, especially when there is a whole process at work in film-making that needs to be taught, that goes beyond how to handle the camera. For example, one has to re-evaluate how to handle sound, how to take a frame.' These practical questions require much thought and discussions. Those who continue with Panh have to 'endure' long and endless daily work sessions, since he has each assistant discuss the day's work at night in a critical and profoundly democratic process.

Panh conjugates several projects concurrently; the one on memory goes on in Cambodia with the help of assistants he trained earlier. This work is especially crucial at this time in history that witnesses the trial of former Khmer Rouge leaders. People according to him are confused with history and truth and believe the truth will come out during these trials. This project is also an important vector in the transmission of history from one generation to the next, to ensure that 'history' is not too distorted during these trials. For the past ten years, he has closely followed Heng Nath, a painter and survivor of a camp, and his former jailer Houy. Their interviews were featured in a segment of *Bophana*.

'People think that these traumas do not transmit themselves to the next generation – 2 million deaths in Cambodia! People are starting to notice the effects of war on children that are born now, in their behaviour etc.' Many cases concern women again, while men who have suffered tend not to talk about it. Panh raises careful questions and investigates the minds of the people to find out why a simple peasant can become a torturer. The comparison with the Holocaust is inevitable in the similarities between the inflicted cruelties.

Production stories

The financing and assistance that the film-maker has received is informative of the way certain films are presently made in France. In the previous discussion of *Les Gens de la rizière*, made on a relatively small 10,500,000 francs budget, I distinguished the different agencies at work. Its financing involved a multi-European group with the largest part originating from a Swiss company, Thelma Films, for a total 2,480,000 francs. The Cambodian assistance was of 200,000 francs and JBA Production, Pahn's major supporter, of 1,480,000 million francs.[27] One of the agencies involved is a governmental agency, Fonds Sud Cinéma, that was created in 1984 during the Mitterrand years and directly subordinated to the Ministère des Affaires Etrangères: 'The Fonds Sud Cinéma created in 1984 is interested in fiction, animation, or documentary films destined to be shown in France and abroad.'[28] The film-makers produced by Fonds Sud come from countries that formerly belonged to the French 'empire' but not necessarily so. Asian countries as Cambodia, Vietnam and Laos are prioritised along other geographic areas in African countries, Latin America, the Middle and Near East, Asia, former Yugoslavia and former Soviet countries. Raphael Millet (1998) has conducted some of the most informative research in this area.[29] Since its creation, Fonds Sud boasts 230 projects that were screened at international film festivals. *Les Gens de la rizière* is one example of such a production, but so is Arturo Ripstein's 1994 film *La Reine de la nuit* and Zhang Yimou's *Shanghai Triad* (1995) and Vietnamese director Dang Nhat Minh's *La Saison des Goyaves* (2002). The list is long and looks prestigious.

JBA, or Jacques Bidou's production house, constitutes another independent effort toward producing new talents and has done so for the past fourteen years. They produced the Algerian director Merzak Allouache's films *Bab El Oued City* (1994) and *Salut Cousin* (1996), as well as *Flame* (1996) by Zimbabwean director Ingrid Sinclair. Such a direction is truly interesting in view of the dominant Franco-French aspects that dominate French film production. Bidou, a graduate from the INSAS (Institut Supérieur des Arts du Spectacle, Brussels) started as a film-maker and moved into politics after 1968 but continued to produce documentary films between 1971 and 1981. Created in 1987, JBA Production started producing documentaries made by young directors from developing countries. It is closely associated with Varan.

Varan

Varan originated in 1978, precisely during the independence of Mozambique, where the then French Cultural attaché, Jacques d'Arthuis, requested that films be made about the country on behalf of the Mozambican government. D'Arthuis asked Jean Rouch, Jean-Luc Godard and Ruy Guerra to participate in this venture. Varan administrator Chantal Roussel recalls that both Guerra and Rouch started on the project. The latter realised that it was not up to them – French directors – to make films there, but instead, they should send young students to train film technicians there who in turn would film 'their own reality'.[30] This worked so well that Jacques d'Arthuis founded Varan right after that experience. He obtained help from the Ministry of Foreign Affairs and subsequently created a non-profit non-governmental association in 1981. For the next decade, Varan received trainees from all over the world and then in turn went to several countries to shoot, backed by the Ministry. Varan went to Bolivia, South Africa, Brazil, the Philippines and Laos. After ten years of support, the Quai d'Orsay (another name for the ministry that designates its location in Paris) detached itself slowly from Varan and all other associations. After what actually corresponded to a change of politics and government, Varan reoriented its position and started the training of French people as well. In its reorganisation, it started its foreign workshops again in Cambodia, Romania and more recently the Mauritius Island and Columbia. The financing of Varan's films has now changed and although it is still backed by the Ministry of Foreign Affairs, they have to secure outside funding.

Varan is composed of a board of professionals, including directors such as Jean-Louis Comolli, Richard Copans and Claire Simon, producers like Jacques Bidou and scriptwriters such as Pierre Baudry. The team works at Varan part-time and participite in a collection of workshops three times a year. Each workshop lasts for two and a half months and comprises a dozen trainees. The principle of the workshop is that each participant realises one film in his/her country of birth and helps other participants closely on their film. The spirit of production is collective and collaborative. The screening of film rushes entails the critical gaze of all participants – a way of thinking clearly adopted by Rithy Panh.

Jean Rouch, who no longer participates in Varan, is influential in the philosophical approach to film-making and the selection criteria of the school. One can differentiate a Varan style that is clearly distinguishable from the rest of documentary production. It entails a theory and practice that goes beyond technical achievements and includes the cultural and political – in its philo-logical sense – as interested and participating in the business of the city and its people and identity concepts. One of the trainees wrote, 'The act of filming is not only a question of intelligence, ability, craftsmanship and aesthetic flair, but also of a certain moral.'[31] In the same tradition as Robert Flaherty and Joris Ivens, one recalls Dziga Vertov's lesson 'to be perpetually awakened'.[32] Varan's primary vocation was to prepare 'young cineastes from developing countries, for the possibility to learn how to read and write in images and sounds, giving them the opportunity to make, with small means, films that escape the inva-sion of standard cultural models and to constitute archives out of popular or ethnic memory'.[33] Varan's reputation has grown and now attracts a growing number of trainees from France who want to acquire a thorough formation of good documentary film-makers.

French governmental agencies and a strong system of European co-pro-ductions solidly endorse the production mode behind Panh's films. If franco-phone funds play a fundamental part in the production of recent French or francophone films, so do non-francophone funds coming from countries such as the United Kingdom, Germany and Italy. A precise study of these funds and their institutions remains to be done. The situation has turned the film-makers into easy targets by critics who are convinced that Panh's films are not 'Cambodian'. The same type of criticisms are directed at Tran Anh Hung.

The debate is important enough that I want to examine it to show a few ideological positions that affect not only Franco-Asian film-makers living in France, but many groups grappling with similar issues. Rithy Panh, Tran Anh Hung and others have been able to make their films because of French – and also European – funding and training. In a *Cahiers du Cinéma* article, David-Pierre Fila argues that francophone African cinema exists thanks to outside funding and that as such it is 'dead' or 'dead-born' (2000: 50–1). His argument contends that no other cinema has been assisted as much as African cinema. According to an assisted regime, such a cinema has to conform to the norm of the country that subsidises its films. One of the specificities of the Fond Sud agency is that their selection must carry a message and reflect a certain quality and a strong cultural identity. Any information relative to the selection criteria of the Fonds Sud Committee is difficult to obtain. Fila views this type of film as producing a 'confidential cinema' or a 'cinema of cinéphiles intello'; roughly speaking, what academics represent (2000: 51). What some of these critiques do not take into account is the special position that film-makers like Rithy Panh or Tran Anh Hung find themselves in. Both film-makers are now French yet, as Panh mentions, they have remained 'culturally' attached to their country of origins. Panh is culturally Cambodian. One should recall that before the late 1980s, he could never have returned to his country and was living in France as an exile. Thanks to the new Cambodian regime and the arrival of Hun Sen, he has been slowly able to return and shoot films.

The postcolonial nature of the relations among producers and film-makers enters the equation and my readings of the films. Following Homi Bhabha's argument, the West flexes its power: 'A large film festival in the West – even an alternative or counter cultural event such as Edinburgh's "Third Cinema" Conference – never fails to reveal the disproportionate influence of the West as cultural forum, in all three senses of that word: as a place of public exhibition and discussion, as a place of judgement and as a marketplace' (1994: 21). The product is 'mostly French' and depends on the good will and authority of the French state along with various French and/or European institutions, organisations and white-collar workers. Millet remarks that these films are deterritorialised or exist outside of their country of origins, which he names 'Southern' countries, a geopolitical term that now qualifies for what once used to be called 'Third World countries' and later 'developing countries': 'Their existence takes place outside of the Southern countries themselves, but yet, like Fespaco in Africa, their first presence is foremost a festival presence' (1998: 150).

However, can we frankly adopt Tarr's position that both Panh and Tran 'sidestep a critique of the effects of empire in their films, concentrating instead on the lived experience of their indigenous subjects?' (1997: 64) This position incriminates the dependency on French funding for the promotion of artsy 'auteurist films' (1997: 60). *Les Gens de la rizière* shows the life of a family on the rice fields, as they fall victims of natural disasters, yet the intervention of the 'snake' ushers a politicised reading of these calamities that befell the family and by extension, the village. *Un soir après la guerre* confronts the demons of a violent society after the war has ended and people have resumed their 'normal' activities. Next to the film production in Cambodia that Panh qualifies as 'rosy-coloured' (or diluted) and next to the habitual fare of American, Hong Kong and East Indian big-budget production, Panh's films must disturb the apparent peaceful surface of a nation of people that 'want dreams'.

France has now become the place where members of the former empire live and make films and constitutes the largest spectatorial reservoir – these films are shown almost exclusively in France. This is the result of the state of cinema worldwide. Vietnam, for example, has barely any filmhouses left and some of them were converted into video arcades. Cambodia shows films from Hong Kong, India, Egypt and the United States. Millet affirms that 'there are more theatres in Paris than in entire black Africa and more theatres on the left bank than in Vietnam' (1998: 150). His analysis is crucial in understanding the mode of production of these films and the constraints placed on film-makers ensuing from such a state of dependency. However, I would question the influence of France on these narratives. Do these film-makers blindly adopt the French iconic system of representation, turning, for instance, African films into Frenchified films, destined to please a certain public as Millet claims? If so, such a punctual analysis has yet to be made. For Millet, these ventures display French presence and culture abroad. Accordingly, *L'Odeur de la papaye verte* and *Cyclo* demonstrate some 'exoticising window-shopping effects aimed at Western consumption' (1998: 141). However, in the global market economy and conditions of cinema, worldwide, I wonder if Millet can firmly believe in and dream up a rejection of financial and technical help or a state of total autonomy, as he seems to suggest.

In an article entitled 'De la difficulté de voir (et faire) des films vietnamiens au Vietnam' ('On the difficulty to see (and make) Vietnamese films in Vietnam'), *Herald Tribune* film journalist Joan Dupont (1996b) discloses that the sole 35mm-equipped theatre in Hanoi shows foreign films. Dupont further adds that without foreign film festivals and investments, Vietnamese cinema would not exist. In 1993, the Vietnamese government helped finance the production of two films. Most film-makers have had to go abroad to obtain film training. The case of Ho Quang Minh, who directed *Karma* (1985), is interesting in that respect. He went to Russia and then France in the 1980s, where he was an assistant on Lam Lê's *Poussière d'empire*. Now living in Switzerland, he has his own Swiss production house and is able to shoot and work in Vietnam. Similarly, Viet Linh, an acclaimed Vietnamese woman director had to train in Moscow (VGIK) before making films in Vietnam. Her latest film, *L'Immeuble* (1999), secured French funding from the ACCT (Agence de la francophonie) and Fonds Sud (Ministry of Foreign Affairs). It became the first Vietnamese film to be commercially distributed in France. Viet Linh is a salaried director of Giai Phong Films studios (Ho Chi Minh City). She made her first film in 1986 (*Là où règne la paix, les oiseaux chantent*). Her next, *La Troupe de cirque ambulant* (1988), has circulated widely in Europe and received many prizes.[34]

Similarly, one of Vietnam's top film-makers, Dang Nhat Minh, could finance some of his films (*Tro Ve* [*The Return*], 1994; *Thuong nho dong que*, [*Nostalgia for the Countryside*], 1995) thanks to the financial support of the UK's Channel 4 and Japan's NHK and, recently, France, with *La Saison des Goyaves* (*Guava Season*, 2002). Film-making has been, and continues to be, a luxurious enterprise, especially in a country whose dominant preoccupation is not the making of fiction. Asked if his films were 'purely Vietnamese', Dang Nhat Minh retorted that without foreign assistance he would not have been able to make them. He is solely interested in producing his own images and claims to finally be able to 'make the kind of film I wanted to'.[35]

In 1990, a crucial time when considering the renewed relations between France and Asia, a Vietnamese film delegation presided by Nguyen Thu came from Hanoi to Paris to secure French investments in Vietnamese cinema. He met with diverse agencies such as the CNC, Gaumont and the Ministry of Foreign Affairs asking for help: 'I asked for help ... in the technical training of Vietnamese film-makers and the assistance with modern equipment' (1990: 10).[36] Nguyen Thu expressed a desire to 'renew' the mutual ties between France and Vietnam.

The alternative to French or European investments and assistance might not be long-lasting. Film-makers from Cambodia and Vietnam, for instance, have to control their own image and any tendency to do otherwise would amount to a renewed and reversed 'exoticism'. These are serious questions that posit the perilous condition of cinema, not just 'Southern' countries' cinema, yet they fail to address the reasons for the deterritorialisation of these film-makers, or the finished products – the films themselves. The state of things has reached a paradoxical situation, which in no way eliminates the fact that there are film-makers able to function with a base in France who have in the Diaspora been able to stay connected to their country of origins. Their primary goal is to maintain the connection. In addition, film-makers are able to finance their films with French or francophone funding. A recent example of such would have to include the American director Jim Jarmush, with *Ghost Dog: Way of the Samurai* (2000). Does his film turn out to be a Frenchified product because of its funding? Maybe one of the paradoxes at the end of the twentieth century is that French spectators are able to watch Cambodian or Vietnamese films in France that the country and other European countries have produced – something that could not have occurred in the early part of the twentieth century.

Perhaps the best approach to maintain, while discussing these films and film-makers, is a concern for their hybrid position, or that of an in-between; in-between two cultures, in-between two types of languages and codes. Panh and, for example, Lam Lê, have been continually renegotiating this position between two cultures. Eurocentric criticism may unfortunately reproduce fossilised notions about Franco-Asian positions and identity, avoiding crucial historical and ideological aspects – not to mention filmic ones – under a liberal disguise.

Panh has never made a film without thinking about the 'dead ones' – those he left behind when he could leave for France, or his family who had died. 'I am one of those who are either fortunate or unfortunate to have two cultures … the administrative word that best qualifies my position when I arrived in France is stateless. When one has lived this once, one no longer belongs anywhere.'[37]

Appendix

Personal Interview with Rithy Panh conducted in 1997 at Atria, a film editing office in Paris, during the final stages of editing *Un soir après la guerre.*

SB: *I am interested in certain points you make in Les Gens de la rizière and your next project … You are now editing your next film I think. My first question is, when did you start being interested in film-making in Cambodia, when you were young?*

RP: Not really. My uncle was making films, but that has nothing to do with that. It came later. There is a magical side to cinema, I never decided – it came much later. I tried to paint and to write, but I was unable to do so. Films fascinated me much more than the other two disciplines.

SB: *When you write, you always write for films – you write all your scripts and dialogues?*

RP: My process is special. At first, I made many documentary films. It was a way for me to approach people and get another idea. That is the reason why in the films I made, characters count a lot. *Les Gens de la rizière* is the adaptation of a novel, but the characters are entirely reworked and confronted to the reality of Cambodian peasants. For instance, in my new film, the script is only possible after all my documentaries have been made; it is the sum of all the images I have encountered.

SB: *What is the title of your next film?*

RP: For the time being, it is *Un soir après la guerre.*

SB: *Have you returned to Cambodia?*

RP: Yes, all my films take place in Cambodia, except for the one I made in Africa, on Souleymane Cissé. The rest take place in Cambodia with Cambodian people. I try to take Cambodian technicians, there are very few left, we really deal with video. For each film, I train for their cinema over there.

SB: *Each time you return, you have a team already trained?*

RP: I take a maximum of ten persons, or eleven … it is a contract, from the start, that they are not there just to make films, but to train other persons, to make a film truly respecting Cambodians, one has to implicate them in the shooting, in the project. They have to be a majority. I am not interested in making a film *about* Cambodia. I make a film *with* Cambodia; it is a process ... I firmly believe in respecting this.

SB: *If you do not want to make a film about Cambodia, you mean...*

RP: What I mean is a film that has nothing to do with Cambodians, that could have been shot anywhere, like you are in Cambodia just for the setting (décor), instead we are with them, it is their story. We help them. We are foreign doctors; we help them express their point of view. Aesthetic considerations do not take priority.

SB: *I watched your film and ... it is still very beautiful...*

RP: Very beautiful, but not with a gratuitous aesthetic. Rice paddies are everywhere, in Thailand, in Vietnam, in France, in Portugal. However, if you choose to film Cambodian rice paddies, it is not the rice paddies that matter, it is the people in the rice paddies.

SB: *I noticed the very large part you give to women in Les Gens de la rizière. In addition, I suppose, but I do not know, that in Buddhist traditions, when the father dies, the older daughter must shave her head?*

RP: In fact, it has to be the older son.

SB: *In all Buddhist countries?*

RP: I do not know, but in Cambodia, yes.

SB: *The film is adapted from a novel that was translated into French?*

RP: Yes. At first, I wrote a script with this story; I was trying to document first. It is a Malaysian writer who has been translated into French. I read the book and decided to meet the author. I bought the rights, telling myself that I would make a Cambodian text out of it.

SB: *You have said that you extracted everything that was tied to religion in the book.*

RP: Yes, I do not exclude anything, but it is an adaptation. It is the Muslim religion in the book, not Buddhism. Therefore, *Les Gens de la rizière* is tied to the rhythm of Cambodian peasants, which is more Buddhist, animist ... One believes in spirit, whereas in Buddhism, there are no spirits. In animism, there is the spirit of the earth, the spirit of rice etc.

SB: *So, toward the end, there is a ceremony enacted by the young girl, it is a benediction...*

RP: It is to send away misfortunes; the water is going to take away the evil spirits. It is a typical animist gesture, not a Buddhist one. It was not in the novel either.

SB: *What was the reception of the film and your other documentary films in Cambodia? Were they shown?*

RP: They were shown. It went very well. City people had a harder time understanding it. A French man took the film and showed it on video, because he was helping to train Cambodian teachers, in the province, in libraries, and each time he screened the film. Sometimes, people ask why it is no longer shown. The reception has been very warm among peasants and teachers.

SB: *Do they have television in the countryside?*

RP: Yes, some people do. That is the reason why it is important to make films.

SB: *When you return home, are you welcome, do people ask you to speak?*

RP: Yes, often. With Varan, we started a training workshop over there. I had trainees. I have an entire crew working with me and they make beautiful documentaries. We first made *Les Gens de la rizière* together then.

SB: *So, it is a team of Cambodians living in France?*

RP: No, they live there. That is what is interesting. It is a project. That is the reason why I make films that way. Pedagogical films, with parallel training. Because, I cannot represent Cambodian cinema all by myself, it is too large; it is pretentious and impossible. If you want Cambodian cinema to exist, other film-makers must exist as well. A film-maker can only exist if you give him/her the necessary training and the means to express themselves. That is what we are trying to do.

SB: *Has there been a moment in Cambodian history where there was a history of film-making and film-makers?*

RP: There are films that are shot, a bit 'à l'indienne' (Indian-style cheap productions) and a bit sentimental, but I believe in the necessity to develop a documentary-type of film-making in Third World countries, so that people can start looking in at their own reality, so that they can see what can be done, what happens, because fiction calls for huge means and with documentaries and fewer means, one can still manage to give one's point of view, one's remarks … that's what is happening. With Varan, we brought in material, cameras, we now have a digital camera and it is a bit more professional. I managed to find credits here and there to send and to avoid training.

SB: *Does the French government or Centre de la Cinématographie help to finance these projects?*

RP: The French ministry in 1994 participated in the workshop. We have asked for another grant, but we have a hard time trying to obtain it. What I am trying to explain does not cost much. It makes good products. You should see the interest in these documentaries in Cambodia. Finally, we have people who make films and it is becoming a democratic instrument, one gives voice to others, documentary films are interested in others. When you are poor, when you have passed through wars, you are afraid, you no longer speak and all of a sudden, you are given the means to express yourself, to analyze the situation, to look at life, it is very important.

SB: *I am going to ask you a naive question. Has the situation improved lately over there? Is there an opening?*

RP: Of course. It is not yet French democracy, but one can shoot films, people can talk.

SB: *Does the Cambodian government help?*

RP: They have no money. However, they support us. They give us a place, everything that they can lend us, they give us.

SB: *Are there women film-makers?*

RP: Yes, there are three women, one of them is working for television, another one works for the ministry of information and another one works for an American NGO. Every week, she broadcasts half an hour on television, in a special program devoted to women. She is someone that we have trained.

SB: *Speaking of Americans, has your film been released in the United States?*

RP: I do not know. I know that it was shown in festivals, but sold, I do not know.

SB: *You have not been there to introduce it?*

RP: No, but I went to Hawaii – people liked the film. I was a bit surprised. There was a huge line of people to see it.

SB: *Why not?*

RP: They like the big 'productions' so much. It is a very intimate film; one must take time and respect time. It is not in their habits. I take frames that last two and a half minutes. If you accept to enter this, you will like the movie, if you refuse this rhythm, you cannot like it.

SB: *Does the French audience appreciate your films, do you have a good reception here?*

RP: Yes, we made a positive score for this film.

SB: *Was it shown at Cannes?*

RP: It was selected at Cannes, but then it was released with a few cuts in France. It is going well. It is the first time that Cambodia has reached this level.

SB: *Yes, until now, there were no Cambodian films made in France.*

RP: No, but ... how can I say this, it is because I am lucky, because of the accidents of history, to find myself in France, while at the same time, I am very unhappy to have lost my country. Either way, one must see the positive side of it. My arrival in France allowed me to meet with French, Swiss and German producers, etc ... We do not have the means to make films. How can you make films in a country when a teacher makes $40? I cannot produce films in Cambodia, so I need a foreign co-production.

SB: *Can I make a comparison and place your situation on the same level as some Vietnamese film-makers in France or would you rather not this comparison?*

RP: I do not know if you can compare. It is a different village. I live half the time in Cambodia, but if you wish, I work on my projects, I write in Cambodia. It is a gaze from the inside on peasants. I made a co-production with European countries because we do not have the means, but we totally master the acting part and the *mise-en-scène...*

SB: *Do you know each other?*

RP: Yes. I saw a few films by Tran Anh Hung. I saw Lam Lê's film, *Poussière d'empire*. He is currently making another one. I cannot say much about Tran Anh Hung. We have so many different ways to look at things. I do not make the same type of films he makes. One cannot compare in that sense. However, I like what he does. He values his country, his culture … one likes it or does not like it but he must have the same problems I encounter, in order to find money in Vietnam.

SB: *I am particularly interested in what was formerly Indochina: Cambodia, Vietnam and Laos. Are there Laotian film-makers in France?*

RP: We try. I met a Laotian film-maker the other day, in Laos; we try to help him. We, Cambodians, do not have the means but we try to tell him that if we get together, we could find something. I even offered my help if he needs it, I would try to produce him. I will help him to look for producers in Europe; we need money but not that much. We especially need equipment.

SB: *It is similar to the situation in Africa?*

RP: Yes, but at the same time, we have to learn to work … each time we learn and do by ourselves. Because the equipment is rented. That is why I am really concerned with this workshop that Varan is putting together in Cambodia, with video equipment, that we financed, so that it continues to make documentary films like that.

SB: *So Varan is an association you helped create?*

RP: No, they've been out for a long time. What I did with them, is create a workshop in Cambodia. That is all Jean Rouch's. Since I believe that their pedagogical method is the best for Cambodia, I participated in the creation of the Atelier Varan in Cambodia.

SB: *Have you kept your Cambodian nationality or did you become French?*

RP: I took the French citizenship because when I came to France, not in exile but as a refugee, I did not want that, history did. After a while in France, as a political refugee, you find it hard to travel inside Europe, each time it was an incredible amount of paperwork and therefore I decided to become French. At that time, I was still a political refugee and could not return to my country … now things have changed, but it is not bad to be French. I have now spent half of my life in France and I love France, but I was born in Cambodia and have a French citizenship. I am very happy.

SB: *Had you learned French in Cambodia?*

RP: No, in France.

SB: *One no longer speaks French in Cambodia?*

RP: It is spoken less and less. It is English now. It is a business and/or tourist language but I am francophone, I like the Vietnamese people.

SB: *When you write your scripts, do you write them in French or Cambodian?*

RP: When I truly write, I write in French. I have also worked with French scriptwriters.

SB: *When were you able to return to Cambodia without any problems?*

RP: After 1989, 1990, I no longer had problems. I even shot a film in 1991. Nevertheless, the fact that you no longer will face problems, that does not happen all of a sudden. Nobody ever forbids you to go home.

SB: *It must have been very difficult, the first time you returned.*

RP: Yes, it is very moving and to find one's friends. Very few people who lived under the Khmer Rouge and Pol Pot ... I found a cousin, in fact the daughter of the famous uncle who was a film-maker and lived nearby, the man I called 'uncle'.

SB: *So your uncle was a film-maker?*

RP: It was not my uncle but an 'uncle'. In Asia, it is that way. It is someone I had called 'uncle' since I was born. Two families that get along together, that's 'my uncle'.

SB: *Is this man still alive?*

RP: No. He was executed. Out of his entire family, there are only two children alive, the two sisters. The youngest one lives in Paris. They were happy to see my 'images'.

CHAPTER SEVEN

Translating Spaces and Positions: Hybridity and Corps Metis

Films are translations and film-makers are translators, whether the culture they show is their own or others ... we are constantly in a state of translator-translated whenever we do anything. The question of translation is not limited to the transfer of meaning from one language to another. It is involved in the very production of meaning within one or across several contexts, mentalities and cultures. (Trinh T. Minh-ha 1999: 60)

This final chapter proposes a reading of the tropes of métissage and translation – a position that, I argue, is central to most artists under scrutiny – albeit sometimes articulated in different forms. In the previous chapters, I suggested that film-makers placed in a diasporic situation perform a balancing act between their community and country of adoption. Located in an interstitial space, these film-makers are 'at the intersection of aesthetic systems, languages, nations, practices, cultures' (Naficy 2001: 291). This involves language and film strategies along his/her various theoretical enunciations and film frames. Some of these notions also apply to contemporary writers of the diaspora.

Hybrid and fluctuating identities

Turning to contemporary fiction written from a diasporic perspective brings us to examine two contemporary French writers; Linda Lê and Kim Lefèvre. I am not conducting an overall survey of contemporary Vietnamese literature written in Vietnam or in the diaspora, nor is it my intention to compare and contrast them. I am most interested in the problematical positioning, stemming from the mostly Eurasian perspective and the rich production that is currently taking place in the West.

Linda Lê is one of France's emergent writers, whose background and origins have become manifest in her recent writing that intersects with a hybrid identity and transcultural experience. Jack Yeager locates her, with Bach Mai and Nguyen Huu Khoa, as breaking 'radically with the work of their predecessors' and as writers who 'show important new fields of examination and present new situations' (1996: 210). Literary critics consider her the first writer of the Vietnamese diaspora[1] and in the context of 'francophonie'. Lê, however, refuses such labeling and stands out at the margins of such discourse.

I too am reluctant to cast her in this position, a labeling of the kind she fundamentally opposes, as it reduces the problematic to a commonly shared denominator. Instead, I prefer to locate her in the recent trend found in contemporary French literature of writing about the self, along with other current authors like Christine Angot, whose novels have been interpreted as confessional and autobiographical (i.e. *Sujet Angot* (1998), *Inceste* (1999)). Yet some of the texts Lê wrote after the mid-1990s, her Vietnamese trilogy for example, show a reclaiming of her roots. These texts, located in a diasporic and shifting Franco-Vietnamese identity, transcend the personal to reach a universal dimension that eschews notions of ethnic boundaries.

The three film-makers previously discussed exhibit dissimilar exilic approaches in their works. Lê's now completed trilogy on Vietnam, constitutes a body of texts that metaphorically and physically returns to Vietnam, the land of the father (not the mother).

Lê was born in Dalat in 1963 and arrived in France with her mother and sisters when she was 14 years old. The three novels written in the mid-1990s – *Les Trois Parques*, *Voix* and *Lettre morte* – form a triptych.[2] The trilogy accomplishes a mourning process starting with the first installment, the foretold visit of the aging father, a destitute 'King Lear' still living in Vietnam. The second installment finds the writer in an asylum. The third and last part of the trilogy ends with the actual death of the father and feelings of guilt and pain over the impossibility to attend to him as he was dying. This 'love story' for the father combines a parallel and destructive love affair between the writer and her lover, Morgue. Chronologically speaking, the first novel, *Les Trois Parques*, was written shortly after the death of the father and concluded with an epilogue on the writer's hospitalisation.

Ghosts and mad characters continuously threaten the narrative with collective insanity while images of decay haunt the novels. Critics have noted the suppressed references to Vietnam and its history usually found in earlier French-language Vietnamese texts (Yeager 1997: 267). The texts, written between 1995 and 1999, constitute a return to her native land, a return that she performs narratively. Some of her textual practices in terms of the position that she ascribes to, and her relationship with both countries, one of them the country of exile, and her rapport with language are different strategies that are essential in reformulating her link with the country of her origins.

The violence of her prose is especially striking when reading *Les Trois Parques*. The conflictual rapport with Vietnam takes several modes. Writing has become the absent space that Lê inhabits to manage the 'pain' of exile, the traumatic loss of her country and father: 'I have the impression that I am carrying a dead body in me. Surely, it is Vietnam that I'm carrying like a dead child.'[3]

Vietnam is 'inside her'. Her space in France is of a diasporic person, who claims to feel foreign to the language in her writing; yet, she feels foreign to both countries: 'I feel like a foreigner writing in French. I am a foreigner to the world, to the real, to life, to the country where I am living, to my own country.'[4]

Her identity occupies a no (wo)man's land, no space/no place. This way of seeing belongs to a poetics of the world, a fitting place for the artist in the postmodern world where the writer is by (her) definition a stateless person or a bad citizen, a double agent and a traitor. Similar to Joseph Conrad, whose example she analyses in one of her essays on literature (1999b), Lê has changed countries and language. The nomadic space is doubly reinforced by exile and writing. The mere evocation of a return home has severe implications and suggests accountability: 'A writer betrays his land, his language, and the name of the father' (1999b: 57).[5]

Lê's short story *Les pieds nus* (*Bare Feet*, 1995) presents a six-year-old girl who has to leave home in the middle of the night with her family because of the war and who, in the flight, forgets her shoes. Her bloodied bare feet leave red traces on the road. The narrative offers a feminine and historically marked reinterpretation of Charles Perrault's *Le Petit Poucet* (*Tom Thumb*), the tale of a small boy who, with his brothers, is abandoned by an impoverished father and drops pebbles to remember the way home. In the revised Franco-Vietnamese version the way home is impossible and images of wartime horror have infiltrated the narrative. When the father returns home to fetch his daughter's shoes, he inadvertently picks up the wrong shoes, one that belongs to her sister, and the other one, her own. She will have to wear shoes that do not fit ('dépareillées') throughout her life. The crippling motif found in later texts (*Les Trois Parques*) is thus already evoked.

Written in the third person, the two-page tale shifts to the first person in its last paragraph: 'I left home bare-foot. If I had continued to walk bare-foot, I could have found my way back home, but I put on shoes that were not mine. French became my only language' (1995: 58).[6] The twist of fate brought by the war forces the separation with one's country. Reconciliation and return are both impractical. Instead, the image of an orphan, now a foreigner carrying her country in her arms, comes out in the final paragraph, 'I keep in mind the image of a child fleeing bare-foot on the road, but I will always be the one who wears mismatched shoes, and these shoes will not take her back home.'[7] The final line shows dislocation between the first and the third person's voice.

The metaphor of unmatched shoes originates from a pool of Western children's tales (*Cinderella*). It sheds light on the artist's state of mind, whose language is now other. In its concise form, the text condenses many themes found in exile literature: war, a night flight, and departure from one's land, the myth of return, and a sense of displacement.

The writer strips herself of all artificiality and sentimentality. Masochist tendencies surface when the central female character speaks of herself in either first or third person as the itching 'Stump' (*Les Trois Parques*). Representations of her amputated limb, whose history one never fathoms except through its potentially horrific origins, turn up and provoke a physical response in attentive readers. Yet signs of decay, putrefaction, and madness contaminate the description of Saigon and human relationships. Most of them speak directly of Vietnam, and the present state of the country. Despite some of these descriptions, the writing is not located in a realist mode. Highly allegorical language sprinkled with scientific terms delineate a modern Saigon, and the organisms that have sprouted on its decayed 'body'. The 'saprophytes', a biological term, stand for parasitical organisms living off decomposing bodies. Here, depending on one's reading, it indirectly or directly speaks of the conditions of Saigon after its new political takeover (*Les Trois Parques*, p. 16). Violence is directed at the country (not often or necessarily named under her pen) that the three female characters fled when the communists entered Saigon. Ambiguous feelings toward the father are expressed as he is the one who stayed alone in his empty kingdom or, as we realise ultimately in *Lettre morte*, he is the Loved One who was abandoned and betrayed.[8]

Lê's writing has the precision of a scalpel that does not hesitate to tear at the most intimate scars. Her critique of the West such as its recently-acquired new age philosophy and Buddhism, a direct import from the East, draws a parallel critique of the country of origins, its religion(s) and some of its affluent members. The aunt's adherence to Buddhism and later Catholicism is dissected.

The text requires an analytical grid as it attests of displacement, mutilation, self-loathing, scars and putrefaction. Lê's voice, characteristic of a 'rage', recalls Nathalie Sarraute's 1939 *Tropismes*, in the description of the latent hidden undercurrents between people. The Stump predicts catastrophic events in a prophetic voice; she is the evil 'bird' compared to an 'albatross' (which Lê derisively calls the 'albatroce', a play on words with the adjective 'atrocious').

The exile's rapport with the country is consummated through language and food. Such a trait is not unusual and enters Tran Anh Hung's scripts, especially the most recent, *A la verticale de l'été* (2000), where cooking reaches the dimensions of a sexual rite. As found in other 'accented films', the artist explores a world of aromatic and sensual experiences in most of his films (Naficy 2001). Vietnamese language has become a 'patois' – a 'barbaric' dialect that 'they' no longer use to communicate, preferring the French language of diplomacy instead. The three cousins – the number three is significant as it designates the three colonial components of Vietnam, the three Ky – are plotting the father's visit to France. They have to translate and interpret the letters that the father has regularly sent from Saigon for the past twenty years: 'After all, it was King Lear's language, therefore our childhood dialect, that I pretended to have forgotten, like my younger cousin, who could not understand a single word of King Lear's letters' (*Les Trois Parques*, p. 13).[9] Unfortunately, the last paternal letter disappears amid cookbooks in the older cousin's sanitised suburban villa. The complex narrative oscillates between past and present, and shifts back and forth between Vietnam and France, the latter representing the grand dreams of high technology and modernism.

Shakespearean references cleverly illustrate the two formidable dramatic characters, the aunt Lady Chacal who saved them by taking them away from Vietnam and the father King Lear. Catholic iconography as well as early Christian references abound, superimposed to the figure of the Stump, a character who has lived a Christ-like martyrdom. Lê grew torn between the father's Catholic religion and the mother's Buddhist practices (Lê 2000: 7). However, pagan imagery is also present and upsets Western world order. The aunt's wandering spirit returns from the dead to haunt them and disrupts the older cousin's wedding banquet in an apocalyptic horror scene. Ghosts are the matrix of many of Lê's stories. Her writing is uncannily reminiscent of cinematic writing. Staging theatrical and nature-morte scenes, she shifts back and forth between several perspectives. Cinema was the one medium she shared with her father, who used to take her to the movies.

French language has become a double-edge sword, a weapon that can be used toward one's country and family. Insisting on her status as a foreigner, in other novels like *Calomnies* ('Slander'), Lê defines herself first as a 'foreigner' writing in French (1993: 12).[10]

Cultural métissage is a term that applies to the dual situation of modern writers and directors of the diaspora. Notions of syncretism and nomadism impact their existence: 'The hybrid diasporic subject is confronted with the 'theatrical' challenge of moving, as it were, among the diverse performative modes of sharply contrasting cultural and ideological worlds' (Shohat & Stam 1994: 42). Usually defined as the biological mixing of races but expanding onto a cultural plane, métissage has been used in theories about racial purity, as Gobineau's in the nineteenth century. His 'Essai sur l'inégalité des races humaines' (1853–55) was based on the theory that racial miscegenation leads to degenerate, intellectually inferior human beings. The same theories would later be used in support of the scientific experiments of the Nazis and forced sterilisation of hundreds of mixed people born of the union between German women and French African soldiers. The Vichy government gladly embraced these theories in implementing the racial discrimination laws of 1940. The nascent 'negritude' movement in France of the 1930s played an important role in reassessing métissage. In the 1950s and 1960s, métissage was re-evaluated and has gained a more positive connotation, specifically in view of the Caribbean literary and theoretical development. The critical debate turned to the concept to redefine the way multiple cultural, ethnic and linguistic backgrounds have enriched textual discourse and praxis.

The métis is located in colonial and postcolonial history. The complexity of the French Eurasians' experience stretches back to the colonial Empire, a socio-political entity that legally ceased to exist in 1954. However, the métis has had to either stay in his/her country of origins or live in exile by relocating to France or elsewhere. Again, the multiple trajectories of formerly colonised people enter a complex debate that goes beyond the biological.

Kim Lefèvre's self-portrait, *Métisse blanche* (*White Metisse*, 1989) articulates in the autobiographical mode a debate on cultural mixing: 'I was born in Hanoi, one spring day, right before the Second World War, from the ephemeral union between a young Annamite woman and a French man' (1989: 17).[11] In their affirmation of their culture of origins, francophone Vietnamese writers have used tales but also autobiographical novels – a format well suited to detail their experience (Pham Dàn Binh 1994–95: 12–13). The opening line of *Métisse blanche* establishes the entire paradigm of her métissage. As a child born of the union between two races all the motifs are established: an identity quest, a migration from Vietnam to France, the quest for the father(land) and therefore her own fluctuating persona. The autobiographical novel, or bildungsroman, exposes in a realist mode the conflict of a mixed child growing up in colonial and postcolonial Vietnam of the 1940s and 1950s. The concept of difference is closely examined. The site and meaning of her 'difference' as inscribed in her body becomes a central element in the text. The autobiographical mode signifies a therapeutic experience and re-examines the survival strategies that both mother and daughter had to perform in a colonised nation.

A more euphoric model of assimilation offered by French society in respect to mixed children is staged in the film *Indochine*. The plot, examined earlier, sanctifies the link that France had established with its colony until the 1954 Geneva agreements. Although the script does not initially cast a métis in the leading role, Eliane (Deneuve), the young female colonial entrepreneur at the head of the plantation, tries to 'pass' for a hybrid or cultural métisse herself in her desire to be treated as a white Asian. The sequence that best exemplifies this occurs when she interacts with her adopted daughter of Vietnamese descent, Camille. Both engage in a debate on Parisian fashion and style when Camille's sense of self comes into questioning. The mother praises her for her beautiful skin and emphatically declares, 'the difference among people is not the skin colour but this…' *This* is actually what the character is biting into: a mango. The film intimates that difference is cultural, not racial. For instance, 'Indochinese people' do not know what an apple tastes like, but instead they know the taste of mangoes. Eliane considers herself part of the same people she lives with and was born with, the colonised: 'I am an Asiate, a mango.' However, to make that distinction, Eliane must have tasted 'the apple'. Eliane is a hybrid – a transplanted person. Again, the reference to a plant that is grafted, an agricultural term, bears multiple ramifications in this analysis with its implied ramifications on food.

Fruit and plant metaphors are deployed in texts that originate in/about the East. Tran Anh Hung reminisced on fruit and vegetable in *L'Odeur de la papaye verte* to recapture childhood memories and devoted many close ups on food preparation and dishes in *A la verticale de l'été*. Cooking and preparing food becomes an extremely sensuous task but is also part of the daily rhythm captured in his films. Fruit and vegetal metaphors regularly expose Lefèvre's mixed condition. Indigenous fruit are appropriated to separate 'bad' seeds from good ones in a female-inscribed scenario: 'I was a tree who could not bear fruit.' As a child of mixed origins, she sees herself as 'the fruit of shame'. When she awakens to her sexuality she represents 'the forbidden fruit', realising that métissage attracts a different response in men (*Métisse blanche* p. 105). In her exile in France she at first excluded people from her country of origins, a population that she could encounter in Paris in a microcosmic form. She chose to ignore the Parisian neighborhood where she could encounter Vietnamese expatriates like herself. Her trip to an unnamed Chinese supermaket, probably Tang (Place d'Italie), in the second novel, *Retour à la saison des pluies* (*Return to the Rain Season*, 1990) instantly reconnects her with her past, as mediated by the durian fruit, a favoured fruit yet disliked by Westerners because of its smell (p. 38).

Sociologist Le Huu Khoa examines the legal problems facing Eurasian children born in colonial and postcolonial Indochina. These have still not been resolved, making it hard for sociologists to isolate and analyse Eurasians as a distinct group. The rapport Lefèvre has with her multiple identities, layered through time until her departure for France, is emblematic of the critical situation of Eurasians throughout history. This is not solely confined to France but extends itself to other (colonial) nations. Lefèvre's mother never married the man who fathered her daughter and later abandoned them because mixed unions between the French and Vietnamese were illegal. However, it was common practice for French soldiers to live with Indochinese women (concubines) and have children. The authorities encouraged such an arrangement as long as it did not directly interfere with the legal system. Although a mock wedding took place, the father never recognised the child.

The absent birth certificate rules her life and determines her access to higher education. Lefèvre does not provide the argument that legally, if her genitor had recognised her, she would have been considered French by the colonial administration. However, as Le Huu Khoa points out, Eurasians that are abandoned or not recognised live a 'double rejection, and a double marginality' (1993: 85).

Besides the biological differences she denotes, and hates herself for, Lefèvre stands out physically. In search of ways to be accepted by her people, she acknowledges her alterity: 'Neither French, nor Vietnamese.' The mirror image literally plays a fundamental role here, as she does not recognise her

Figure 11 Parisian kiosk, August 1999 (© S. Blum-Reid)

'self'. Her sense of self is mostly mediated through the gaze of 'Others' – here a concept used in the Sartrean sense.

Her crisis is that she is the product of two races, two cultural backgrounds, and centuries of stereotypes coming from both sides about children of mixed race. Next to the image of her country, Lefèvre is divided. The novel pays homage to the mother whom she thanks for her courage to keep her first-born Eurasian child. Another child was born to her, a boy, who was whisked away by his French father, never to be seen again. It is thanks to the mother's obstination and the essentially matriarchal structure of the family, and despite an authoritarian repressive Chinese stepfather that the family remains together.

Lefèvre returns to Vietnam after a thirty-year absence. *Retour* is the painful evocation of a return that for thirty years could not take place and which the act of writing, somehow, activated.

Both narratives can be read independently but form a pendant. The situation of the métisse, a person who reflects the image of colonisation to others, is traumatic. Such a person, or its representation, was not welcomed, especially at the rise of nationalism and newly acquired independence. References to such difference mark her as 'the enemy'. Curiously, Lefèvre does not question the fact that she always ran into other mixed people when she was growing up. Their proximity did not in turn lead to any concerted union. Probably due to her own confusion over her identity, her struggle remained solitary.

Ultimately the métis is foreign, not Vietnamese and not French. He/she is a fusion of different elements, or 'metals'.[12] This condition is at the heart of cultural métissage. Ostracised in Vietnam, Lefèvre is now a lucid observer of increased racism from within France. Lefèvre's personal desire to blend in is almost realised once, when she briefly lived in the countryside. Yet her French Catholic education reinforces her marginalisation from, and rupture with, her own Buddhist family. In the tension to prove herself, higher education seems the only outlet. This perception comes close to Confucian ideals regarding education as open to all.

The departure from Vietnam to France took place in 1960. Lefèvre's autobiographical tale participates in immigrant women's 'travel stories' and projects an intimate vision of her culture, and native country. Her family story follows the tragic events of colonial history, and the many displacements people experienced. The word 'syncretism' explains a condition which in 'postcolonial writing calls attention to the multiple identities generated by the geographical displacements characteristic of the post-independence era' (Shohat & Stam 1994: 41). Leaving Vietnam meant abandoning the mother or betraying her – a scenario that has other traumatic implications, since earlier in life Lefèvre was left in an orphanage at the age of five. France represents the absent father, the one who abandoned both mother and daughter. The more recent return to that space awakens repressed memories and blockages, with the symbolic rejection of her native language that took place for twenty to thirty years, and her refusal to mix with the French Vietnamese community.

However, once the first book came out and she appeared on *Apostrophes,* France's leading literary television programme, conducted by Bernard Pivot (renamed *Bouillon de Culture* until 2000) figures and ghosts from the past materialised. A circular return is affected in special ways, the initial one being through language. Lefèvre is now a prominent translator of Vietnamese fiction into French.

Michel Ragon's 1982 (auto)biographical novel *Ma Soeur aux Yeux d'Asie* (*My Sister with Asian Eyes,* untranslated as yet) gives another treatment of the mixed identity of the colonial métisse. The narrative relates the tragic ephemeral life of Ragon's half-sister, Odette, a product of his father's union with a Cambodian woman during his stay as a soldier in Indochina. Ragon, a proletarian writer and art critic, reflects on the obscure origins of his older sister, who was whisked away to orphanages and distant members of the father's family once in France. Her Asian roots and identity are established once for all, when the father takes her as a young child to the 1931 Colonial exhibition in Vincennes to show her the Cambodian pavilion. The father, a peasant from Vendée, at first a pure product of the French colonial system and its preconceived notions of difference and superiority, conveyed his impressions of Indochina through letters to his family. Michel (Ragon) and Odette retrieve their father's past as a soldier in Indochina as well as her origins through the letters he wrote his family in Vendée. Perceived as a foreigner, an exotic and fragile 'island bird', Odette will succumb to tuberculosis ('taken by the ogre') during the Occupation in France.

Translating Acts

Film-makers reclaim their past in images, and sounds. Musicians perform analogue tasks with music, and combine several musical traditions as Nguyen Lê recently did. *Tales of Vietnam* is a Jazz composition that borrows from Vietnamese folk music and as such constitutes a journey home. Lê, trained in jazz, discusses this composition as a 'recreation of one's roots in the midst of a dominant Western culture' (Lê 1998):[13]

> For a long time I had dreamt of a band mixing jazz musicians with vietnamese traditional musicians, playing a music inspired by the songs my mother used to sing me. Born in Paris from vietnamese parents, I lost the vietnamese language when I began school … It is a journey back into my childhood, a return to lost roots. But it also means the creation of an imaginary folklore that stems from a crossroad of contemporary influences.[14]

Similarly, Marc Marder, an American classically-trained musician who now lives in France combines both Eastern (Cambodian) musical instruments and tunes, and Western jazz in his 1997 original score for Rithy Panh's *Un soir après la guerre* and the earlier *Les Gens de la rizière*.[15] Panh had suggested that Marder write 'a musical emotion', not an illustrative score. Marder was supposed to compose his 'own story' once he had read the script of *Les Gens de la rizière*. Eventually, Marder traveled to Cambodia and 'lived' in the culture before composing these original scores.

Lam Lê's *Poussière d'empire* embraced and tackled the entire colonial history between Vietnam and France. Tran Anh Hung's fictions have shown a facet of postwar Vietnam that has become Westernised. His own positioning remains at the centre of critical debates, as one who is no longer Vietnamese

Figure 12 Parisian kiosk, July 2002 (© S. Blum-Reid)

enough for Vietnam and not exactly French for his critics. Despite his own effort to paint 'the Vietnamese soul', he has been catalogued as representing contemporary *Vietnamitude* in France, a position that he has had to frequently justify – a difficult task for an artist of his generation who defied traditionalism and prejudices to become a film-maker. Film-making and acting go against traditions – a notion that is culturally exported to France.

During the course of my research, I ran across this labeling. My debate is informed by the sources that animate each director and originate from their native country. For Panh, Cambodian people call him and motivate his desire to continue his work. Lê's epic task of dealing with the entire history of the colonisation of Vietnam was a personal response to his exilic situation in France and performs a 'return narrative' in both a literal and physical sense though he acknowledges he could no longer live there. This responsibility may be too much to carry on. Yet, he facilitated the way for younger directors like Tran.

The theory that best describes the 'hybrid' position that each artist finds himself/herself in is of the *translator*, or in French, *passeur*. The term denotes a passing of information, a transmission of missing elements between countries, people, and nations with the figure of a mediator involved in the exchange. The role of the *passeur* is emblematic of these narratives. In his history of nomadism, Michel Maffesoli explains the social role of the foreigner as 'a passeur' in our societies. According to his reading, the foreigner, or passeur, is a person in constant circulation and flux. In many ways, these figures are crucial in the exchange of ideas, and communications, among and within cultures (1997: 42).

Hamid Naficy's study on 'accented cinema' tries to establish a list of common components and a general style. Even though Franco-Asian directors do not enter his study, and might not entirely fit his description of an accented film-maker, there are some common denominators to be found. Various intermediary figures stand out in the narratives under analysis. *Poussière d'empire* is the story of a message that will take over twenty years to reach its destination thanks to several messengers; one of them is a young deaf mute boy. Ideally, the child represents the future one places in one's country and its newly acquired independence. A similar figure of a deaf-mute child surfaces in Panh's *Un soir après la guerre,* a reading of the contemporary situation in Cambodia, after the war, in a post-Khmer Rouge era. Parenthetically, the mediator is the film-maker, whose message even if received may or may not be understood by an audience. Other aspects shared would point to the recurrent theme of displacement, and journey home, hybridity, and the juxtaposition of different times not to mention the loneliness of the director.

The task of the translator can be tedious. For example, often a Franco-Asian director finds himself/herself locked in the position of making films dealing solely with Asian themes (people, landscapes). Similarly, a writer of Asian origins will be struggling to define her/his roots in an ethnographic way. Comparable incidences arise when for example, African and first- or second-generation Franco-Arab film-makers depart from 'assigned territories' with the recent example of Idrissa Ouedraogo's *Le Cri du coeur* (1995) or Rachid Bouchareb's *Poussières de vie* (1995), a fiction about Amerasian children in Vietnam adapted from Anh Duyen's book, *La Colline de Fanta* (1995). Bouchareb's interest in pursuing such a topic was criticised because of his ethnic origins: 'How can a French director, born of Algerian parents, take on an American-style film, with the concerns and modesty of a Western director' (Péron 1995: 35).[16] However, seen from Bouchareb's perspective, it was precisely his position as a cultural métis in France, which enabled him to direct the film and understand the situation.

Alternatively, a Franco-Asian director is found in the automatic position of casting an 'Asian' gaze on objects and people that in turn influences every film take. Critics and reviewers frequently invoke the notion of difference i.e. Asian perspective. For instance, reviews of *A la verticale de l'été* invariably single out the director's 'Asian use of time'. The binary oppositions between East and West are at work and even if a French film-maker of Asian origins or background casts a gaze that is shaped by his/her origins, such a reading will be ultimately reductionist. Admittedly, in a Franco-Asian bi-cultural problematic, a Western part needs to be acknowledged or people of his/her community, in his country of birth, eventually will raise the point.

Sociologist Le Huu Khoa, in his edited anthology of exile literature, observes that writers located in Vietnam consider their diasporic counterparts of no interest and vice-versa: 'One can read under the pen of South Vietnamese writers now exiled in the West that "the literature of writers who stayed home is not literature". And those who stayed in the North share the opinion: "The literature of Vietnamese exiles in the West has no interest"' (Le Huu Khoa 1995: 19).[17] Exchanges among diasporic communities and Vietnam are constant and publication is now taking place in the West, with European and American countries actively publishing contemporary Vietnamese writing or reprinting earlier texts. Georges Boudarel (1998) notes that rare, out of print books that were first published in South Vietnam are now reprinted by American publishers. The French Sudestasie Company also circulates many out of print texts.

Is 'ethnic labeling' a way to reassure oneself that the director (or writer) will uniquely deal with the assigned territorial space and not anything beyond what is not related to his (her) culture? Would the alternative endanger the Western neo-colonial domination of the East or the strategic position France is trying to maintain in the East? Such boundaries may play a determinant role in film scripts that in turn will or will not ensure funding from the multiple state agencies involved depending on its subject. However, in the twenty-first century, the situation will soon embrace artists who are born in France and know of their parents' past as a remote yet highly symbolic place. The reactivation of the 'place of origins' will take a different symbolic stage. Differences among generations are important factors when examining the position of these artists. For example, first-generation Franco-Vietnamese people claim a Vietnamese identity whereas second-generation youth is indifferent to such labeling (Le Huu Khoa 1987: 77).

Trinh T. Minh-ha claims and celebrates a hybrid position. Her task as a film-maker and cultural theorist is a constant negotiation between two positions. When she was initially attacked for making films about Western francophone Africa (*Reassemblage*, Senegal, 1982; *Naked Space*, West Africa, 1985), she had to explain herself. This predicament would probably not apply to a Western film-maker who decides to make a film in Japan, for instance.[18] Minh-ha opposes this labeling: 'We have been herded as people of colour to mind only our own cultures. Hence, Asians will continue to make films about Asia, Africans on Africa, and Euro-Americans on … the world.'[19] She concedes that in many instances Africa and Asia meet because of the shared colonial experience. Indeed their interrelated path has come up more than once in this study, for instance when analysing Claire Denis' *Chocolat,* or Rithy Panh's *Souleymane Cissé*. Such an area of research needs to be further examined.

Minh-ha's notion of 'in betweenness' gives rise to 'an elsewhere within', a space that is difficult to classify that some may view as a 'third space' (Bhabha 1994). She bridges together various parts of the former empire like East and West, or East and South, yet because of her ethnic origins, she has had to justify her ethnographic film practice – something that Jean Rouch probably never had to consider while making films in West Africa. However, Amie Karp (1999) helps clarify the fact that 'Jean Rouch's scientific documents were not even officially criticised until he screened *Les Maîtres fous* at the Musée de l'Homme'.

The translation practice, likely to be found at the heart of any immigrant or native other, is not bound to Franco-Asian communities in France and extends itself to other groups, like writers. Despite exposure to France's ethnic population and its products, the 'majority' population, largely out of ignorance and misinformation (both terms are connected), still uses the old stereotypical labeling and misreading: 'The filmic experience must inevitably be inflected by the cultural awareness of the audience itself, constituted outside the text and traversed by sets of social relations such as race, class and gender' (Stam & Spence 1985: 646). There is a set of possible approaches to 'Third World cinema', and in front of 'other' films, the spectator sometimes resorts to 'aberrant readings' that go against the grain of the discourse.

Some film-makers working in the diaspora opt to disrupt Western preconceived notions on film-making and create a distanciation effect. Minh-ha's ethnographic approach reconsiders documentary cinema. She emulated the Jean Rouch's interview practice in her film *Surname Viet Given Name Nam* (1989) where she presents Vietnamese women being interviewed. Upon second viewing, the spectator realises that despite the language barrier, the interviews are indeed staged; Minh-ha re-enacted previously done interviews, conducted by Mai Thu Van, and disrupted the normally invisible structure of documentary film-making. In opening a 'critical space in the viewing of the film', she questions the conventions of documentary film-making.

The film-maker or writer as translator can be taken literally and figuratively. The film-makers' translated acts come in their interpretation of different cultural texts and beliefs. Their images translate, or at least help translate, cultural concepts that may be foreign to a Eurocentric culture. However, one should note that even in one's nation, especially in France, foreignness takes different or pluralistic aspects depending on one's regional and local position. The director may not do this consciously, or according to a plan. Images may translate other experiences and feelings. In so doing, film-makers are reaching out for a larger audience. This reversal is interesting in that in the past we had to deal with Western monolithic interpretations of an Asian otherness (in films, literature and essays), sometimes fueled by a fascination for Asia that in turn threatened to become a new orientalism, especially in the 1970s and again in the 1990s. A fascination for the East does not reflect a proper understanding of its cultures, languages or people. Or as Gina Marchetti emphasises in her study of Hollywood's representation of Asians in film, which I apply here to mainstream French cinema, this attraction becomes 'a flirtation with the exotic rather than an attempt at any genuine intercultural understanding' (1993: 1). Instead it produces what Barthes qualified as a 'colourisation' or 'assimilation' of the East by Western (ethnographic) directors, whereby films they made would obliterate the cultural traits of these countries by trying to Westernise them (1957: 64).

European or Euro-American films attempting to interpret Asian cultures may miss some of the codes. These films may in turn be interpreted in a different way depending on the audience, and their particular cultural and ethnic background. A Western audience might not be able to appreciate the difference between say, a Malaysian person and a Vietnamese or Cambodian person or their habitus, which James Clifford characterises as 'rather than a place, a cluster of embodied dispositions and practices' (1997: 69). Although cultural awareness is gradually changing, films stemming from a Eurocentric gaze give a one-dimensional look, when they do not directly speak in a paternalistic way for 'the other' as *Indochine* or *L'Amant* did. Transnational or transcultural perspectives and trajectories revise these notions informing us of other cultural experiences and encounters that speak (to us) in several languages.

Minh-ha works from what is now an American perspective; the problematic of 'translation' runs through her film:

> Instead of going back to Vietnamese for more authenticity, I rather deal with the notion of translation itself, and not claim any authentic retrieval. There is no real desire to make people believe that what they have on screen happened (or did not happen) in Vietnam, so to have the interviews in Vietnamese would just be using the cliché … Whereas the use of English in the context of Vietnam and of Vietnamese in the context of the US already creates a displacement, and a tension arises because not only do you have to listen to these Vietnamese faces speaking English, but you also have to understand a different sound of English.[19]

On a linguistic level, the act of translating implies a language that will be shared by all spectators. Observers note that diasporic people speak the language 'of the master'. This implies French language and sometimes the tendency to include a French aesthetic, especially in terms of film quotations. However, the fact that most films analysed in this study speak in their native language undermines this notion. Until now, Panh's films do not speak French, Tran's films are entirely shot in Vietnamese (although a French dubbed version of the film is released as well), and Lê's films speak Vietnamese, except when it comes to the French colonial figures of the soldier and the nun, obviously grotesque figures that are mocked by the village translator – a métis in *Poussière d'empire*. Unlike films produced about the colonial other, where the absence of the language of the colonised stands out, these films ignore the language that they had to learn at the French colonial school or in exile. However, were these films to speak French, as they likely will in the future, if not English, I am sure that French will not remain 'the master's language' but more like a weapon, deconstructing narratives from within.

The film subtitles may elude the spectator. This in turns somewhat shakes up the notion of film as a universal language that I appropriated in my earlier reading. Speaking of translation between French and Vietnamese, translator Phan Huy Duong (also series editor at Picquier) carefully specifies the various difficulties between both languages and the richness of the Vietnamese language; he also invokes the notion of linguistic métissage. I incidentally noticed differences between English and French translations originating from Vietnamese texts, especially regarding Duong Thu Huong:

> There is no correspondence between concepts. The relation between men and their environment differs according to each country. Vietnamese language is so musical that there are hundreds of words to qualify one object, whereas in French, the same word would have only two or three synonyms. In Vietnamese, the word translates a real sound, or sensual feelings … In the linguistic structure, there is a métissage (Vietnamese, Chinese and French). French conjugation is linked to universal time.[20]

A system of codes from a different country and culture otherwise begs explanations. This is exactly when the spectator and director may land in a difficult area. Subtitles transcribe content, yet certain codes may be unknown. Most film spectators in the age of entertainment will not make the effort to read up and analyse every shot – this area may be the favourite ground for film professors and film students. Tran intentionally makes films that speak directly to a person of Vietnamese origins and, as a result, non-speakers may miss some of it.

Some of the references that the spectator misses are of a cultural, philosophical and ideological kind. These may include film adaptations of original Vietnamese folktales and literature. I spoke earlier of the folk tales of *The Married Woman of Nam Xuong* and *The Stone of the Waiting* as the literary and cultural foundations of three film adaptations. These tales culled from Vietnamese legends are reworked into modern situations, yet they elicit a meaning for Vietnamese spectators abroad. Implicit messages abound in some of the Vietnamese texts written under communism, and are part of a way of thinking and writing, so that the critic or avid reader (and spectator) must remain attentive to 'implicit' signs. I documented a Vietnamese response to a scene in *L'Odeur de la papaye verte*, more specifically the allusion to the family's dead daughter and the polemical reading performed by a Californian Viet-Kieu spectator. This type of careful reading and interpretation demands a skillful interpreter, trained in the culture and language, but also in the (sometimes dissident) ideology of the country of origins.[21]

Some themes are transcultural; for instance, the wait for one's husband who is at war may find its equivalence in French medieval literature. Similarly, the 'stone of the waiting' found in Vietnamese legends and beliefs based on the sacredness of stones, interfaces with those of the Celtic past (of Brittany). Lê bridges both cultures under the poetic mode, by quoting Breton poet Guillevic, at the opening of *Poussière d'empire*. The 'encapsulated' message conveys hope for his compatriots, at home and abroad. It also activates the 'myth' of a return to one's country, a permanent desire for people whose migration for a long time was 'temporary'. Poetry is recited at intervals and combines with certain chants intimately linked to the country of origins and its nostalgia. The same occurs with music and the use of certain tunes. In Vietnam, it is common to see people recite entire poems, sometimes long epic ones. Poetry connotes strong affinities between Vietnamese and French people and may be one way to preserve one's identity while in exile (Condominas 1995: 30).

Cultural rituals dedicated to food preparations, healing practices or funerary rites may need to be contextualised and explained to a non-familiar audience. Native fruit, trees and flowers also abound and may inscribe themselves in a certain ritual or tradition that needs to be transmitted and explained if one wishes a multi-cultural exchange. For instance, during my research, I ran across important symbolism related to fruit or trees; the examples of the arec tree, the papaya, and the betel nut come to mind, as they do not have any equivalent in France. Dang Nhat Minh's 2002 film *La Saison des Goyaves*, located in Hanoi, is structured around a guava tree whose spiritual symbolism becomes clear. Tran, Lê and Panh have all expressed their respective intentions in press kits that were released to accompany their films, or if they were fortunate, the volume that was published with *Cyclo* or *Les Gens de la rizière* published script. Producer Rossignon worked hard to ensure some sort of shared language between Tran Anh Hung and (French) spectators. Journalists in their reviews take up these explanations. Film-makers sometimes choose to give us keys to enter their film, yet sometimes the spectator does not need any keys. However, this may limit the films to a selective group of spectators who either regularly attend 'art movies' or are part of the Euro-Asian community, although this point is exteremely difficult to research.

Certain signs evidently escape the non-native speaker. Some of them of a linguistic nature are traceable in accents that can instantly be detected by native speakers. The difference between a Northern and Southern Vietnamese accent is essential when discussing the national history of a country that was partitioned for decades; this cannot be 'heard' by the non-speaker. Yet, the inscription of a northern accent in a Southern city can inflect a script. The importance of the role of women in Vietnamese and Cambodian societies may not be known in the West: these cultures knew a matriarchal system before colonial rule. Their role as resistance fighters is fundamental to the understanding of films and texts. Minh-ha combined voices of women from the diaspora to evoke a poetics of a lost space/country that she sees as maternal and feminine. In an interview with Judith Mayne, she explains the importance of heroines as figures of resistance in the history of Vietnam – a history that she thoroughly explores in her films.

Other signs may be of an anthropological nature, that only a native person, or trained ethnographer could discern. I am referring to gestures, and the more global concept of the 'habitus', which I used in my discussion of *L'Odeur de la papaye verte* earlier. Storytelling constitutes an ongoing field of exploration, a rich reservoir of tales that Franco-Vietnamese and Vietnamese directors tap into. To illustrate a hybrid position, Minh-ha tells of the weaving of Zen into her texts, which she compares to a tree grafting and not as a 'return to her roots'.[22] Again, the agricultural image is invoked, as it aptly weaves aspects of hybridity:

> Zen was recuperated into a dualistic and compartmentalised worldview. Speaking again of classifications and borders, you are here either 'holistic' or 'analytical', but you cannot possibly be both, because the two are made into absolute antithetical stances. Zen has the gift to frustrate and infuriate the rational mind, which hurriedly dismisses it as simply one more form of mystification. Therefore, Zen's tenets are a real problem for a number of academics; but I myself do not operate within such divisions, and I don't see why I have to be bound by them. Spirituality cannot be reified. It's difficult to talk about it, not only because it escapes the principles of logic but also because 'spiritual' itself is an impossible term: disinherited and vacated in this society of reification, hence not easy to use without exacting negotiations (1992: 141).

Minh-ha cautions the West against the recuperation of Zen, an oriental philosophy. Tran openly adheres to Zen and all his films touch upon this. *L'Odeur de la papaye verte* combines Zen influences when the discourse revolves around the permanence of things. As such, it may determine the way a shot is constituted. It also plays with the function of time on a larger scale.

Ultimately, the complexity of the translating act in film does not involve language, but on the contrary, silence and sometimes music. Most films stemming from the Asian point of view, especially fiction films have minimalist dialogue and long segments of silence. Many times, during the analytical process of adding words when there were none, I found myself in the awkward classifying position denounced by Surrealist André Breton as the 'tendency to make known what is unknown' (1984: 17–18).[23] French cinema has a tendency to speak a great deal, and to make plenty of noise. Silence then will not accommodate some spectators used to wordy films. However these films have to be treated as poetic texts whose meaning may even escape the film-maker.

Film-makers and writers compose with their diverse bilingual, multi-lingual, cultural and transnational experiences. Walter Benjamin (1969) gave a warning to the function of the translator who has to convey a 'message' that in turn has to be trusted by an audience. Yet, translatability eludes certain works. Tran has expressed his intentions to deal with time and memory in an effort to reclaim his past and his country. As a film-maker of 'desire,' he early suggested that Asian seduction oppose Western seduction. As a representative of an Asian voice in France and therefore as a *translator*, the audience has to believe (and usually wants to do so) that indeed what is portrayed filters an Asian essence and that for example, seduction is performed differently in his culture. Some of these claims, were they articulated by a Western voice, would come under attack. After all, sexuality and Asia are two necessary ingredients of Euro-centred exotic plots.

With respect to writers and directors of the Asian diaspora, defining their position from within shows the fragility and complexity of their situation. As artists they have to first prove themselves, compromise and negotiate for practical purposes, especially in the business of publishing and film production. Their texts are often pre-empted by critics and placed in a convenient corner that excludes further investigation. However, in this extremely productive area an opening has taken place. Films are made by French people of various ethnic ancestries who speak in two voices. These texts (fiction/autobiography/documentary) sometimes escape definitions and categories and debunk some of the most ferocious Western myths about the East. The stage is set where the 'Orient' takes multiple meanings, and sites, and when its actual location(s) needs to be revised.

A Franco-Asian artist cannot solely be viewed as a single voice, gaze or mold exemplary of his/her culture, ethnicity and race. Western imagination has nurtured its dreams upon such generalisations and essentialisms. It is necessary to look at the way the Orient is present in the West and manifests itself in different iconographic modes or, again, what Michel Maffesoli designates 'the orientalising of the world' (1997: 64).[24] It is also urgent to interrogate the way that France has finally revisited its past in Asia, as never before, and has crudely corrected some of its amnesia. *Indochine*, *L'Amant* and *Diên Biên Phû* were mega-film productions and cultural icons of the 1990s whose influence is still felt. More has been written on the 'return to Indochina' in terms of a possible 'reconquista'. However, in an effort to locate itself in its post colonialism, French cinema raises questions about the identity of the Asian other, opening a door, and possibly enabling fictions produced now, and earlier, to (re)surface and be fully explored. As suggested throughout this study, the time has come to acknowledge the (colonial) past in Asia and France and time for the Western metropolis (and country) to 'confront its postcolonial history, told by its influx of postwar migrants and refugees, as an indigenous or native narrative internal to its national identity' (Bhabha 1994: 6). The complexity of this task lies at the intersections of France's multi-ethnic, multi-racial and multi-gender map. The various paths it has already taken and will continue to take in the future point to an engaging opening and exchange.

Introduction

1 The term Vietnam or Vietnamese was rarely used in France until the 1950s. People were referred to by the colonial terms of 'Annamites' or 'Indochinese'. (Alain Ruscio (1962) *La décolonisation tragique*. Paris: Messidor/Editions sociales, 231.)

2 'L'Agent orange, une bombe à retardement', *Bulletin d'Information et de Documentation Association d'Amitié Franco-Vietnamienne*, 26 (November 1998), 2–3. 'La guerre américaine tue encore au Vietnam, et tue aussi aux Etats-Unis. Ce que, depuis longtemps, on pouvait redouter, explose aujourd'hui. Des enfants anormaux naissent de parents touchés, autrefois, par l'épandage de produits chimiques et particulièrement du plus terrible, l'Agent Orange.' ('The American war still kills in Vietnam and also in the United States. What one could fear, for a long time, is now exploding. Abnormal children are born from parents that were affected, sometime ago, by chemicals, and more particularly by the most horrible one, Agent Orange.')

3 Christophe Bataille (1993) *Annam*. Paris: Seuil; Régine Deforges (1994) *Rue de la Soie*. Paris: Fayard; Jean-Luc Coatalem (1995) *Suite Indochinoise*. Paris: Kailash.

4 Eurasie. Available at www.eurasie.net.

5 Hoàng Bich Son, 'Si, par le passé, les partants espéraient le retour de la paix au pays pour y revenir, la plupart d'entre eux aujourd'hui se sont fixés pour longtemps là où ils vivent. Ce qui caractérise ces communautés vietnamiennes de l'extérieur, c'est le fait que, bien qu'elles doivent s'adapter à la vie du pays où elles se trouvent, elles conservent toujours le caractère vietnamien.' (If in the past, those who were hoping for the return of peace to the country in order to come back, most of those have now settled down in the country where they live. What characterises Vietnamese communities on the outside, is the fact that, even if they have to adapt to the life of the country where they are, they always maintain a Vietnamese character.) Cited in G. Boudarel (1988) 'La Diaspora et les exils vietnamiens', *Relations internationales*, 54, 249–50.

6 'Beur' is a slang term that designates second or third generation children born of parents who emigrated from North Africa to France.

7   For example, *Voix Boudhistes*, broadcast every Sunday morning on Antenne 2 (a 15-minute segment consisting of interviews and reportage on Buddhist activities and books in France).

8   'L'Orient m'est indifférent.' Barthes, *L'Empire des signes*, 7.

9   For a detailed history of the French venture in India, see Rose Vincent (1998) *L'Aventure des Français en Inde: XVIIe–XXe* siècles. Paris: Editions Kailash.

10 'L'objet de la recherche de la jeunesse occidentale est une notion nouvelle de l'homme. L'Asie peut-elle nous apporter quelque enseignement? Je ne le crois pas. Plutôt une découverte particulière de ce que nous sommes.' André Malraux (1985) 'André Malraux et l'Orient' (1926) *Mélanges Malraux Miscellany*, 17, 53–4.

Chapter One

1   Paula Ahmad's dissertation project (University of Chicago) is entirely devoted to the archives. She has been able to access some of the archives that are not visible to the public.

2   'Déshabillage et habillage d'une jeune viêtnamienne.' Printout museum collection, film #142. The date is in question.

3   The numbers here are used as identification numbers in the Albert Kahn catalogue of the Archives (e.g. #143). The viewing system is interactive and allows visitors to select the entire collection.

4   'Le site d'Angkor Thom ancienne capitale kmèr (IXe au XVe s.) resta livré à l'abandon pendant cinq siècles. Ses monuments étaient envahis par la végétation lorsqu'en 1908 le Service archéologique de l'Ecole d'Extrême Orient fut chargé, par le Gouvernement d'Indochine, de la conservation de ces édifices médiévaux.' *Guides Madrolles* (c. 1925) Paris: Hachette, 52.

5   'La conquête coloniale … c'est une organisation qui marche. Son procédé, c'est de manifester la force pour en éviter l'emploi; son but, ce ne doit pas être la destruction de l'adversaire, mais son attirance.' *Le Matin*, 7 May 1931, n.p.

6   'La France n'a peut-être pas les plus belles colonies du monde, elle peut se vanter d'avoir les plus beaux colonisateurs. Ils sont là, tant en Asie qu'en Afrique, une petite élite qui sut unir à l'ardeur latine la tenace réflexion batave et l'audace anglo-saxonne, en y ajoutant une chaleur d'âme, un don de sympathie spécial à la race française.'

7   'Les colonialistes employaient le cinéma pour dénigrer notre peuple. Ainsi, à la foire-exposition de Marseille, en dehors des affiches représentant une foule de mandarins annamites se confondant en prosternation devant le roi fantoche et son molosse, le gouverneur général et le résident supérieur en plus des coolies au torse nu qui tiraient le pousse-pousse, il y avait encore le cinéma. Dans les films, on voyait de vieilles femmes aux dents laquées mâchant du bétel, des paysans décharnés et déguenillés, des hommes en langouti qui grimpaient sur les cocotiers…tout cela baptisé Images d'Annam.' 'L'itinéraire du film de Fiction Vietnamien', *Le Film Documentaire Vietnamien* (1984) Hanoi: Editions en Langues étrangères, 4.

8   'Voir dans Indochine un regard nostalgique sur le monde colonial serait un contresens: le film dit au contraire la fracture inéluctable entre la France et l'Indochine, pays que symbolisent les deux personnages féminins.'

9   See Truffaut's 1954 article in translation 'A Certain Tendency of the French Cinema', in Bill Nichols (ed.) (1976) *Movies and Methods, Vol. I*, Berkeley, Los Angeles: University of California Press, 224–37.

10 'Il y a ensuite ce déchirement (à la fois progressif et soudain) qui se répercute en écho d'un bord de l'Atlantique à l'autre: des sixties à Mai 68, la guerre du Vietnam et tout ce qu'elle entraîne et symbolise, ses effets de déstabilisation, de politisation, aux Etats-Unis, comme en France ou en Allemagne'. 'Then, there was this progressive and sudden rupture, which had its repercussions from one side of the Atlantic to the other: from the sixties to May 68, the Vietnam war, and all that it brought and symbolized, its destabilizing effects, and politicization in the U.S., in France or in Germany.' Raymond Bellour (ed.) (1980) *Le Cinéma américain. Analyses de films.* 2 vols. Paris: Flammarion, 7–8.

11 For a discussion of recent films made in Vietnam, see Karen Jaehne (1989) 'Cinema in Vietnam: When the Shooting stopped ... And the Filming Began', *Cineaste*, XVII, 2, 32–7.

A discussion of recent Vietnamese literature is in 'Les cent fleurs du Vietnam', *Le Monde*, 22 July 1994, VII.

12   'J'étais parti en Indochine pour faire du cinéma et j'y ai découvert quelque chose de bien plus vaste que ma propre ambition. ... Aujourd'hui encore, je puise dans l'expérience de ce monde vietnamien...' 'I had left for Indochina to make films, and I found there something much bigger than my own ambition. ... Still today, I draw from my experience of Vietnam...' *En Lumière: Les directeurs de la photographie vus par les cinéastes* (2001) Interviews by Dominique Maillet, Photographs by Sylvie Biscioni. Paris: Editions Dujarric, 74–8.

13   'la représentation indochinoise est très 'en retard' dans le cinéma français (c'est le cas aussi de l'Afrique noire coloniale), alors que la période algérienne de la France a donné lieu à plus de vingt films classés dans le genre fiction.' 'the Indochinese representation in French cinema comes very late (such is also the case for colonial 'black' Africa) whereas the French Algerian period has given more than twenty fiction films.' Benjamin Stora (1992) 'Indochine, Algérie, autorisations de retour,' *Libération*, 30 April, 5.

14   'Le Japon est, de tous les pays asiatiques, celui dont le cinéma possède le plus d'attraits pour moi. Les films japonais m'envoûtent littéralement, me plongent dans une eau dense et sensuelle. ... Je vois, je vis les films japonais comme des rêves érotiques.' 'Of all Asian countries, Japan has a cinema that is most attractive to me. Japanese films literally haunt me and plunge me in a dense and sensual water. ... I see, and live Japanese films as erotic dreams.' Ado Kyrou (1957) *Amour – Erotisme et cinéma*. Paris: Le Terrain Vague, 129.

15   'Tout prépare le monde des Blancs en Asie, qui s'étale dans les marges du scénario; maisons immenses de coloniaux, serviteurs pour coloniaux, piscines pour coloniaux, voiture coloniale qui s'avance en fendant la foule des enfants curieux, boys érotiques coloniaux.' Catherine B. Clément (1975) 'Emmanuelle et la commande sociale: Sur un an de succès', *Le Monde*, 12 June, 25.

16   Thanks to Alain Oudin for providing this biographical information.

17   Jean-Jacques Annaud, *L'Amant* Press Kit.

18   During the 1995 Sarasota French Film festival, after the premiere of *Une Femme Française*, I asked Wargnier about his personal interest in Indochina, which I see as a backdrop in most of his films. He reacted to this question by explaining how important Indochina (and the war) has been for French people. He also promised that he would not use this source in his next film.

19   'The coolie was on his knees, the hands tied behind his back. "You wanted to escape; you are a deserter. You forced me to beat you. However, you are my child. Do you think a mother likes to beat her children?" The coolie bowed down. "You are my father and my mother."' Christian de Montella, *Indochine*, 36–7.

20   'Des enfants français doivent manger des pommes. Ils grimacent et les recrachent. Ils disent qu'ils étouffent avec ça: c'est sans jus, on dirait du coton.' Frédérique Lebelley (1994) *Duras ou le poids d'une plume*. Paris: Grasset, 17.

21   I have seen three different versions of the film *Indochine*. The American video-released version cut one important scene out of the film in which the father bribes the young navy lieutenant with money in exchange for leaving his daughter. Without this scene, the father does effectively appear lame (emasculated). However, in the newly-released DVD version, part of the scene between the father and lover has been reinstated.

22   Christian de Montella (1992) *Indochine*. Paris: Arthème Fayard. After the film written by Catherine Cohen, Louis Gardel, Erik Orsenna and Régis Wargnier.

23   In 1993, a French Vietnamese film-maker made one low-budget film in a French studio. It won an award at the Cannes' Film Festival. *L'Odeur de la papaye verte* (*The Scent of Green Papaya*) by Tran Anh Hung recreates in a suburban studio an atmosphere among Indochinese people during colonial times, just before the independence of Vietnam.

24   Pierre Schoendoerffer (1992) *Dien-Bien-Phu: De la bataille au film*. Paris: Fixot/Lincoln: 128.

25   'l'apothéose de l'Empire colonial et l'apogée de l'idée coloniale en France se situeraient, tous deux, dans les années 1930 et 1931.' Charles-Robert Ageron (1984) 'L'Exposition coloniale de 1931', in Pierre Nora (ed.) *Les Lieux de Mémoire*. Paris: NRF: 561.

26 Chirat's Catalogue of films produced in the 1930s reports that out of 1,305 fiction films made only 85 were located outside France with 53 films in Africa – mostly North Africa – and only 13 in Asia (Nesterenko 1986: 127).

Chapter Two

1   Lê is effectively considered to represent Franco-Vietnamese cinema. Paris-Hanoï, a French Institute conference and retrospective that took place in New York in March 1997, invited him to discuss Vietnam and cinema with Dang Nhat Minh, the most important film-maker in today's Vietnam. *Poussière d'empire* was the opening film.
2   'Un OVNI, un film étrange, oeuvre d'un Vietnamien disparu sans laisser de traces, comme son héroïne: *Poussière d'empire*.' (A UFO, a strange film, the work of a Vietnamese man who disappeared without leaving any traces, like his heroine.) Guy Gauthier (1992) 'Indochine, Rêve d'empire,' *La Revue du Cinéma*, 483, 50–61.
3   Lam Lê, interview with the author, Paris, 30 May 1997. 'J'étais le premier Vietnamien à être dans le métier professionnellement parlant, le premier réalisateur à formation vraiment de base.'
4   *Là où vont les nuages: Art et Identité de la diaspora vietnamienne* (Olivier Grégoire & Laurent Van Laucker, Brussels, 1999. Productions Polymorfilms). I will discuss this film in the chapter 'Documenting Vietnam'.
5   Jean-Pierre Mocky (1977) *Le Piège à cons*. Lê was a set designer.
6   His generation is also called 'the Vietnamophones'. This aspect is covered by Louise Ernct's film *Double-Je* (see chapter 5).
7   'Vendre des gros plans comme dans *Indochine*, c'est impossible, c'est pas mon genre.' Lam Lê, Interview with author, Paris 30 May 1997.
8   *Port Djema*. Dir. Eric Heuman. Script Eric Heuman, Jacques Lebas, Paradis Films, Orly films, La Générale d'Images, Italie: Classic S.R.L., Greece: Theo Angelopoulos. 1997.
9   'Je viens de relire *Le Lotus bleu* d'Hergé, auteur qui … a marqué toute mon enfance au Vietnam, et j'ai été frappé par sa perfection. Il y a par exemple une image qui occupe la moitié d'une planche et où l'on voit Tintin sur un pousse-pousse dans les rues de Shangai. La question qui m'intéresse, c'est: pourquoi Hergé décide-t-il à ce moment-là de faire une grande case plutôt que quatre ou cinq petites?' Benoît Peeters, Jacques Faton & Philippe de Pierpont (1992) *Story Board-Le Cinéma dessiné*. Paris: Editions Yellow Now, 65.
10 Lam Lê, interview with author, Paris 30 May 1997.
11 *Rencontre des nuages et du dragon: Long Van Khan Hoi*. Script by Henri Colomer and Lam Lê, music by Tran Quang Hai. 1980.
12 *Rencontre des nuages et du dragon* actually opened a conference on Vietnamese cinema in New York and was featured at a film festival in Aix-en-Provence (February 1995). It was officially selected at Cannes film festival in 1981.
13 'La mousson divine est tombée le jour où on vous a pris, tes mains habiles savent changer les visages, tu refuses de manger des lézards, Oncle printemps, tu es un homme puissant. Pinceau magique, tu dois m'aider.'
14 Barbara Bui, now a famous fashion designer, plays this character.
15 'On s'interroge alors soi-même: et si ces objets, dont nous voulons à tout prix faire des questions…n'étaient que des particularités historiques et géographiques, des idiotismes de civilisation? Nous voulons qu'il y ait des choses impénétrables pour que nous puissions les pénétrer: par atavisme idéologique, nous sommes des êtres du déchiffrement, des sujets herméneutiques: nous croyons que notre tâche intellectuelle est toujours de découvrir un sens.' Barthes (1974) 'Alors la Chine?', 1, 14.
16 'C'est la première fois qu'on voit un Vietnamien faire un film sur le Vietnam en parlant vraiment de toute l'histoire du Vietnam, depuis la France jusqu'à nos jours.' Lam Lê, Interview with author, Paris 30 May 1997.
17 'Dans leurs déclarations solennelles, les Vietnamiens se sont toujours désignés comme les fils du Dragon et de la Fée.' Philippe Franchini (1994) *Tonkin 1973–1954. Colonie et Nation: Le delta des mythes*. Paris: Autrement, 80.

18   'La face est seulement: la chose à écrire; mais ce futur est déjà lui-même écrit par la main qui a passé de blanc les sourcils, la protubérance du nez, les méplats des joues, et donné à la page de chair la limite noire d'une chevelure compacte comme de la pierre.'

19   'Imaginer, fabriquer un visage, non pas impassible ou insensible ... mais comme sorti de l'eau, lavé de sens, c'est une manière de répondre à la mort.'

20   '*Rencontre des nuages et du dragon*, l'histoire d'un retoucheur photographe qui a le pouvoir de réaliser le désir des gens. ... Mais l'histoire n'est qu'une excuse. Je voulais faire une métaphore sur l'avenir du Vietnam et si possible sur le Tiers-Monde? Comment l'aider? Dans une première phase, je crois, en le faisant mieux connaître.' Hervé Guibert (1983) 'Je suis né en 1948, à Haiphong, Indochine', *Le Monde*, 8 September, 18.

21   'Le Ciel, ou *Trò'i* n'est pas seulement une voûte qui est au-dessus de notre tête; considéré sous l'aspect de principe des forces naturelles, le ciel est transcendant et personnifié. On dit en vietnamien 'Monsieur le Ciel'... car dans l'esprit du peuple le ciel est un génie respectable qui est le maître des phénomènes atmosphériques ... Le Ciel est aussi un génie puissant qui voit, qui rend justice, qui aide, qui punit, qui sait ce qui se passe sur terre.' Agustoni-Pham (1997) *L'Esprit du Vietnam: Croyances, Culture et Société*. Genève: Editions Olizane, 58.

22   'L'être humain asiatique a souvent été représenté sur les estampes chinoises ou japonaises comme un tout petit élément perdu dans l'immensité de la nature. Ceci signifie que l'homme est totalement dominé par le cosmos, à l'intérieur duquel il est seul pour méditer sur son propre état d'âme et sur l'humanité.' Agustoni-Pham (1997), 58.

23   *Poussière d'empire* (1983). Dir. Lam Lê, script Henri Colomer, Lam Lê. Music Nguyen Thien Dao. Production: Bernard Lorain/Uranium Films, FR3. 1h 43.

24   Lam Lê, 'Dans le scénario, je voulais que Dominique Sanda descende de la montagne comme le Christ en Galilée.' My translation. Yann Lardeau & Alain Philippon (1983) 'Le Jeu des quatre coins. Entretien avec Lâm Lê', *Cahiers du cinéma*, 352, 29–33.

25   'Les Tonkinois sont beaucoup éloignés de l'orgueil des Chinois et ont un naturel merveilleusement disposé à suivre la raison et à croire les vérités de l'autre vie,' cited in Philippe Franchini (ed.) (1994) *Tonkin 1873–1954. Colonie et Nation: le delta des mythes*. Paris: Autrement, 17.

26   'Que ne puis-je avec un baton magique, raccourcir les distances/ ou comme cette immortelle changer un châle en pont/Faut-il attendre que je sois transformé(e) en pierre/ou que je n'aie plus de larmes en montant la tour.'

27   Vladimir Propp, *Morphologie du Conte*.

28   *Poussière d'empire* press kit.

29   *Ibid.*

30   'Lorsque l'inhumation est à demi-achevée ... cette âme en soie est remplacée dans son rôle par la tablette. A ce moment, l'écrivain désigné pour cet office donne un léger coup de pinceau et trace, sur la tablette, un petit point qui complète le dernier caractère de l'inscription, dont les autres traits avaient été tracés précédemment.' My translation.

31   'Les classes instruites, les artisans qui manient les puissantes machines modernes, les étudiants initiés aux disciplines occidentales, n'échappent pas à cette emprise du surnaturel; des faits d'expérience prouvent que la croyance ancestrale peut sommeiller au fond de leur coeur, mais qu'elle se réveille ... à la première occasion.'

32   'Le film nous entraîne de la sacralité de l'Orient, traitée de façon un peu théâtrale, à la futilité de l'occident', Pierre Guerrini, *Cinéma 83*, 298.

Chapter Three

1   *L'Odeur de la papaye verte* (*The Scent of Green Papaya*) was a relatively low-budget film costing 18,000,000 francs. By comparison, *L'Amant* had a budget of 122,000,000 francs.

2   Ecole Louis Lumière, 4 June 1997. Thanks to the Louis Lumière film school, I was able to screen *La femme mariée de Nam Xuong* which at that time had not yet been released on video. The Louis Lumière film school trains its students to a professional career in two years; they obtain the BTS (Brevet), now in three years, after two years at a University. It trains *chef opérateur, cadreur* – film technicians. The final goal is not to direct films. Each student's final

project usually lasts about 11 minutes. Tran made an exceptionally long final project that ran 20 minutes.

3   *L'Odeur de la papaye verte*, press kit, productions Lazennec 1993: 3. My translation.

4   Alain Ruscio, (1989)' 'Le seul endroit où il y (a) une véritable confrontation (est) au Viet Nam. Maintenant que nous avons un problème pour essayer de faire croire ... notre puissance, le Viet Nam me parait le bon endroit pour ça' affirme Kennedy.''The only place where there is a true confrontation is in Vietnam. Now that we have a problem trying to make believe … our power, Vietnam seems to me to be the best place for that' states Kennedy.' 'Viet Nam et Occident: Le Cycle des guerres', 136.

5   Emmanuel Moreau, *Le Mékong*, 4 juillet 1993. n.p. Thanks to Joel Luguern for sending me the article of this now rare journal.

6   Press kit. My translation.

7   'C'est une permanence de notre histoire: les femmes ont toujours moins facilement accepté les coutumes de l'occupant que les hommes. C'est vrai pour la façon de se vêtir. C'est vrai pour les coutumes familiales. Cela est éclatant dans le domaine linguistique. Qui conserve la langue si ce n'est la femme.' Hoang Xuan Han. He was born in 1908, came to France, and was first to be admitted at Polytechnic. Engineer of Ponts et Chaussée, he has a degree in mathematics, and has taught both in Vietnam and France. In Ruscio 1989: 61.

8   'Oui, Khuyen est partagé entre deux cultures.' ('Yes, Khuyen is torn between two cultures.') Bernard Génin (1993) 'Une intense douceur', *Télérama*, 2265, 9 juin, 35.

9   A mo gia tri or 'a ball-shaped wooden instrument … used by monks during recitation of their litanies'. Barbara Cohen (1990) *The Vietnam Guidebook*. New York: Harper & Row, 113. Debussy, Clair de lune & Chopin, Préludes 23 & 24. Improv. Jazz, by Ton That An. Original score by Thôn-Thât Tiêt.

10 'Dans la *papaye*, il y a beaucoup d'éléments issus de la culture japonaise, parce que j'ai une admiration illimitée pour la culture japonaise,' '*Papaya* has many elements borrowed from Japanese culture which I deeply admire'. Tran Anh Hung Interview with Alexis Charpenet and Arnaud Leveau, and Sean James Rose (1995) 'Cyclo Story,' *Xích Lô, Bulletin bilingue d'information sur le Viêt-nam*, Septembre,11.

11 'Dès que l'on parle du Vietnam, au cinéma, on voit des images de guerre. La violence masque, depuis des années, l'humanité de mon peuple.' Interview with Tran Anh Hung (1993) *Télérama* 2265, 9 juin, 35.

12 '*L'Odeur de la papaye verte* est un exemple réussi et un produit parfait de la politique d'intégration des nouveaux Français d'origine étrangère…' Lam Lê (1993) 'La petite Cosette du delta du Mékong', *Libération*, 9 June, 42.

13 Leur éducation les a imprégnés des préceptes du vénérable Livre des poèmes chinois: 'Des garçons naîtront à l'empereur, ils seront couchés sur des lits, vêtus de belles robes, et auront pour jouets des tablettes de jade … Des filles naîtront à l'Empereur, elles seront déposés à terre, on les enveloppera de langes, on leur donnera pour jouet une tuile.' Philippe Franchini (1995) *Continental Saigon*. Paris: Editions Métailié, 11.

14 'Dans le film, le père dit à son épouse à propos de leur petite fille décédée qu'elle est peut-être mieux là où elle est maintenant. Par cette phrase, insinuez-vous qu'il est préférable d'être mort dans le Viêt-nam d'aujourd'hui?' Tran Anh Hung Interview with Alexis Charpenet and Arnaud Leveau, and Sean James Rose (1995) 'Cyclo Story', *Xích Lô, Bulletin bilingue d'information sur le Viêt-nam*, Septembre, 8–11.

Chapter Four

1   Tran Anh Hung, 'The *Cyclo* Press Conference', New York Film Festival, 1995.

2   *Cyclo*. Venice Golden Lion (1995), Eperon d'or – best film at Flanders film festival (1995), Georges Delerue Prize for composer Ton Thât Tiêt – best film music (1995).

3   'Le cyclo-ici le terme désigne aussi bien l'homme que son instrument de travail-s'est imposé naturellement comme le meilleur véhicule qui soit puisqu'il est en mouvement. A travers lui, je pourrais parler du monde du travail, de la fatigue, de la transpiration, de la nourriture, de l'argent.' *Cyclo* press kit.

4   'Les Français ne me proposent que des rôles stéréotypés d'Asiatiques faisant fantasmer les hommes.' Monique Pantel (1995) 'L'Odeur du succès,' *France-Soir*, 27 September, 15.

5   Tran Anh Hung (1995) *Cyclo*. Paris: Actes Sud.

6   'Il ne faut pas oublier que *Cyclo* n'est pas totalement français.'('One should not forget that Cyclo is not totally French.') Christophe Rossignon (1995: 11).

7   Production plan of *Cyclo*: total budget of 35,004,000 francs. Lazennec=7,830,000 francs, Lumière=3,000,000 francs. SFP Cinema 1,006,000 francs, La Sept Cinéma 3,800,000 francs. Advance upon receipt from the CNC=2,650,000 francs., Sofica=9,500,000 francs, Canal+=6,000,000 francs, La Sept/Arte=1,200,000 francs, 'Plan de Financement' (1995) Ecran Total 96, 27 september: 15.

8   'Il n'y a pas grand-chose qui m'intéresse dans ce pays. Ce qui se passe en ce moment au Viet-nam est beaucoup plus intéressant et plus intense.' 'Cyclo Story' (Xích Lô!), *Bulletin bilingue d'information sur le Viêt-nam*, September 1995, 8.

9   '*Cyclo* parle du Viêt-nam d'aujourd'hui, du travail, de la nourriture, de l'argent, de la tentation du mal, de l'innocence, de l'héritage spirituel des ancêtres, mais surtout, il est un voyage intérieur à l'intérieur d'un pays qui est constitué de la substance concrète de mes rêves.' Tran Anh Hung (1995) *Cyclo*, 8.

10   'Mais ça, ce n'est pas grave, si c'est une dimension qui échappe aux Occidentaux. C'est plus un clin d'oeil aux Vietnamiens. Je ne donne pas le mode d'utilisation.' *Ibid*. 8.

11   Tran Anh Hung in Cross (1994: 36): 'What I think I have understood of the Vietnamese people is that they do not have to talk to one another in a rational way to communicate. Rather there is this notion that they somewhat mentally impregnate or penetrate one another. They understand things without being precise, without using words.'

12   'Et puis je voulais parler de la séduction. Comment la montre-t-on à l'écran? A l'américaine: un homme et une femme se rencontrent, immédiatement il y a rapport de forces. Ca ne se passe pas comme ça en Asie. Deux Asiatiques attirés l'un par l'autre se frôlent, s'évitent, créent des instants de hasard où ils vont pouvoir se revoir et, petit à petit, devenir indispensables l'un à l'autre. La douceur, toujours la douceur.' ('I wanted to speak about seduction. How does one show it on screen? American style: a man and a woman meet, and immediately there is a power struggle. It does not happen like this in Asia. Two Asians, attracted by one another, barely touch one another, avoid one another, and create chance encounters where they can see each other again, and slowly, become indispensable to teach other. Softness, always softness.') 'Tran Anh Hung, Interview with Télérama' (1993) *Télérama*, 2265, 9 June, 35.

13   Cyclo Press Conference, Online posting by Henri Béhar, Tuesday 10 Oct 1995. <http://www/filmscouts.com/festivals/ny95/interv/cyclo.html>

14   *Ibid*.

15   'Est-ce qu'un jour, vous porterez votre regard sur la France qui est quand même votre société, votre pays? -Cette question, je me la pose et je ne trouve pas de réponse. Ce que je sais c'est que pour moi, c'est un énorme handicap de tourner ici en France, parce que je ne vois pas comment je peux faire un cadre dans un appartement…je veux dire par là, c'est une interrogation liée à l'écriture filmique, à ce qui est propre au cinéma, et je me pose la question, j'ai du mal. Le Viet-nam me donne cette liberté-là, cette variété de cadre, me permet de rendre totalement crédible, qu'on ne se dise pas mais pourquoi cette hauteur de caméra, pourquoi cet angle si bizarre, parce que ça ne paraîtra pas bizarre, à cause du décor, à cause de nos repères par rapport au décor. Tandis qu'ici c'est toujours l'horizontalité, la verticalité, on obéit donc à certaines règles, à une certaine habitude et quand on fait un plan un peu différent, ce n'est pas acceptable et d'ailleurs moi je n'ai pas envie de faire ce plan différent d'appartement, et pour moi, ça me limite trop, énormément, par rapport à l'écriture filmique.' M. Makki: 'Will you one day turn your gaze to France which is your country now? Tran Anh Hung: 'I have thought a lot about this question but I cannot find an answer. What I know is that it is a real handicap for me to shoot in France, since I do not see how to take a frame in an apartment. What I mean remains an interrogation linked to filmic writing, to what is specific to cinema. I ask myself but cannot find an answer. Vietnam gives me this freedom, this multiplicity of frames, which enables me to make it credible so that one will not ask me why the camera is at such a height, or at such an odd angle, since it will not look strange, because of the film

set, and our ties to it. Whereas here, it is always all about horizontality, verticality, one must obey certain rules, certain habits, and when one takes a different frame, it is not acceptable, and in anycase, I do not feel like taking a different frame of an apartment, and I feel extremely limited in relationship to filmic writing.' Tran Anh Hung, Interview with Mona Makki (1995) 'Le Vietnam dans l'objectif', *Espace Francophone*. television program. Le Magazine télévisé de la francophonie. ICAF (Institut pour la coopération audiovisuelle francophone). Dominique Mallet and Mona Makki, Channel 5, 1995.

16   *A la verticale de l'été*, released 24 May 2000. After 10 weeks in Paris, 1,694 entries daily, and a total of 86,573 entries for Paris.

17   I was struck by the resemblance between the painted scenes found in the mentioned artworks located in the Hanoi Fine Arts Museum, and those involved in the film regarding three sisters together, and one young woman washing her hair.

18   In an interview with Vietnamese film-maker Viet Linh (Autumn 2000) I asked about the possible Vietnamese correspondence of his title, but she explained that it was not a 'Vietnamese' phrase, but a poetic license adopted by Tran Anh Hung.

19   'Comme le titre l'indique, la grande affaire des trois héroïnes, c'est d'inverser la tendance géométrique de leur vie: à la verticale de l'été, elle rêvent de tisser des liens horizontaux, entre elles, et vers leurs hommes....' ('As indicated by the title, the main business of the three heroines, is to invert the geometrical tendency of their life: A la verticale de l'été (In the verticality of summer, they dream of weaving horizontal links, between them and toward their men.') Marine Landrot, 'A la verticale de l'été', *Télérama*, 2628, 62–3.

20   Thanks to artist and painter Vuong Trong Duc who gave me this information in Hanoi (Summer 2001).The film-maker does not include the name of the artist in the credit sequence.

21   'Ce qui fait la singularité du cinéma asiatique, et tout particulièrement de *A la verticale de l'été*, c'est une conception et un traitement cinématographique du temps très différent de ceux des Occidentaux. Pour Tran Anh Hung, il n'est pas une fatalité, bien au contraire; il participe à ce bonheur de se sentir être avec le monde. Et plutôt que de réinventer un temps, celui du récit, le réalisateur préfère juxtaposer des scènes avec le moins d'ellipses possibles, pour le rendre intact.' O.V. (2000) '*A la verticale de l'été*, Review. *Jeune Cinéma*, 263, 47–8.

22   Tran Anh Hung (1996) *Autour de Cyclo*. Film about the film (Postface), Arte video.

Chapter Five

1   Louis Malle, *Calcutta* (1968–69) Prod. Nouvelles Editions de films (105 mins), *L'Inde fantôme: Réflexions sur un voyage*, a seven-part television series (378 mins).

2   Claude Mauriac (1969) rev. *Calcutta*, Le Figaro Littéraire, 5 May, 42. 'Calcutta en tant que film est le point de départ d'une réflexion, mon voyage en Inde est pour moi le commencement d'un mouvement qui va m'entraîner vers une direction que j'ignore.'

3   *Les Hommes des trois ky*. Dir. Dzu le lieu. Hulot Productions, Ellipse/Imako. Television vietnamienne. 1996. Distributed by la Médiathèque des Trois Mondes (Paris).

4   *140,000 Chinois pour la Grande Guerre*. Documentary by Olivier Guitton, Véronique Izambart and Gilles Sionnet (1997). Aired on Arte, August 2000 (La Sept-Arte, Alif productions), 52 minutes.

5   'Un milieu porteur de modernisation: Travailleurs et tirailleurs vietnamiens en France pendant la première guerre mondiale,' Thèse pour l'obtention du diplome d'archiviste-paléographe, Ecole Nationale des Chartes, 1986, 382pp. 'La guerre de 14-18 déclenche, à partir de 1915, la première émigration massive et organisée de main-d'oeuvre indochinoise à distance: près de 90 000 hommes, recrutés essentiellement parmi les paysans les plus pauvres du delta tonkinois et du Nord-Annam, sont amenés en métropole de 1915 à 1919' (Favre 1986: 1).

6   Cited in Favre 1986, reference to J. Lugand (1924) *L'Immigration des ouvriers étrangers en France et les enseignements de la guerre*. Paris, 39. n.p. 'On louera l'habileté (due à la finesse de ses mains), la "douceur" et la résignation de cette main d'oeuvre "quasi féminine" (16).' ('One will praise the skills (due to the thinness of their hands), the "softness" and the resignation of

this "almost feminine" workforce', 42.)

7 'Maintenant je suis au cœur de l'aventure, avec le Tonkin tout autour de moi … le bibelot de porcelaine de mon enfance … ces photographies au-dessus de nos lits … je tends la main et je les atteins.' (Now, I am at the heart of adventure with Tonkin all around me … the China of my childhood … these photographs above our beds, I reach out and touch them with my hand.') Clara Malraux (1992) *Nos Vingts ans*. Paris: Grasset & Fasquelle, 99.

8 'Viollis … a parlé de ce que fut la traite des Jaunes. Il y a aussi les Jaunes qui ont fait la guerre en France et qui se souviennent – car s'ils ne sont pas français, du moins sont-ils bons à défendre la France.' ('Viollis talked about the Yellow trade ... There are also Yellow people who fought the war in France who remember – for if they are not French, at least they are good enough to defend France.') *Ibid.*, p. 131.

9 'Ce film retrace (ce dont ne fait pas état le synopsis) une grève déclenchée par les dockers de Marseille, sous un prétexte syndical, pour mener une action contre la guerre d'Indochine. Il contient des scènes de résistance violente à la force publique. Sa projection est de nature à présenter une menace pour l'ordre public.' Edouard Waintrop (1990) 'Le Deuxième "Rendez-vous des quais"', *Libération*, 13 February, 39–40.

10 Françoise Audé, 'Le cinéma retrouvé: Trente-cinq ans après (*Le Rendez-vous des quais*),' *Positif* 349 (March 1990), 73–4. 'Etre le premier public d'un film conçu en pleine guerre froide, sous la IVe Republique colonialiste, est une expérience à hauts risques critiques.'

11 *Hoa Binh*. Dir. Raoul Coutard. 1970. UTA, Madeleine films, Parc films. 1h.30. Assistant dir. Nguyen Van Lan, Pierre Roubaud.

12 'Eviter de faire 'les Misérables' ou un "Sans famille" asiatique, un mélo au sens péjoratif du mot,' Raoul Coutard (1970) Maquette/Synopsis of the film entitled in French 'Mi-Automne'. Bibliothèque du film, Paris.

13 'Je pense que c'est une question de forme cinématographique. Une difficulté peut surgir du fait que pour un occidental auquel le film est destiné, l'identification au personnage vietnamien de l'histoire ne sera pas simple. Pour surmonter cet obstacle, nous garderons les enfants toujours présents … Nous montrerons la vie au Viet-Nam sans tomber dans le folklore, la misère des enfants abandonnés, sans sombrer dans le fantastique social.' *Ibid.* 12.

14 'Seigneur, faites que ces yeux se rouvrent un jour sur un monde où les hommes ne rajouteront pas de la douleur à celle que vous avez mise dans notre création, en particulier, dans vos plaines d'Asie.' Raoul Coutard, script, 56.

15 'Comment ne pas éprouver un certain malaise-voire s'indigner- quand on voit que loin de contester la présence d'un demi-million de soldats américains qui jour et nuit tuent, pillent, incendient, violent et massacrent femmes, vieillards et gosses vietnamiens, le film donne des vues élogieuses de cette présence.' Nguyen Vinh Ba (1970) 'A propos du film 'Hoa Binh' un Vietnamien nous écrit, *L'Humanité*, 8 April, 8.

16 'On met en scène des Vietnamiens, au Vietnam, aujourd'hui, c'est faire encore de la politique.' Claude Mauriac (1970) 'Le Vietnam de la nuit et du silence, *Hoa-Binh* Review, *Figaro Littéraire*, 9 March, 36–7.

17 'C'était le Vietnam même. Un film vietnamien? C'est un bon juge, oui.' *Ibid.*

18 *Point de départ* (1993) Dir. Robert Kramer. La Sept/Film d'Ici, Association des Cinéastes Vietnamiens, Channel Four. USA: distributed by Interama Video Classics. NY. (1996) Aired on French television Arte.

19 Other films include *Ha Noi Co Cau Long Bien* (*A Hanoi, il y a le pont Long Bien*) Dir. Pham Cuong, 35mm., 19'; *Ban Toi* (*Mon ami*) Dir. Trinh Le Van, 35mm., 18'; *Chu Be 'Cu Li'* (*Le petit Coolie*) Dir. Pham Nhue Giang, 35mm., 16'.

20 'Le film n'est pas vraiment 'sur' le Vietnam. Il concerne plutôt le passage du temps, avec l'oubli, avec les grands changements qui se sont produits, et comment l'espérance est devenue quelque chose d'autre … Je crois que je fais un film à propos de l'absence.' Jean-Michel Frodon (1993) 'Tourner, retourner au Vietnam,' *Le Monde*, 7 August, 17.

21 'Je me demande comment se souviennent les gens qui ne filment pas, qui ne photographient pas, comment faisait l'humanité pour se souvenir.' (*Point de départ*, 1993, film)

22 For Kramer's observations on his experience during the shooting of the film, relating to language, translation and some form of censorship, see Bernard Eisenshitz (1997) *Points de*

départ: Entretien avec Robert Kramer. Aix-en-Provence: Institut de l'image, 118–20.

23 Duong Thu Huong, *Paradise of the Blind* (New York: Penguin books, 1988).

24 Duong Thu Huong, 'Nous avions alors quinze ans. Nous étions jeunes, la révolution aussi était jeune et fraîche. Nous chantions sans discontinuer d'un combat à l'autre le *Chant des camarades* … Belles paroles, n'est-ce pas? Elles ont fleuri, elles ont donné leurs fruits. Maintenant commence la dégénérescence. C'est une loi universelle. La révolution, comme l'amour, s'épanouit pour se décomposer. Simplement, la révolution pourrit plus vite que l'amour … Quand les relations réelles entre ceux qui partagent le même combat n'ont plus rien `a voir avec la camaraderie, les gouvernants se doivent de propager le mot le plus largement possible, de la façon la plus dithyrambique … C'est justement votre devoir, les hommes de cultures, les éducateurs. On vous donne un salaire pour cela.' *Roman sans titre*, 142–3.

25 'Nous avions vécu trop longtemps la guerre, nous nous étions complètement noyés dans la beauté des temps de feu et de sang. Etait-il possible qu'un jour nous retrouvions les origines, la beauté de la création, l'ivresse d'une vie paisible?' *Ibid*. 170–1.

26 'J'ai soudain imaginé une colline verte, un homme jeune embrassant son amante et roulant dans l'herbe. C'était peut-être une femme des villes comme sur les étranges photos que j'avais vues. Ou bien une paysanne comme de chez nous…. La guerre s'achève. On n'est plus dans la jungle.' *Ibid*. 250.

27 'Le Vietnam est un pays francophone, non seulement par le nombre d'individus qui pratiquent le français, mais aussi par les valeurs héritées de la Révolution française, le goût assimilé de la littérature française et, sans doute, par des structures mentales qui se sont infiltrées dans sa culture à travers le processus de rationalisation de sa langue par des écrivains et des intellectuels imprégnés de culture française.' Phan Huy Duong (1994) *Terre des Ephémères*. Arles: Philippe Picquier, 10.

28 *Là où vont les nuages. Art et identité de la diaspora vietnamienne.* Dir. Olivier Grégoire and Laurent Van Laucker, Production Polymorfilms, Brussels, 1999.

29 *Double-Je.* (1991) Dir: Louise Ernct and Béatrice Ly Cuong. Approx. 27 mins. Vidéothèque de Paris (now renamed Forum des Images).

30 *Saigon sur Seine* (1980) Dir. François Debré and Jacques Kaprielan, 13 mins; *Quand on navigue sur un fleuve* (1997) Dir. Sylvie Gadmer, 56 mins, Forum des images, Paris.

Chapter Six

1 'Que savions-nous d'autre du Cambodge que ce que nous en avait appris Loti, l'Inventaire et les récits de moines Chinois dont l'expérience était vraiment trop lointaine pour nous être encore utile! Il y faisait chaud, il y régnait des maladies étranges, le pays était 'protégé' par la France et nous avions vu, six mois plus tôt, de délicates danseuses venues de là-bas, accompagnées de musiciens les uns et les autres avaient fait fuire, après quelques éclats de rire, le public des habitués de l'Opéra. Réduite à cette faible documentation, j'imaginais le pays plus difficile à atteindre qu'il ne l'était, même à cette époque.' (My translation)

2 Rithy Panh was in charge of Atelier Varan Cambodge. Thanks to Catherine Dussart Productions for giving me access to material concerning Panh's films and career and thanks to Rithy Panh for taking time off for an interview that took place in June 1997 at Atria, Paris.

3 'Ayant vécu la même série d'épreuves que beaucoup de mes compatriotes, il m'est apparu vital dès mon arrivée en France en 1979, ou plutôt dès que j'ai pu maîtriser la langue, de faire connaître mon expérience en la mettant en images.' Rithy Panh (1987) 'Aux abords des frontières', *Scenario/Script*. Bibliothèque du film: Bifi archives.

4 *Bophana: Une Tragédie Cambodgienne.* Dir. Rithy Panh, 1996. Production: France 3, CDP, Ina. Awards: Prix du Jury Planète Cable, Marseille: 1996, Médaille d'Argent, Grand Prix du Documentaire de Création de l'URTI, Monte Carlo, 1997.

5 *Les Gens de la rizière*, 2 hours 05 mins. Budget of 10,502,418 French francs. Prize of L'Office Catholique du Cinéma à Cannes, 1994. Won Best Script prize, 1993.

6 'Norodom Sihanouk, La Permanence de l'identité khmère' (*The Permanent Nature of Khmer Identity*), *Espace Francophone* television programme, Le Magazine du monde d'expression

francophone, with Mona Makki, I.C.A.F. Institut (Institut pour la coopération audiovisuelle de France) INA, 1986.

7 'Look back in Pain': Rithy Panh talks to Bruno Jaeggi and Martial Knaebel (1994) *Cinemaya* 24, 44–7.

8 'Le réseau des rizières devenu comme une seule et immense respiration du corps entier de tout le village ... commença à changer de couleur.' Shahnon Ahmad (1987) *Le Riz*. Paris: Actes Sud-Unesco, 134.

9 'Sensibilité malaise en tout cas, relevant d'une représentation du monde commune aux pays de l'Asie du Sud-Est. Tout autant qu'entre les catégories des êtres vivants eux-mêmes, les frontières s'estompent et le passage se fait en continu entre les vivants et les morts. Ce qui explique la familiarité avec les uns et les autres.' (Biros, postface to *Le Riz,* n.p.)

10 *Les gens de la rizière* (1994) Press kit. Paris: ARP.

11 Rithy Panh (1987), 'Aux Abords des frontières', script. SCEN Paris: Bibliothèque du film.

12 I pointed this out again in my recent interview with Rithy Panh (6 September 2000) and he agrees, yet it is done mostly 'involuntarily' in his films. It is not a deliberate attempt to locate women.

13 Rithy Panh, *Souleymane Cissé: Cinéaste de notre temps*, Channel 4, 1991.

14 'Ceux qui sont venus filmer ici n'ont jamais montré des êtres humains ... Ils sont venus pour nous montrer comme des animaux à leur public ... Le cinéma des blancs montre que les Africains n' appartiennent pas à la communauté humaine ... les fauves ils les filment avec plus de respect.' *Souleymane Cissé*.

15 'Les femmes khmères ont perdu la valeur, la place, le respect que leur accordaient la culture et la religion. Si la guerre et la résistance concernent plus les hommes qui combattent avec des armes, ce sont les femmes qui en subissent les conséquences ... Elles sont démunies de tout ce qui faisait leur force: la terre, la maison, la vie familiale stable.' Script 'Aux abords des frontières', Bifi.

16 'Le risque était important, d'autant que le Cambodge, est une 'terre martyre envers laquelle, vu notre passé colonial, nous éprouvons un sentiment latent de culpabilité.'

17 'Un assistant de production était persuadé qu'il y avait le mauvais oeil sur le tournage parce qu'on avait rasé la tête de la fille aînée, qui est en deuil dans le film, alors qu'en réalité personne de sa famille n'était mort. Quand des gens de l'équipe cambodgienne, que l'on sait être instruits, cultivés, intelligents, viennent nous dire: 'Si on ne brûle pas de l'encens, demain on ne pourra pas tourner la scène' on entre dans des relations irrationnelles que seul Rithy, étant cambodgien, était à même de pouvoir comprendre.'

18 *La Terre des âmes errantes*, 1999, Prize of festival du cinéma du réel (Visions du Réel, festival du cinéma documentaire de Nyon, Switzerland).

19 I wish to thank Atelier Varan for allowing me to screen the entire Varan Cambodge films made under the supervision and training of Rithy Panh. These films will soon be available for screening at the Grande Bibliothèque de France (Paris).

20 I am making a parallel reference to and play on words with Hélène Cixous's play on Cambodia, *L'Histoire Terrible mais inachevée de Norodom Sihanouk roi du Cambodge*, Théâtre du Soleil, 1985.

21 'La réalité quotidienne ne peut être dite, ni racontée dans sa totalité sans qu'elle ait été vécue.' Rithy Panh (1987) 'Aux abords des frontières,' Scenario/Archives, Bibliothèque du film, Paris.

22 'Une génération ...est en train de se battre pour retrouver l'imaginaire...En toute modestie, on essaie de filmer l'âme de ce pays et de mettre en avant la dignité des gens.' Panh, Personal Interview, 6 September 2000. Quotations below are from this interview unless stated otherwise.

23 'C'était une époque de bouleversements. La peur et la misère nous avaient tous corrompus, jusque dans l'amour et l'amitié.'

24 'Que la barque se brise, que la jonque s'entrouvre...' ARTE production (summer 2000) had a budget of 5 million francs. Jean-Marie Le Brun (2000) 'Que la barque se brise': Rithy Panh tourne son 1er téléfilm pour Arte', *Le Film français*, 8 September.

25 Panh spoke in the interview of two cases of infanticide. One took place in Cambodia, the

other one took place in provincial France. In each instance, the mother cut off the head of her child, reproducing an act that she had seen done to her family by the Khmer Rouge.

26   'J'ai besoin de la fiction pour me libérer du documentaire, j'ai besoin du documentaire pour me libérer de la fiction.' (Personal interview 2000)

27   Budget for *Les Gens de la rizière*: JBA Productions 1,480,00 francs, La Sept/Cinéma 1,100,000 francs, Thelma Film 2,480,000 francs, CNC 1,060,000 francs, Ecrans du Sud, 150,000 francs, Channel Four 380,000 francs (sales abroad). *Ecran Total* 57, 30 November 1994.

28   'Le Fonds Sud Cinéma créé en 1984 concerne des projets de films de fiction, d'animation ou de documentaires de création destinés à une exploitation en salle en France et à l'étranger.' Ministère des Affaires Etrangères, Fonds sud. Available at: www.cooperation.gouv.fr/culture/france/index3.html

29   I wish to thank Chris Holmlund for bringing out this important article to my attention.

30   Chantal Roussel, personal interview with the administrator at Atelier Varan, 8 September 2000.

31   Varan documentation, Calendar 1999–2000, 7.

32   'Etre perpétuellement en éveil.' *Ibid.*

33   'La vocation de Varan était d'aménager, pour de jeunes cinéastes des pays en voie de développement, la possibilité d'apprendre à lire et à écrire en images et en sons, avec des moyens peu onéreux, des films qui échappent à l'envahissement des modèles culturels standards et de constituer des archives de mémoire populaire et ethnique.' *Ibid.* 2. My translation.

34   Viet Linh, *La Troupe de cirque ambulant*, 1988. Best Film, Best Direction, Vietnamese film cinema, 1990. Audience prize for children's film, Uppsala, 1991. Best Film, Women's Film Festival, Madrid, 1991, Grand Prize of Third World Films, Fribourg, 1992.

35   Dang Nhat Minh (1996) 'Interview with film-maker', *Cinemaya*, 31, 20.

36   'J'ai demandé une aide … pour la formation technique de cinéastes viêtnamiens et l'apport de matériel moderne.'

37   'Je fais partie de ceux qui ont la chance ou le malheur d'avoir deux cultures … Quel était le mot administratif pour me qualifier quand je suis arrivé en France? Ah oui … apatride. Quand on a vécu ça une fois, on est à jamais de nulle part.' Cécile Maveyraud (2000) 'La route des fantômes', *Télérama*, 2621, 5 April, 82.

Chapter Seven

1   Linda Lê's first text, *Un si tendre vampire*, locates her in this position.

2   Linda Lê (1997) *Les Trois Parques*. Paris: Christian Bourgois éditeur; (1998) *Voix*. Paris: Christian Bourgois éditeur; (1999) *Lettre morte*. Paris: Christian Bourgois éditeur.

3   'J'ai l'impression de porter en moi un corps mort. C'est sûrement le Vietnam que je porte comme un enfant mort.' Linda Lê (1999) 'Interview with Catherine Argand', *Lire*, April, 28–33, 31.

4   'Je me sens comme une métèque, écrivant en français … Je suis une étrangère au monde, au réel, à la vie, au pays dans lequel je vis, à mon propre pays.' *Ibid.* 7. The word 'métèque' is particularly difficult to translate into English. As far as the dictionary goes, 'wog' is the Harrap's dictionary version. Jack Yeager translated it as 'an interloper'. The word brings to mind Greek exile singer Georges Moustaki's 1970's song 'Avec ma gueule de métèque' (*With my foreigner's face*). It invariably corresponds to 'the foreigner'. Jennifer Howard's review of Lê's novel *Calomnies* (1993), proposes 'dirty foreigner'. Jennifer Howard (1996) 'French as a Weapon', *New York Times*, 1 December: VII – 23: 2.

5   'Mais un écrivain ne rend jamais de comptes. Il trahit la terre, la langue, le nom du père.'

6   'J'ai quitté la maison pieds nus. Si j'avais continué à marcher pieds nus, j'aurais peut-être trouvé le chemin du retour, mais j'ai mis des chaussures qui ne sont pas à moi. Le français est devenu ma seule langue.'

7   'Je garde en tête l'image d'une enfant fuyant pieds nus sur la route, mais je serai toujours celle qui porte des chaussures dépareillées et ces chaussures ne la ramèneront pas à la maison.' Lê,

'Les pieds nus,' 58.

8 By capitalising the word 'Loved One' I faithfully reproduce Linda Lê's own emphasis on names in the novel, most of them being capitalised.

9 'Après tout, c'était la langue du roi Lear, et donc notre patois d'enfance, que je disais avoir oublié, tout comme ma jeune cousine, qui ne comprenait jamais un traître mot aux bafouilles du roi Lear.'

10 'En ce qui la concerne, elle, le français est devenu sa seule langue, son outil, son arme. L'arme qu'elle dirige contre sa famille, contre le Pays. Grâce à cette arme, elle sera toujours seule. Elle est métèque écrivant en français. La langue française est pour elle ce que la folie a été pour moi: un moyen d'échapper à sa famille, de sauvegarder sa solitude, son intégrité mentale.' ('As for her, French has become her only language, her tool, her weapon. The weapon she directs against her family, against the country. Thanks to this weapon, she will always be alone. She is a foreigner, writing French. The French language is for her what madness has been for me: a way of escaping her family, of preserving her solitude, and her mental integrity.')

11 'Je suis née, paraît-il, à Hanoi, un jour de printemps, peu avant la Seconde Guerre mondiale, de l'union éphémère entre une jeune Annamite et un Français.'

12 'Tu es un alliage, ni or ni argent.' ('You are a mix, neither gold nor silver.') *Métisse blanche*, p. 49.

13 Nguyen Lê (1998) Interview. 'L'Ethno-jazz de Nguyen Lê', *Cyclo*. n.p.

14 Nguyên Lê (1996) *Tales from Viêtnam* (CD booklet).

15 Marc Marder is a New Yorker who has lived in Paris since 1978. He started writing musical scores for Charles Lane's *Sidewalk Stories* (1989).

16 'Comment un cinéaste français, né de parents algériens, envisage un film à l'américaine … avec des soucis et des pudeurs d'auteur occidental.' Didier Péron (1995) 'Viet-nam, enfants de naguère, 19 January, 35.

17 'On peut lire de la plume des écrivains exilés du Sud du Vietnam maintenant en Occident que "la littérature des écrivains qui restent au pays, n'est pas la literature". Et ceux qui restent dans le Nord tiennent à peu près le même discours: "La littérature de l'exil vietnamien en Occident n'a aucun intérêt."'

18 I am referring to Jean-Pierre Limosin's *Tokyo Eyes* (1998), a Franco-Japanese film.

19 Trinh T. Minh-ha, 'Why a Fish Pond?': Fiction at the Heart of Documentation', Interview with Laleen Jayamane and Anne Rutherford, *Framer Framed*, 165.

20 'Il n'y a pas de correspondance entre les concepts. Les rapports entre les hommes et leur environnement diffèrent selon les pays. La langue vietnamienne est tellement musicale qu'il y a des centaines de mots pour qualifier une chose quand en français le même mot n'a que deux ou trois synonymes. En vietnamien, le mot traduit un son réel ou des sensations charnelles. … Dans la structure de la langue, il y a le métissage (vietnamien, chinois, français). La conjugaison française est liée au temps universel.' Emmanuel Deslouis, 'Quand la Littérature effraie le pouvoir.' Interview with Phan Duy Huong, *Eurasie*, www.eurasie.net.

21 'La pensée littéraire vietnamienne véhicule souvent le sens latent, la signification morale souterraine ou tout simplement le savoir collectif dissimulé face au contrôle et à la censure du régime. Cette expérience de l'implicite dans la littérature vietnamienne demande aux lecteurs l'effort supplémentaire de prévoir et deviner le non-dit autour du dit.' ('Vietnamese literary thought often carries a latent moral underground meaning, or simply, a collective knowledge hidden from the regime's control and censorship. The experience of the 'implicit' in Vietnamese literature requires additional effort from its readers, in predicting and guessing what is unsaid around what is said.') Le Huu Khoa (ed.) 1993: 21–2.

22 Trinh T. Minh-ha, *From a Hybrid Place*, 141: 'Not a return to my roots, but a grafting of several cultures onto a single body – an acknowledgment of the heterogeneity of my own cultural background.'

23 'L'intraitable manie qui consiste à ramener l'inconnu au connu, au classable, berce les cerveaux. Le désir d'analyse l'emporte sur les sentiments.'

24 'Les divers syncrétismes religieux ou philosophiques en témoignent, les pratiques du New Age le montrent à loisir, les recherches spiritualo-corporelles en font foi, nous sommes bien confrontés à une sorte d'orientalisation du monde.'

FILMOGRAPHY

Jean-Jacques Annaud

L'Amant. d. Jean-Jacques Annaud. fiction. Script Gérard Brach, Jean-Jacques Annaud based on Marguerite Duras's novel *L'Amant.* Perf. Jane March, Tony Leung Kar Fai, Frédérique Meininger, Arnaud Giovaninetti, Melvil Poupaud. Cinematography Robert Fraisse. Music Gabriel Yared. Prod. Renn Films, Burill Productions, Films A2, Giai Phong Film, 1992. 110 min.
César for best music written for a film, best cinematography, best costume design, 1993.

La Victoire en chantant (*Black and White in Colour, Noirs et Blancs en couleurs*). d. Jean-Jacques Annaud. fiction. Script Georges Conchon, Jean-Jacques Annaud. Perf. Jean Carmet, Jacques Dufilho, Catherine Rouvel, Jacques Spiesser, Cinematography Claude Agostini. Music Mat Camison, Pierre Bachelet. Prod. Reggane Films, Société Française de Production, Artcofilm, Société Ivoirienne de Production. 1976. 100 min.
Oscar for Best Foreign Language Film, 1977.

Patrick Barbéris

Chroniques du Coq et du Dragon (*Chronicles of the Rooster and Dragon*) d. Patrick Barbéris. documentary. With Truong Công Tin, Nguyen Khanh Hoi. Cinematography Eric Pittard. Prod. Lapsus, La Cinquième, Dérives, RTBF, 1997. 52 min.

Rachid Bouchareb

Poussières de vie (*Bui Doi, Dust of Life).* d. Rachid Bouchareb. fiction. Script Bernard Gesbert, Rachid Bouchareb, adapted from novel by Duyên Anh, *La Colline de Fanta.* Cinematography Youcef Sahraoui. music Safy Boutella. Perf. Daniel Guyant, Gilles Chitlaphone, Jéhan Pagès, Eric Nguyen. Prod. 3B Productions, 1994. 87 min.

Paul Carpita

Le Rendez-vous des quais. d. Paul Carpita. fiction. perf. Roger Manunta, Jeanine Moretti, Albert Mannac, Annie Valde. music Jean Wiener. Prod. Profilim, Les Films du Soleil, Cinéma Alhambra Marseille. 1955. Video Editions Montparnasse 1996. 75 min.

Raoul Coutard

Hoa-Binh, d. Raoul Coutard. fiction. Script Raoul Coutard based on Françoise Lorrain's 'La Colonne de cendres'. Perf. Danièle Delorme, Phi Lan, Huynh Cazenas, Le Quynh. Music Michel Portal. Cinematography Georges Liron, Assistant directors Nguyen Van Nhan, Pierre Roubaud, Prod. UTA Film, Madeleine Films, Parc Films, Gueville, C.A.P.C.A. (Compagnie Artistique de Productions et d'adaptations Cinématographiques, distribution: Warner Bros. Pictures. 1970. 93 min.
Best Picture, London Film Festival and Cannes, 1970.
Oscar nomination for Best Foreign Film, 1970.
Best First Work, Cannes, 1970. Prix Jean Vigo.

Dang Nhat Minh

La Saison des Goyaves. d. Dang Nhat Minh. fiction. Script Dang Nhat Minh, based on his short story entitled "L'ancienne demeure." Perf. Bui Bai Binh, Nguyen Lan Huong, Pham Thu Thuy, Le Thi Huong Thao. Cinematography Vu Duc Tung, music Dang Huu Phuc. Prod. Studio de la jeunesse (Vietnam), President Films, Ministère de la Culture et de l'information, et L'Office du Cinéma du Vietnam. Fond Sud Cinéma (France), Fondation Montecinemaverita (Locarno, Switzerland), Francophonie et Production Service (Toronto, Canada), Fonds Francophone de production audiovisuelle du Sud, Agence intergouvernementale. 2002. Prize: Don Quichotte (Locarno), Mention spéciale, (Festival de Namur), Mention spéciale (Festival de Rotterdam). 100 min.

François Debré, Jacques Kaprielan

Saigon sur Seine. d. François Debré, Jacques Kaprielan. documentary. Series L'Evénement. prod. TF1. Forum des Images, 1980. 13 min.

Claire Denis

Chocolat. d. Claire Denis. fiction. Script Claire Denis, Jean-Pol Fargeau. Perf. Isaach de Bankolé, Giula Boschi, François Cluzet, Jean-Claude Adelin. Cinematography Robert Alazraki. Music Abdullah Ibrahim. prod. Electric/Cinemanuel/MK2/Cerio/Wim Wenders Producktion/ TF1/ Sept/Caroline/Fodic, 1988. 105 min.

Marguerite Duras

India Song. d. Marguerite Duras. fiction. Script Marguerite Duras. Perf. Delphine Seyrig, Michael Lonsdale, Mathieu Carrière. Cinematography Bruno Nuytten, Music Carlo D'Alessio, Prod. Films Armorial, Sunshine Production. 1975. Prix de l'Association française des cinémas d'art et d'essai (art film house prize) Cannes, 1975. 120 min.

Des Journées entières dans les arbres (Entire Days Spent in Trees). d. Marguerite Duras. fiction. Script Marguerite Duras. Perf. Madeleine Renaud, Bulle Ogier, Jean Pierre Aumont. Cinematography Nestor Almendros, Music Carlos D'Alessio. Prod. dist. Gaumont, 1976. 95 min.

Dzu le lieu

Les Hommes des trois Ky. d. Dzu le lieu. documentary. Cinematography Jacques Tchao, Dominique Tripier, music Jean-Marc Pedoussant. Prod. Ellipse, Imako, Hulot Production. Cerravhic, TLT, Télévision Nationale Vietnamienne. 1996. 52 min.
Distributed by the Médiathèques des trois mondes, Paris. 1997.

Louise Ernct

Double-Je. Dir. Louise Ernct and Béatrice Ly Cuong. documentary. co-prod. Louise Ernct & Béatrice Ly Cuong. 1991. Paris: Forum des Images. 28 min.

Sylvie Gadmer

Quand on navigue sur un fleuve. d. Sylvie Gadmer.documentary. Cinematography Thomas Rouard. Prod. Io Production, C9 television. Forum des images, Paris, 1997. 56 min.

Jean-Luc Godard
Letter to Jane. d. Jean-Luc Godard, Jean-Louis Gorin. documentary. Script Jean-Luc Godard, Jean-Louis Gorin. Perf. Jane Fonda, Jean Luc Godard, Jean-Louis Gorin. 1972. Prod. 52 min.

Olivier Grégoire
Là où vont les nuages: Art et identité de la diaspora vietnamienne (Where Clouds Go: Art and Identity of the Vietnamese Diaspora). d. Grégoire, Olivier and Laurent Van Laucker. documentary. Brussels: Production Polymorfilms, 1999.

Olivier Guitton
140,000 Chinois pour la Grande Guerre (One hundred thousand Chinese for the Great War). d. Olivier Guitton, Véronique Izambart and Gilles Sionnet. documentary. Prod. La Sept-Arte, Alif productions. 1997. ARTE, August 2000.

Eric Heuman
Port Djema. d. Eric Heuman. fiction. Script Eric Heuman and Jacques Lebas. Story board Lam Lê. Perf. Jean-Yves Dubois, Nathalie Boutefeu, Christophe Odent. Cinematography Yorgos Arvanitis. Music Sanjay Mishra. Prod. Paradis Films, Orly films, La Générale d'Images, Italie: Classic S.R.L., Greece: Theo Angelopoulos, 1997. 95 min.
Silver Bear for Best Director, Berlin Film Festival

Just Jaekin
Emmanuelle (Emmanuelle: The Joys of a Woman). d. Just Jaekin. fiction. Script Emmanuelle Arsan, Jean-Louis Richard, adapt. from E. Arsan's 1954 novel *Emmanuelle*. Perf. Sylvia Krystel, Alain Cuny, Christine Boisson, Daniel Sarky, Marika Green. Music Pierre Bachelet, Francis Lai. Cinematography Robert Fraisse. Prod. Orphée, Trinacra. Dist. Parafrance, 1974. 105 min.

Robert Kramer
Point de Départ (Starting Place). d. Robert Kramer. documentary. Script Robert Kramer. Cinematography Robert Kramer. Prod. Les Films d'Ici/La Sept. The Association of Vietnamese Filmmakers, Channel Four, C.N.C. 1993. Interama Video Classics, 1996. 80 min.

Lam Lê
Poussière d'empire (Hon Vong Phu, Dust of Empire). d. Lam Lê. fiction. script Lam Lê and Henri Colomer. Perf. Dominique Sanda, Jean-François Stévenin, Thang Long, Hang Lan, Lam Lê, Myriam Mézières. Cinematography Gérard de Battista. Music Nguyen Thien Dao. Sound François Waledisch. Prod. Uranium Film, FR3. 1983. 103 min.

Rencontre des nuages et du dragon (Long Van Khan Hoi). d. Lam Lê. fiction. script Henri Colomer, Lam Lê. Cinematography Gérard de Battista.Music Tran Quang Hai. Perf. Thang Long, Van Lê, Van Dê, Yann Roussel, Ticky Holgado, Barbara Bui. Prod. Cad Productions, 1979. 32 min. Official selection Cannes, 1981.

Louis Malle
Calcutta. d. Louis Malle. documentary. Prod. N.E.F. (Nouvelle Editions des Films), Cinematography Etienne Becker. 1969. 105 min.
Nominated for Golden Palm, Cannes 1969.

L'Inde Fantôme: Réflexions sur un voyage (Phantom India). d. Louis Malle, documentary. Prod. N.E. F. Nouvelles Editions de Films. 1969. 378 min. *And the Pursuit of Happiness*. d. Louis Malle. TV documentary, Prod. Pretty Mouse Films. 1986. 80 min.

Alamo Bay. d. Louis Malle. fiction. Script Louis Malle, based on a novel by Alice Arlen. Perf. Amy Madigan, Ed. Harris, Ho N'Guyen. Cinematography Curtis Clark, Music Ry Cooder. Prod.

Louis Malle, Vincent Malle. 1985. 98 min.

Alain Resnais
Loin du Vietnam (*Far from Vietnam*). d. Alain Resnais, Joris Ivens, Claude Lelouch, Chris Marker, William Klein, Agnès Varda, Jean-Luc Godard, Michele Ray, and Marceline Loridan. documentary. Prod. Sofracima, 1967. Les Films de ma vie video. 130 min.

Prôm Mesar
J'ai quitté la guerre (*I left the war*). d. Prôm Mesar. Documentary. Prod. Varan Atelier Cambodge, 1994-1995. 26 min.

Euzhan Palcy
Rue Case-nègres (*Sugar Cane Alley*). d. Euzhan Palcy. adapted from Joseph Zobel's novel. Perf. Garry Cadenat, Darling Legitimus, Douta Seck. Cinematography Dominique Chapuis, Music: Malavoi. Prod. NEF, Orca, Su. Ma. Fa, 1983. 103 min.
Prix du Public Fespaco, 1985. Venice Mostra: OCIC, Lion d'Argent. 1983.

Rithy Panh
Site 2, d. Rithy Panh, documentary. Grand Prix du documentaire du Festival International d'Amiens, Grand Prix de la SCAM du Meilleur Documentaire de Création de l'année 1989, Mention spéciale, Festival du Réel, 1989.

Souleymane Cissé. d. Rithy Panh. documentary. Cinéma de notre temps series. Prod. Channel 4, 1991.

Cambodge, entre terre et paix (*Cambodia between War and Peace*). d. Rithy Panh. documentary, 1991.

Bophana, Une Tragédie Cambodgienne (*Bophana, A Cambodian Tragedy*). d. Rithy Panh. documentary, adapted from "Les Larmes du Cambodge" by Elisabeth Becker. Coprod. France 3, CDP, INA. France 3, CDP, Ina. Awards: Prix du Jury Planète Cable, Marseille: 1996, Médaille d'Argent, Grand Prix du Documentaire de Création de l'URTI, Monte Carlo, 1997. 59 min.

Les Gens de la rizière (*Rice People*). d. Rithy Panh. fiction, Script Rithy Panh, Eve Deboise. adapted from Shahnon Ahmad's novel *Rice*. Perform. Peng Phan, Mom Soth, Chhim Naline. Cinematography Jacques Bouquin. Composer Marc Marder. Prod. JBA Productions. Thelma Film AG, La 7 cinéma, Canal +, EDI-DEH (Bern) ZDF, RTSR (Radio Télévision Suisse Romande), Channel Four, Ecrans du Sud, 1994. 125 min.
Prix International du film, Prix du jury oecuménique, Cannes 1994.

Un Soir après la guerre (*One Evening after the War*). d. Rithy Panh. fiction. Script Rithy Panh, Eve Deboise, Perf. Chea Lyda Chan, Narith Roeun, Ratha Keo, Peng Phan, Cinematography Christophe Pollock, Composer Marc Marder, Prod. JBA productions, la Sept Cinéma, Thierry Abel & Eliane du Bois, Thelma Film AG, Compagnie Méditerranéenne de cinéma, La Direction du cinéma au Cambodge, 1998. 108 min.

La Terre des âmes errantes (*Land of the Wandering Souls*). d. Rithy Panh. documentary, Prod. ARTE, 1999.
Golden Matchstick, Amnesty International Film Festival 2001, Best Documentary, Cinéma du Réel Award, 2000, TV5 Documentary Award, Namur, Goden Gate Award, San Francisco 2001. Best Documentary, Vancouver International Film Festival, 2001.

Que la barque se brise, que la jonque s'entrouvre. . . (*Let the boat break, let the junk open*). d. Rithy Panh. script Rithy Panh. Perf. Vantha Talisman, Eric Nguyen, Molica Kheng, Thang-Long. Music Marc Marder. Fiction, Prod. ARTE France, CDP, 2001. 90 min.

Brigitte Rouan

Outremer (Overseas). d. Brigitte Rouan. script B. Rouan. Philippe Le Guay, Christian Rullier, Cédric Kahn. Perf. Nicole Garcia, Brigitte Rouan, Marianne Basler, Philippe Galland, Yann Deded, Bruno Tedeschini. Cinematography Dominique Chapuis. Prod. Paradise Prod., Lira Films. 1990. 98 min.
Nominated for best first work, Cannes 1991.

Pierre Schoendoerffer

Diên Biên Phú. d. Pierre Schoendoerffer. Script Pierre Schoendoerffer. Perf. Donald Pleasance, Jean Rochefort, Patrick Catalifo, Ludmila Mikael, J. F. Balmer, Eric Do, Cinematography Nguyen Thu. music G. Delerue, Prod. Mod Films, Antenne 2, Flach Films. Production Marcel Dassault, GM Aviation Services, Seco Film. 1992. 140 min.

La 317eme section (317th Platoon). d. Pierre Schoendoerffer, Script P. Schoendoerffer. Perf. Jacques Perrin, Bruno Cremer, Bouramy Tio Long. Cinematography Raoul Coutard. Prod. Rome, Paris Films. 1965. 100 min.
Best Screenplay, Cannes 1965.

Dai Sijie

Chine, ma douleur (China, my Sorrow/Niu-Peng). d. Dai Sijie, script Dai Sijie, Yan Zhu Shan. Perf. Liang Yi Guo, Quan Nghieu Tieu, Han Lai Vuong, Sam Chi-Vy, Loi Truong, Souvannapadith Vivareth. Prod. Titane, La Sept Cinema, Flach Film. Cinematography Jean-Michel Humeau, Music Qui Gang Chen. Consultant Jean Rouch. 1989. Grand Prix Jean Vigo, 1989. 86 min.
Mention spéciale, Locarno Film Festival, 1989.

Tran Anh Hung

La femme mariée de Nam Xuong (The Married Woman of Nam Xuong). d. Tran Anh Hung. perf. Lam Lê, Tran Nu Yên Khê. Prod. Ecole Louis Lumière. 1987. 20 min.

La Pierre de l'attente (Hong Vong Phu, The Stone of Waiting). d. Tran Anh Hung. Perf. Lam Lê, Tran Nu Yên Khê. Prod. Lazennec tout court. 1991. Forum des images. 20 min.

L'Odeur de la papaye verte (Mui Du Du Xanh, The Scent of Green Papaya). d. Tran Anh Hung. Script Tran Anh Hung. Perf. Tran Nu Yên Khê, Lu Man San, Nguyen Anh Hoa, Vuong Hoa Hi, Truong Thi Loc. Cinematography Benoît Delhomme. Music Tôn Thât Tiêt. Prod. Lazennec, SFP Cinema, Sept Cinema. 1993. 104 min.
Camera d'or, Prix de la Jeunesse. Cannes 1993

Cyclo (Xich Lo). d. Tran Anh Hung. Script Anh Hung Tran, Nguyen Trung Binh. Perf. Le Van Loc, Tran Nu Yên Khê, Tony Leung Chiu Wai, Nhu Quynh Nguyen. Cinematography Benoît Delhomme. Music Tôn Thât Tiêt. Prod. Lazennec, Canal +, Lumiere, La Sept Arte, SFP Cinema. 1995. 120 min.
Venice Mostra: Golden Lion, 1995. Georges Delerue prize for composer Ton That Tiet, Festival International du film de Flandre (Belgium).

A la verticale de l'été (The Vertical Ray of the Sun). d. Anh Hung TranTran. Script Tran Anh Hung. Perf. Trân Nû Yên Khê, Nguyên Nhû Quynh, Lê Khanh, Cinematography Pin Bing Lee. Music Tôn Thât Tiêt. Prod. Lazennec, Arte, Canal +, zdf/Arte, Hang Phim Truyen Vietnam, 2000. 112 min.

Trinh T. Minh-ha

Surname Viet Given Name Nam. d. Trinh T. Minh Ha. semi-documentary. Cinematography Kathleen Beeler. Perf. Khien Lai, Ngo Kim Nhuy, Tran Thi Bich Yen, Tran Thi Hien, Lan Trinh, Sue Whitfield. Prod. Jean-Paul Bourdier. 1989, 108 min.

Viet Linh

Là où règne la paix, les oiseaux chantent (*Noi binh yen chim hot*). d. Viet Linh. Prod. Giai Phong Films Studios, Vietnam 1986.

La Troupe de cirque ambulant (*Gang Xiec rong*). d. Viet Linh. fiction.Prod. Giai Phong Films Studios, 1988.
Mention spéciale du jury UNICEF, Berlin Film Festival 1991
Best film, Women's film festival, Madrid, 1991. Grand Prize, Third World Films, Fribourg, 1992.

L'Immeuble (*Chung Cu*). d. Viet Linh. fiction. Adapted from Hô Nguyen's novel. Perf. Mai Thanh, Hong Anh, Dong Dyong, Minh Trang, Quyeu Linh. Cinematography Bao Hai. music Quang Phu. Prod. Giai Phong Films Studios, Le Bureau, ACCT, Fonds Sud, 1998. 90 min.
Prix de la réalisation de l'ACCT, Namur Festival, 1999.

Régis Wargnier

Indochine. d. Régis Wargnier. Script Régis Wargnier, Catherine Cohen, Erik Orsenna, and Louis Gardel. Perf. by Catherine Deneuve, Vincent Perez, Linh Dan Pham, Jean Yanne, Dominique Blanc. Cinematography François Catonne. Music Patrick Doyle. Prod. Eric Heuman,Paradis Films, Générale d'Images, BAC Films, Orly Films, Ciné Cinq, 1992. 158 min.
Oscar Best Foreign Film, 1993.
Césars for best actress, cinematography, production design, sound, and best director.

Wong Kar-wai

In the Mood for Love (*Hua Yang Nian Hua*). d. Wong Kar-Wai. fiction. Perf. Maggie Cheung, Tony Leung. Cinematography Christopher Doyle, Pin Bing Lee (Mark Lee), Music Mike Galasso, Shigeru Umebayashi. Prod. Block 2 Pictures (Hong Kong), Paradis Films. 1999. Released in France in 2000.
Best Actor, Technical Grand Prize, Cannes 2000.
César Best Foreign Film.

Achard, Maurice (1992) 'Extreme et oriental', *Première*, February, 109.

Adler, Laure (1998) *Marguerite Duras*. Paris: Gallimard.

Ageron, Charles-Robert (1984) 'L'Exposition coloniale de 1931: Mythe républicain ou mythe impérial', in Pierre Nora (ed.) *Les Lieux de Mémoire*. Paris: NRF, 560–91.

Agustoni-Phan, Hung (1997) *L'Esprit du Viêt-Nam: Croyances, culture et société*. Genève: Olizane.

Ahmad, Shahnon (1987) *Le Riz*. Ranjau Sepanjang Jalan. Trans. by Nicole Biros. Paris: Actes Sud-Unesco [1966].

Airault, Régis (2000) *Fous de l'Inde*. Paris: Payot.

Annaud, Jean-Jacques (1992) *L'Amant*. Press Kit.

Armes, Roy (1985) *French Cinema*. New York: Oxford University Press.

Arsan, Emmanuelle (1999) *Emmanuelle. Livre I: La leçon d'homme*. Paris: La Musardine.

Audé, Françoise (1990) 'Le cinéma retrouvé: Trente-cinq ans après (*Le Rendez-Vous des quais*)', *Positif*, 349, 73–4.

Austin, Guy (1996) *Contemporary French Cinema: An Introduction*. Manchester: Manchester University Press.

Baignères, Claude (1995) 'Impressionnisme oriental', *Le Figaro*, 27 September, 22.

Bataille, Christophe (1993) *Annam*. Paris: Seuil.

Barthes, Roland (1957) 'Continent perdu', in *Mythologies*. Paris: Seuil, 163–5.

___ (1970) *L'Empire des signes*. Paris: Flammarion.

___ (1974) 'Alors la Chine?', *Le Monde*, 24 May, 1, 14.

Baudry, Jean-Louis (1975) 'Le dispositif: approches métapsychologiques de l'impression de réalité', *Communications*, 23, 56–72.

Béhar, Henri (1995) *Cyclo* Press Conference. Online Posting. Tuesday Oct. 10, 1995. Film Scouts. Webcast Multimedia. Available at: *http://www/filmscouts.com/festivals/ny95/interv/cyclo.html*

Bellour, Raymond (ed.) (1980) *Le Cinéma américain: Analyses de Films*. 2 vols. Paris: Flammarion.

Benjamin, Walter (1969) 'The Task of the Translator. An Introduction to the Translation of Baudelaire's Tableaux Parisiens', in Hannah Arendt (ed.) *Illuminations*. Trans. Harry Zohn. New York: Schocken, 69–82.

Bhabha, Homi K. (1994) *The Location of Culture*. London: Routledge.

Blot, Jean (n.d.) 'Repères', in *Poussière d'Empire*. Ts. Le Cinéma Municipal Louis Daquin. Blanc-Mesnil.

Blum, Sylvie (1997) 'Returning to Indochina: *The Lover* and *Indochine*', *Jump Cut*, 41, 59–66.

Blum-Reid, Sylvie (2000) 'L'Odeur de la papaye verte. Take One', *Europe Plurilingue*, May, 147–54.

Bonnewitz, Patrice (1997) 'L'homo sociologicus bourdieusien', *Premières leçons sur la Sociologie de P. Bourdieu*. Paris: PUF.

Borgé, Jacques & Nicolas Viasnoff [Photographs by Roger Viollet] (2001) *Archives de l'Indochine*. Pantin: Editions de Lodi.

Boudarel, Georges (1988) 'La Diaspora et les exils vietnamiens', *Relations internationales*, 54, 231–54.

Boulanger, Pierre (1975) *Le Cinéma colonial: De l'Atlantide à Lawrence d'Arabie*. Paris: Seghers.

Bourdieu, Pierre (1990) 'La Domination masculine', *Actes de la Recherche en Sciences Sociales*, 2–31.

Bradley Winston, Jane Ollier & Leakthina Chau-Pech Ollier (eds) (2001) *Of Vietnam: Identities in Dialogue*. New York: Palgrave.

Breton, André (1984) *Manifestes du Surréalisme*. Paris: Gallimard/Idée [1924].

Brunhes, Jean (1952) Human Geography. Trans. Ernest F. Row. London: G. G. Harrap [1910].

Cadière, Léopold (1992) *Croyances et pratiques religieuses des Viêtnamiens*. Paris: Ecole Française d'Extrême-Orient [1919].

Charpenet, Alexis, Arnaud Leveau & Sean James Rose (1995) 'Cyclo Story. Entretien avec Tran Anh Hung', *Xích Lô. Bulletin bilingue d'information sur le Viêt-nam*, September, 8-11.

Chaubon-Cevran, Gil (2000) 'Cinéma vietnamien: regard de femme', *Bulletin de l'Association d'Amitié Franco-Vietnamienne*, 33, 20–1.

Cheng, François (1994) *Empty and Full: The Language of Chinese Painting*. Trans. Michael H. Kohn. Boston and London: Shambhala.

Cheng, Scarlet (1994) 'Tran Anh Hung and the Scents of Vietnam', *Cinemaya: The Asian Film Quarterly*, 24, 4–7.

Chesneaux, Jean (1987) *China in the Eyes of the French Intellectuals*. The Forty-eighth George Ernest Morrison Lecture in Ethnology. Canberra: The Australian National University.

Cixous, Hélène (1985) *L'Histoire Terrible mais inachevée de Norodom Sihanouk roi du Cambodge*. Tours: Théâtre du Soleil.

Clément, Catherine B. (1975) 'Emmanuelle et la commande sociale: Sur un an de succès', *Le Monde*, 12 June, 25.

Clifford, James (1997) *Routes. Travel and Translation in the Late Twentieth Century*. Cambridge and London: Harvard UP.

Coatalem, Jean-Luc (1995) *Suite Indochinoise*. Paris: Editions Kailash.

Cohen, Barbara (1990) *The Vietnam Guidebook*. New York: Harper & Row.

Condominas, Georges (1995) 'Le Quotidien du Peuple: Chanter la Poésie. Questions à Georges Condominas', in Le Huu Khoa (ed.) *La Part d'Exil*. Provence: Publications de l'Université de Provence, 27–31.

Coutard, Raoul (1970) 'Mi-Automne'. Bibliothèque du film, Paris.

Cross, Alice (1994) 'Portraying the Rhythm of the Vietnamese Soul: An Interview with Tran Anh Hung', *Cinéaste*, 35, 20, 3, 35–7.

Cyclo (1995) Plan de financement, *Ecran Total*, 96, 27 September, 15.

'Cyclo Story' (1995) Entretien avec Trân Anh Hùng. A.C., A.L. and S.J.R. *Cyclo! (Xích Lô!)*. *Bulletin bilingue d'information sur le Viêt-nam*, September, 8–11.

Daney, Serge (1986) *Ciné journal 1981–1986*. Paris: Cahiers du cinéma, 178–81.

___ (1992) 'Falling out of Love', *Sight and Sound*, July, 14–16.

Dang Nhat Minh (1996) 'Interview with filmmaker', *Cinemaya*, 31, 20–1.

Deforges, Régine (1994) *Rue de la Soie*. Fayard, Paris.

Deleuze, Gilles (1986) *Cinema 1: The Movement Image*. Trans. Hugh Tomlinson & Barbara Habberjam. Minneapolis: University of Minnesota Press.

De Montella, Christian (1992) *Indochine*. Paris: Arthème Fayard.

De Roux, Emmanuel (1995) 'Les merveilleuses collections d'Albert Kahn, mécène utopiste', *Le Monde*, 16 December, 27.

Deslouis, Emmanuel (2000) 'Quand la Littérature effraie le pouvoir'. Interview with Phan Huy Duong, *Eurasie*. Available at: www.eurasie.net/articles/entretiens/phan_huy_duong.html

Dinh, Thúy (1994) '*The Scent of Green Papaya*. Ambiguity of the Vietnamese Essence.' *Amerasia Journal*, 20, 3, 81–5.

Dumas, Danièle (1994) Interview with Jacques Bidou. 'Les risques du métier', *L'Avant-Scène cinema*, 435, 75.

Duong, Thu Huong (1992) *Roman sans titre*. Trans. Phan Huy Duong. Paris: des femmes.

___ (1993) *Paradise of the Blind*. Trans. Phan Huy Duong and Nina McPherson. New York: Penguin.

___ (1991) *Les Paradis aveugles*. Paris: des femmes.

___ (1991) *Histoire d'amour racontée avant l'aube*. La Tour d'Aigues: Editions de l'Aube.

___ (1995) *Novel without a Name*. Trans. Nina McPherson and Phan Huy Duong. New York: William Morrow.

___ (1996) *Au-delà des illusions*. Trans. Phan Huy Duong. Arles: Editions Philippe Picquier.

Dupont, Joan (1996a) 'De la difficulté de voir (et faire) des films vietnamiens au Vietnam', *Le Monde*, 15 February, 26a.

___ (1996b) 'Bringing Vietnam Back to the Vietnamese', *International Herald Tribune*, 21 February, 22.

Duras, Marguerite (1984) *L'Amant*. Paris: Minuit.

Durney, Daniel (1998) 'Le révolutionnaire et le sage', *Cyclo*, July.

Duyen, Anh (1995) La Colline de Fanta. Trans. Pierre Tràn Van Nghiem & Ghislain Ripault.

Edwards, Penny (1998) 'Womanizing Indochina: Fiction, Nation and Cohabitation in Colonial Cambodia, 1890–1930', in Julia Clancy-Smith & Frances Gouda (eds) *Domesticating the Empire: Race, Gender, and Family Life in French and Dutch Colonialism*. Charlotte, London: University Press of Virginia.

Eisen Bergman, Arlene (1968) *Femmes du Vietnam*. Paris: Editions des femmes.

Eisenschitz, Bernard (1997) *Points de départ. Entretien avec Robert Kramer*. Aix en Provence: Institut de l'Image.

Eurasie. Available at: *www.eurasie.net*

Favre, Mireille (1986) 'Un milieu porteur de modernisation: Travailleurs et tirailleurs vietnamiens en France pendant la première guerre mondiale'. Thesis. Ecole Nationale des Chartes.

Férenczi, Aurélien (1992) 'Cinema français: Comment ça va?' *7 à Paris* 547. 13 May. n.p.

___ (1994) Review of *L'Odeur de la papaye verte*, *Télérama*, 2318, 117.

___ (1999) Review of *Indochine*, *Télérama*, 2569, 138.

Ferro, Marc (1994) *Histoire des colonisations: des conquêtes aux indépendances XIIIe – XXe siècle*. Paris: Seuil.

Fila, David-Pierre (2000) 'Dépendances africaines', *Cahiers du cinéma*, 551, 50–1.

Fonds Sud. Ministère des Affaires étrangères documentation.
http://www.cooperation.gouv.fr/culture/france/index3.html

Fourgeau, Catherine (1998) 'L'Insertion en France des communautés asiatiques. Fidélité au pays d'origine et inclusion des diasporas dans le monde', *Migrations Etudes*, 80, 1–26.

Fourniau, Jean-Michel (1989) 'Les Echanges extérieurs du Viet Nam' in Alain Ruscio (ed.) *Viet Nam: La terre, l'histoire, les hommes*. Paris: Editions de l'Harmattan.

Franchini, Philippe (1994) 'L'or et le sang de la France', in Philippe Franchini (ed.) *Tonkin 1973–1954. Colonie et Nation: Le delta des mythes*. Paris: Autrement, 13–80.

___ (1995) *Continental Saigon*. Paris: Editions Métailié.

Frandjis, Stelio & Pierre Cassan (1997) 'Asie et Francophonie', *Les Cahiers de la Francophonie*, 5, 13.

French, Philip (1993) *Louis Malle on Louis Malle*. London: Faber and Faber.

Freud, Sigmund (1963) 'Fetishism', in *Sexuality and the Psychology of Love*. New York: Collier Books, McMillan, 214–19.

Frodon, Jean-Michel (1993) 'Tourner, retourner au Vietnam', *Le Monde*, 7 August, 17.

Gabriel, Teshome (1989) 'Towards a Critical Theory of Third World Films', in Jim Pines & Paul Willemen (eds) *Questions of Third Cinema*. London: BFI, 30–52.

Gauthier, Guy (1992) 'Indochine, Rêve d'empire', *La Revue du Cinéma*, 483, 50–61.

Génin, Bernard (1993) 'Une intense douceur', *Télérama*, 2265, 34–5.

Gott, Richard (1996) 'Vietnam mon amour', *The Guardian*, 14 March, 10.

Guibert, Hervé (1983) 'Je suis né en 1948, à Haïphong, Indochine...', *Le Monde*, 8 September, 18.

Guillebaud, Jean-Claude & Raymond Depardon (1993) *La Colline des anges. Retour au Vietnam*. Paris: Seuil.

Grewal, Inderpal (1996) *Home and Harem: Nation, Gender, Empire, and the Cultures of Travel*. Durham: Duke University Press.

Ha, Marie-Paule (2000) *Figuring the East: Segalen, Malraux, Duras, and Barthes*. Albany: State University of New York Press.

Halberstadt, Michèle (1994) 'Entretien avec Rithy Panh', *L'Avant-Scène Cinéma*, 435, 1–3.

Hall, Stuart (1992) 'European Cinema on the Verge of a Nervous Breakdown', in Duncan Petrie (ed.) *Screening Europe: Image and Identity in Contemporary European Cinema*. London: BFI, 45–53.

Hargreaves, Alec G. & Mark McKinney (eds) (1997) *Postcolonial Cultures in France*. New York: Routledge.

Hayward, Susan (1993) *French National Cinema*. London: Routledge.

Heung, Marina (1997) 'The Family Romance of Orientalism: From *Madame Butterfly* to *Indochine*', in Matthew Bernstein & Gaylin Studlar (eds) *Visions of the East: Orientalism in Film*. New Brunswick: Rutgers University Press: 158–83.

Holmlund, Christine Anne (1991) 'Displacing Limits of Difference: Gender, Race, and Colonialism in Edward Said and Homi Bhabba's Theoretical Models and Marguerite Duras' Experimental Films', *Quarterly Review of Film and Video*, 13, 1–2, 1–24.

Hougron, Jean (1989) *La Nuit Indochinoise*. Paris: Robert Laffont [1953].

Howard, Jennifer (1996) 'French as a Weapon', *New York Times*, 1 December, 2.

Hue, Bernard (ed.) (1992) *Indochine. Reflets Littéraires*. Rennes: Presses Universitaires de Rennes.

Informations C.N.C. (1984) 201.

INSEE (2000) France, portrait social, 2000–2001/Statistique publique. Paris: INSEE.

Interim, Louella & Olivier Séguret (1983) 'Le Cinéma cosmogonique de Lam-lê', *Libération*, 7 June: 27.

Irigaray, Luce (1999) *Entre Orient et Occident: De la singularité à la communauté*. Paris: Grasset.

'L'Itinéraire du film de fiction vietnamien' (1994) Hanoi: Editions en Langues étrangères, 3–7

Jaeggi, Bruno and Martial Knabbel (1994) 'Look back in Pain', *Cinemaya*, 24, 44–7.

Jaehne, Karen (1989) 'Cinema in Vietnam: When the Shooting stopped ... And the Filming Began', *Cineaste*, XVII, 2, 32–7.

Jameson, Fredric (1983) 'Postmodernism and Consumer Society', in Al Foster (ed.) *The Anti-Aesthetic: Essays on Postmodern Culture*. Washington: Bay Press, 111–25.

Jeancolas, Jean-Pierre (1992) 'La Guerre d'Indochine dans le cinéma français', *Positif*, 375–6, 86–91.

___ (1993) 'L'Odeur de la papaye verte. Un Viêt-nam mental', *Positif*, 389–90, 22–3.

Joly, Martine (1993) *Introduction à l'analyse de l'image*. Paris: Nathan Université.

Kanapa, Jérôme (1989) 'Le Cinéma', in Alain Ruscio (ed.) *Viet Nam: La terre, l'histoire, les hommes*. Paris: L'Harmattan, 287–8.

Kaplan, Ann E. (1987) 'Mothering, Feminism and Representation: The Maternal in Melodrama and the Woman's Film 1910–1940', in Christine Gledhill (ed.) *Home is where the Heart is*. London: BFI.

Karp, Amie (1999) 'Jean Rouch: Cinematic Griot or Western Exploiter?', Undergraduate thesis. University of Florida.

Kong Sothanrith & Frédéric Amat (2000) *Avoir 20 ans à Phnom Penh*. Paris: Editions Alternatives.

Kyrou, Ado (1957) *Amour – Erotisme et cinéma*. Paris: Le Terrain Vague.

Kramer, Robert (1994) 'Notes autour de "Point de depart"', *Positif*, 398, April, 35-40.

Kristeva, Julia (1974) *Des Chinoises*. Paris: des femmes.

'L'Agent orange, une bombe à retardement' (1998) *Bulletin d'Information et de Documentation Association d'Amitié Franco-Vietnamienne*, 26.

L'Odeur de la papaye verte (1993) Press Kit. Les Productions Lazennec.

Lancelin, Aude (2001) 'La Sagesse de l'Orient' *Le Nouvel Observateur*, 3–9 May, 136.

Landrot, Marine (2000) 'A la verticale de l'été', *Télérama*, 2628, 62–3.

Lardeau, Yann and Alain Philippon (1983) 'Le Jeu des quatre coins', *Cahiers du cinéma*, 352, 29–33.

Le Huu Khoa (1985) *Les Vietnamiens en France. Insertion et identité*. Paris: L'Harmattan, C.I.E.M.

___ (1993) *L'Interculturel et l'Eurasien*. Paris: L'Harmattan.

___ (ed.) (1995) *Littérature vietnamienne. La Part d'exil*. Aix-en-Provence: Université de Provence.

Lê, Lam (1993) 'La petite Cosette du delta du Mékong', *Libération*, 9 June, 42–3.

Lê, Linda (1993) *Calomnies*. Paris: Christian Bourgois éditeur.

___ (1995) 'Les pieds nus', in Le Huu Khoa (ed.) *Littérature vietnamienne. La Part d'exil*. Aix en Provence: Université de Provence, 57–8.

___ (1997) *Les Trois Parques*. Paris: Christian Bourgois éditeur.

___ (1998) *Voix*. Paris: Christian Bourgois éditeur.

___ (1999a) *Lettre morte*. Paris: Christian Bourgois éditeur.

___ (1999b) *Tu écriras sur le bonheur*. Paris: Presses Universitaires de France.

___ (1999c) 'Interview with Catherine Argand', *Lire*, April, 28–33.

___ (2000) *L'Evangile selon saint luc*. Preface. Paris: le serpent à plumes & mille et une nuits.

Lê, Nguyên (1996) 'Tales from Viêt-nam.' CD. ACT-World Jazz.

'Le Cinéma français et le Viet-Nam'. Available at: *http:///wwwparis.enpc.fr/-nguyen-t/france.html*

Lebelley, Frédérique (1994) *Duras ou le poids d'une plume*. Paris: Grasset.

Lebrun, Jean (1983) 'Lâm lê: L'oeil écoute', *La Croix*, 13 October, 20.

Lefèvre, Kim (1989) *Métisse blanche*. Paris: Bernard Barrault.

___ (1990) *Retour à la saison des pluies*. Paris: Bernard Barrault.

Leonardini, Jean-Pierre (1994) *L'Avant-Scène cinema*, 435, 67.

Leprohon, Pierre (1945) *L'Exotisme et le cinéma: Les Chasseurs d'images à la conquête du monde*. Paris: Editions J. Susse.

Leridon, Henri (ed.) (1996) *Populations. L'état des connaissances. La France, L'Europe, Le monde*. Paris: Editions la Découverte.

'L'Itinéraire du film de fiction vietnamien' (1994) Hanoi: Editions en Langues étrangères.

Loti, Pierre (1990) *Madame Chrysanthème*. Paris: Flammarion [1885].

___ (1995) 'Un Pélerin d'Angkor, Indochine', in Alain Quella-Villéger (ed.) *Un rêve d'Asie*. Paris: Omnibus [1912], 47–103.

Lowe, Lisa (1991) *Critical Terrains: French and British Orientalisms*. Ithaca and London: Cornell University Press.

Maffesoli, Michel (1997) *Du Nomadisme: Vagabondages initiatiques*. Paris: Librairie Générale Française.

Mai Thu Vân (1983) *Viêtnam: Un peuple, des voix*. Paris: Pierre Horay.

Maillet, Dominique (2001) *En Lumière: Les directeurs de la photographie vus par les cinéastes*. Photographs by Sylvie Biscioni. Paris: Editions Dujarric.

Malraux, André (1935) Préface, *S.O.S. Indochine*. Paris: Gallimard. vii-xi.

___ (1985) 'André Malraux et l'Orient' [1926], *Mélanges Malraux Miscellany*, 17, 53–4.

Malraux, Clara (1992) *Nos Vingts ans*. Paris: Grasset et Fasquelle.

Mam, Teeda Butt (1994) 'Worms from Our Skin', in Kim DePaul (ed.) *Children of Cambodia's Killing Fields: Memoirs by Survivors*. New Haven and London: Yale University Press, 10–17.

Marchetti, Gina (1993) *Romance and the 'Yellow Peril': Race, Sex, and Discursive Strategies in Hollywood Fiction*. Berkeley, Los Angeles, London: University of California Press.

Mauriac, Claude (1969) Review of *Calcutta, Le Figaro Littéraire*, 5 May, 42.

___ (1970) 'Le Vietnam de la nuit et du silence', Review of Hoa-Binh, *Figaro Littéraire,* 9 March, 36-37.

Maveyraud, Cécile (2000) 'La route des fantômes', *Télérama*, 2621, 82.

Mayne, Judith (1992) 'From a Hybrid Place', in *Framer Framed*. New York, London: Routledge, 137–48.

Memmi, Albert (1965) *The Colonizer and the Colonized*. New York: Orion Press.

Ménil, Alain (1992) 'Rue Case-Nègres or the Antilles from the Inside', Trans. Oumar Kâ, in Mbye Cham (ed.) *Ex-Iles: Essays on Caribbean Cinema*. Trenton: Africa World Press, 155–75.

Mérigeau, Pascal (1995a) 'A Venise, les stars américaines face à l'ambition d'un jeune cinéaste franco-vietnamien', *Le Monde*, 8 September, 24.

___ (1995b) 'Christophe Rossignon, producteur atypique', *Le Monde*, 28 September, 28.

Metz, Christian (1982) *The Imaginary Signifier. Psychoanalysis and the Cinema* (1973–1976). Trans. Celia Britton, Annwyl Williams, Ben Brewster and Alfred Guzetti. Bloomington: Indiana U.P.

Millet, Raphael (1998) '(In)dépendance des cinémas du Sud &/vs France, l'exception culturelle des cinémas du Sud est-elle française?', in Laurent Creton (ed.) *Théorème: Cinéma & (In)dépendance*. Paris: Sorbonne Nouvelle, 141–77.

Mondière, A. T. (2001) 'Monographie de la femme de Cochinchine', in Jacques Borgé and Nicolas Viasnoff (eds) *Archives de l'Indochine*. Pantin: Editions de Lodi, 98–104.

Montella, Christian de (1992) *Indochine*. Paris: Arthème Fayard.

Murphy, Kathleen (1993) 'Scented Memories, Whiffs of Bad Faith', *Film Comment*, 29, 6, 66–7.

Naficy, Hamid (2001) *An Accented Cinema: Exilic and Diasporic Filmmaking*. Princeton: Princeton University Press.

Narkunas J. Paul (2000) 'Streetwalking in the Cinema of the City: Capital Flows Through Saigon', in Mark Shiel & Tony Fitzmaurice (eds) *Cinema and the City: Film and Urban Societies in a Global Context*. Oxford: Blackwell, 147–57.

Nesterenko, Geneviève (1986) 'L'Afrique de l'autre', in Michèle Lagny, Marie-Claire Ropars & Pierre Sorlin (eds) *Générique des Années 30*. Vincennes: Presses Universitaires de Vincennes, 127–76.

Ngo Phuong Lan (1995-96) 'Dang Nhat Minh's *Nostalgia for the Countryside*', *Cinemaya*, 31, 18–21.

Nguyên Du (1961) *Kim-Vân-Kiêu*. Trans. Xuân-Phuc and Xuân-Viêt. Paris: Gallimard. Unesco, 1961.

___ (ed.) (1962) *Vaste Recueil de Légendes merveilleuses.* Paris: Gallimard.

Nguyen Thu (1990) 'Le Cinéma Viêtnamien en quête d'investissements', *Le Film Français*, 28 February, 10.

Nguyen, Vinh Ba (1970) Letter. 'A propos du film "Hoa Binh" un Vietnamien nous écrit', *L'Humanité*, 8 April, 8.

Norindr, Panivong (1996) *Phantasmatic Indochina: French Colonial Ideology in Architecture, Film and Literature*. Durham: Duke University Press.

___ (2001) '*The Postcolonial Cinema Of Lam Le*: Screens, the Sacred, and the Unhomely in *Poussière d'Empire*', in Jane Bradley Winston and Leakthina Chau-Pech Ollier (eds) *Of Vietnam. Identities in Dialogue*. New York: Palgrave, 143–57.

Ostria, Vincent (1983) 'Une cabane indochinoise dans une laiterie', *Cahiers du cinéma* 33, mai, v.

O.V. (2000) Review of *A la verticale de l'été*, *Jeune Cinéma*, 263, 47–8.

Panh, Rithy (1987) 'Aux abords des frontières.' Scenario/Script. SCEN 0220 B65.Bibliothèque du film Paris, archives.

Panh, Rithy (1994) 'Look back in Pain', *Cinemaya*, 24, 44–7.

Pantel, Monique (1995) 'L'Odeur du succès', *France-Soir*, 27 September, 15.

Peeters, Benoît, Jacques Faton and Philippe de Pierpont (1992) *Story Board – Le Cinéma dessiné*. Paris: Editions Yellow Now.

Péron, Didier (1995) 'Viêt-nam, enfants de naguère', *Libération*, 19 January, 35.

Pham Dán Binh (1994–95) 'Ecrivains Vietnamiens de langue française. Création et créativité', *Cahiers d'Etudes Vietnamiennes*, 11, 9–17.

Phan, Huy Duong (ed.) (1994) *Terre des Ephémères*. Arles: Philippe Picquier.

Piault, Marc Henri (2000) *Anthropologie et Cinéma: Passage à l'image, passage par l'image*. Paris: Nathan Cinéma.

Pomonti, Jean-Claude (1994) 'Les cent fleurs du Vietnam', *Le Monde*, 22 July, VIII.

'Poussière d'Empire' (1983), press kit.

Portuges, Catherine (1996) 'Le Colonial Féminin: Women Directors Interrogate French Cinema', in Dina Sherzer (ed.) *Cinema, Colonialism, Postcolonialism*. Austin: University of Texas Press, 80–102.

Powrie, Phil (1997) *French Cinema in the 1980s: Nostalgia and the Crisis of Masculinity*. Oxford: Clarendon Press.

Pratt, Mary Louise (1992) *Imperial Eyes: Travel Writing and Transculturation*. New York and London: Routledge.

Propp, Vladimir (1973) *Morphologie du conte*. Paris: Poétique/Seuil.

Quella-Villéger, Alain (ed.) (1995) *Indochine: Un rêve d'Asie*. Paris: Omnibus.

Ragon, Michel (1982) *Ma Soeur aux yeux d'Asie*. Paris: Albin Michel.

Raulin, Anne (2000) *L'Ethnique est quotidien: Diasporas, marchés et cultures métropolitaines*. Paris: L'Harmattan.

Rayns, Tony (1995) 'Here and Now', *Sight and Sound*, 19, April, 18–20.

Reid, Mark A. (1996) 'Colonial Observations. Interview with Claire Denis', *Jump Cut*, 40, 67–73.

Ronsin, Francis (1997) *La Population de la France de 1789 à nos jours: Données démographiques et affrontements idéologiques*. Paris: Seuil.

Ross, Kristin (1995) *Fast Cars, Clean Bodies: Decolonization and the Reordering of French Culture*. Cambridge, London: MIT Press.

Rossignon, Christophe (1995) 'Entretien', *Le Film français*, 2577, 22 September, 11.

Roussel, Chantal (2000) Personal interview. Atelier Varan, Paris. 8 September.

Rousso, Henri (1987) *Le Syndrome de Vichy: de 1944 à nos jours*. Paris: Seuil.

Ruscio, Alain (1987) *La décolonisation tragique: Une histoire de la décolonisation française, 1945–1962*. Paris: Messidor/Editions sociales.

___ (ed.) (1989) *Viet Nam: La Terre, l'histoire, les hommes*. Paris: L'Harmattan.

___ (1995) *Le Credo de l'homme blanc: Regards coloniaux français. XIXe-XXe siècle*. Paris: Editions Complexe.

Russier, Henri (1931) *L'Indochine Française*. Hanoi-Haiphong: Imprimerie d'Extrême-Orient Editeurs.

Sadoul, Georges (1949) *Histoire du cinéma mondial: Des Origines à nos jours*. Paris: Flammarion.

Schoendoerffer, Pierre (1992) *Dien-Bien-Phu: De la bataille au film*. Paris: Fixot/Lincoln.

Séguret, Olivier (1983) '*Poussière d'Empire*', *Libération*, 7 June, 26–7.

Shiel Mark and Tony Fitzmaurice (eds) (2001) *Cinema and the City. Film and Urban Societies in a Global Context*. Oxford: Blackwell.

Shohat, Ella & Robert Stam (eds) (1994) *Unthinking Eurocentrism: Multiculturalism and the Media*. New York: Routledge.

Silverman, Max (1999) *Facing Postmodernity: Contemporary French Thought on Culture and Society*. London and New York: Routledge.

Sklar, Robert (1993) *Film: An International History of the Medium*. New York: Prentice Hall.

Sorlin, Pierre (1991) 'The fanciful Empire: French feature films and the Colonies in the 1930s', *French Cultural Studies*, 2, 2, 5, 135–51.

Sothanrith, Kong and Frédéric Amat (2000) *Avoir 20 ans à Phnom Penh*. Paris: Editions Alternatives.

'Souvenirs d'Indochine' (1992) *Les Cahiers de la cinémathèque*, 57.

Spivak, Gayatri Chakravorty (1988) 'French Feminism in an International Frame', in Spivak (ed.) *In Other Worlds*. New York, London: Routledge, 134–53.

Stam, Robert & Louise Spence (1985) 'Colonialism, Racism, and Representation: An

Introduction', in Bill Nichols (ed.) *Movies and Methods, Vol. II*. Berkeley, Los Angeles, and London. University of California Press, 632–49.

Sterritt, David (1994) 'Beauty Rather Than Depth', *The Christian Science Monitor*, 26 January, 16.

Stoler, Ann Laura (1997) 'Making Empire Respectable: The Politics of Race and Sexual Morality in Twentieth-Century Colonial Cultures', in Anne McClintock, Aamir Mufti & Ella Shohat (eds) *Dangerous Liaisons: Gender, Nation and Postcolonial Perspectives*. Minneapolis: University of Minnesota Press, 344–73.

Stora, Benjamin (1992) 'Indochine, Algérie, autorisations de retour', *Libération*, 30 April, 5.

___ (1997) 'Voyage au bout de la mémoire', *Télérama*, 2462, 22–5.

Tarr, Carrie (1997) 'French Cinema and Post-Colonial Minorities', in Alex Hargreaves and Mark McKinney (eds) *Post-Colonial Cultures in France*. London and New York: Routledge, 59–83.

Tobin, Yann (1983) 'Idéogramme', *Positif*, 273, 9.

Tobing Rony, Fatimah (1996) *The Third Eye: Race, Cinema, and Ethnographic Spectacle*. Durham and London: Duke University Press.

Toroni, Janine (1993) 'Le Vietnam au 46eme Festival International du Film de Locarno', *Association Amitié Franco Vietnamienne: Bulletin d'Information et de documentation bimestriel*, 7, 10–11.

Tran, Anh Hung (1993) Interview with Bernard Génin. 'Une intense douceur', *Télérama*, 2265, 9 June, 34-35.

___ (1995a) Interview with Mona Makki. 'Le Vietnam dans l'objectif', *Espace Francophone: Le Magazine télévisé de la Francophonie*. ICAF. Channel 5.

___ (1995b) Interview with Alexis Charpenet, Arnaud Leveau and Sean James Rose. 'Cyclo Story.' *Xích Lô!* Bulletin bilingue d'information sur le Viêt-nam, September, 8–11.

___ (1995c) 'The Cyclo Press Conference', New York Film Festival. Film Scouts. Webcast Multimedia.

___ (1995d) *Cyclo*. Paris: Actes Sud.

Trémois, Claude-Marie (1970) Review of *Hoa-Binh*, *Télérama*, 1054, 29 March, 65.

Tribalat, Michèle (1996a) 'Combien y a-t-il de Français d'origine étrangère?', in Henri Leridon (ed.) *Populations. L'état des connaissances. La France, L'Europe, Le monde*. Paris: Editions la Découverte, 63–4.

___ (1996b) 'L'Immigration aujourd'hui', in Henri Leridon (ed.) *Populations. L'état des connaissances. La France, L'Europe, Le monde*. Paris: Editions la Découverte, 64–70.

Trinh, T. Minh-ha (1992) 'Why a Fish Pond?': Fiction at the Heart of Documentation', Interview with Laleen Jayamane and Anne Rutherford in *Framer Framed*. New York and London: Routledge, 161–78.

___ (1992) 'Surname Viet Given Name Nam' Script of 1989 film, in *Framer Framed*, New York and London: Routledge, 49-94.

___ (1992) 'From a Hybrid Place' interview with Judith Mayne, in *Framer Framed*, New York and London: Routledge, 137-148.

___ (1999) *Cinema Interval*. New York and London: Routledge.

Truffaut, François. (1954) ' A Certain Tendency of the French Cinema' in (1976) *Movies and Methods* I, Bill Nichols Ed., Berkeley, Los Angeles, 224-237.

Vân, Mai Thu (1983) *Viêtnam un peuple, des voix*. Paris: Pierre Horay.

Vincendeau, Ginette (1993) 'Fire and Ice', *Sight and Sound*, 3, 4, April, 20–4.

Vincent, Rose (1998) *L'Aventure des Français en Inde: XVIIe-XXe siècles*. Paris: Editions Kailash.

Viollis, Andrée (1949) *Indochine S.O.S.* Paris: Les Editeurs français réunis.

Waintrop, Edouard (1990) 'Le Deuxième "Rendez-vous des quais"', *Libération*, 13 February, 39-40.

Wieviorka, Michel (1995) *The Arena of Racism*. Trans. Chris Turner. London: Sage.

Williams, Sherley Anne (1990) 'Some Implications of Womanist Theory', in Henry Louis Gates, Jr. (ed.) *Reading Black, Reading Feminist. A Critical Anthology*. New York: Penguin, 68–75.

Yeager, Jack A. (1987) *The Vietnamese Novel in French: A Literary Response to Colonialism.*

Hanover and London: New England University Press.

___ (1996) 'Blurring the Lines in Vietnamese Fiction in French: Kim Lefèvre's *Métisse Blanche*', in Mary Jean Green & Karen Gould (eds) *Postcolonial Subjects: Francophone Women Writers*. Minneapolis: University of Minnesota Press, 210–26.

___ (1997) 'Narrative Texts of Linda Lê', in Alec G. Hargreaves & Mark McKinney (eds) *Postcolonial Cultures in France*. New York and London: Routledge, 255–67.